Counselling Survivors of Childhood Sexual Abuse

Third Edition

Claire Burke Draucker
and
Donna Steele Martsolf

⑤SAGE

Los Angeles • London • New Delhi • Singapore

First edition published as *Counselling Survivors of Childhood Sexual Abuse* 1992
Reprinted 1993, 1994, 1996, 1998
Second edition published 2000
Reprinted 2001, 2002, 2005
This third edition first published 2006
Reprinted 2008

SAGE Publications Ltd
1 Oliver's Yard
55 City Road
London EC1Y 1SP

SAGE Publications Inc
2455 Teller Road
Thousand Oaks
California 91320

SAGE Publications India Pvt. Ltd
B 1/I 1 Mohan Cooperative Industrial Area
Mathura Road, New Delhi 110 044
India

SAGE Publications Asia-Pacific Pte Ltd
33 Pekin Street #02-01
Far East Square
Singapore 048763

British Library Cataloguing in Publication Data

A catalogue record for this book is available from the British Library

ISBN 978-1-4129-2239-5 (hbk)
ISBN 978-1-4129-2240-1 (pbk)

Library of Congress Control Number Available

Typeset by C&M Digitals (P) Ltd, Chennai, India
Printed in Great Britain by Cpod, Trowbridge, Wiltshire
Printed on paper from sustainable resources

Contents

1 Introduction

Childhood sexual abuse (CSA) is often a significant trauma that may have a lifelong impact on survivors. When adult survivors of childhood sexual abuse seek counselling for any reason, counsellors must be prepared to explore with them the role the abuse has played in their development and the effect it might be having on their present concerns. Due to the prevalence of childhood sexual abuse in the histories of individuals who seek counselling, and its possible pervasive and long-term effects, it is important that all counsellors become adept at addressing the unique and complex needs of survivors.

This chapter will address several basic issues related to the phenomenon of childhood sexual abuse. Topics include the definition of childhood sexual abuse, the recognition of sexual abuse as a significant social problem, and empirical research findings related to adult survivors. In addition, several fundamental counselling issues are addressed, and finally the structure of the book is outlined.

Definition of childhood sexual abuse

Defining childhood sexual abuse has been problematic for both researchers and clinicians. Definitions in the literature vary according to the types of activities considered to be 'sexual' and the circumstances considered to constitute abuse. Finkelhor (1997) suggested that the following definition, formulated by the National Center on Child Abuse and Neglect, is consistent with most legal and research definitions of child sexual abuse:

> Contacts or interactions between a child and an adult when the child is being used for the sexual stimulation of the perpetrator or another person. Sexual abuse may also be committed by a person under the age of 18 when that person is significantly older than the victim or when the perpetrator is in a position of power or control over another child. (NCCAN, 1978: 2)

Finkelhor argued that this definition has several essential components. It includes both intra-familial and extra-familial abuse, as well as contact and non-contact activities. The definition also emphasizes the exploitation of adult authority and addresses the maturation advantage of the perpetrator over the child. Because this broad definition has important clinical relevance, it is appropriate for a book that focuses on childhood sexual abuse as a counselling concern.

The recognition of sexual abuse as a significant social problem

The phenomenon of child sexual abuse was historically denied by the public and by mental health professionals. Herman (1981) outlined three 'discoveries' of the prevalence of sexual abuse in our society. The awareness of the occurrence of sexual abuse as a traumatic experience in the lives of children is usually traced to Freud, who is credited with the first 'discovery' of incest. When female patients in large numbers revealed to Freud that they had childhood sexual experiences with adult men in their families, Freud initially suggested that these traumatic experiences were the cause of hysteria; this became known as the seduction theory. In the service of protecting the patriarchal family structure, Freud identified the perpetrators of the sexual abuse as other children, caretakers, or more distant relatives – but not fathers. In response to peer pressure, however, Freud eventually repudiated the seduction theory and claimed instead that his patients' frequent reports of sexual abuse were incestuous fantasies rather than actual childhood events.

Herman (1981: 10) reported that for decades following Freud's repudiation of the seduction theory, professionals maintained a 'dignified silence' on the topic of incest and the public continued to deny the reality and the prevalence of childhood sexual abuse. It was not until the 1940s that incest was 'discovered' for a second time by social scientists conducting large-scale survey studies of sexual practices, including the now famous Kinsey study (Kinsey et al., 1953). These studies documented that between 20 and 30 per cent of the women who responded to the surveys reported having had a sexual experience as a child with a male, between 4 and 12 per cent reported a sexual experience with a relative, and 1 per cent reported a sexual experience with a father or stepfather. Although the sexual abuse of boys was not addressed in several of these studies, one researcher (Landis, 1956) reported that 30 per cent of the male participants in his survey reported a childhood sexual experience with an adult, who was most typically a male.

Despite the substantiation of childhood sexual abuse provided by these studies, the reality of the phenomenon continued to be denied. For example, most of the sexually abused women in the Kinsey study reported being disturbed by the experience. The researchers indicated, however, that the women's distress resulted from social conditioning rather than from the sexual act itself. Herman concluded that Kinsey and his colleagues, in their attempt to encourage enlightenment and tolerance of sexual attitudes, 'failed to distinguish between essentially harmless acts committed by consenting adults, "nuisance acts" such as exhibitionism, and frankly exploitative acts such as the prostitution of women and the molesting of children' (Herman, 1981: 17).

Herman (1981) dated the 'third discovery' of incest to the 1970s, and credited the feminist movement with bringing the problem of childhood sexual abuse into public awareness, along with other taboo issues such as wife battering and rape. This was followed by legitimate, scientific studies of the problem and public revelations of incest survivors who chose to tell their stories.

Knowledge and public policy related to the sexual abuse of males, however, has lagged behind that for women. While academic researchers and social movements have focused on the sexual abuse of girls perpetrated by adult males, the sexual abuse of boys was ignored until recently (Speigel, 2003). King and Woollett (1997), for example, indicated the forced sexual penetration of a man was not considered rape by English law until 1994. Researchers have documented that mental health professionals rarely inquire about sexual abuse in male patients, are not well informed about the prevalence rates of male sexual abuse, and often have not had specific training in the assessment/treatment of sexually abused males (Campbell and Carlson, 1995; Lab et al., 2000).

Empirical research
related to childhood sexual abuse

Research related to childhood sexual abuse has focused primarily on determining its prevalence in the population and in clinical subgroups, identifying long-term effects that stem from the abuse, relating specific abuse characteristics to long-term effects, and exploring what factors might mediate the relationship between abuse characteristics and adult functioning. This research will be briefly reviewed and summarized.

Prevalence

Researchers now generally agree that the occurrence of childhood sexual abuse is much more frequent than originally believed. Studies have reported, however, a wide variation in prevalence rates – that is, the proportion of the population that has experienced childhood sexual abuse. Wurtele and Miller-Perrin (1992) reviewed several large-scale studies involving college and community samples and found that the prevalence rates of childhood sexual abuse ranged from 7 per cent to 62 per cent for women and 3 per cent to 16 per cent for men. In clinical and forensic samples, these rates are often much higher (Gordon and Alexander, 1993). Prevalence rates are affected by the way sexual abuse is operationally defined (e.g. the types of sexual activities included), the characteristics of the sample studied (e.g. college samples versus random national samples), and variations in research methodology (e.g. face-to-face interviews versus surveys).

In a national US telephone survey of 2,626 adults, 27 per cent of the women and 16 per cent of the men reported having experienced sexual abuse involving physical contact during their childhood (Finkelhor et al., 1990). The Third National Incidence Study on Child Abuse and Neglect (NIS-3) (US Department of Health and Human Services, 1996) indicated that in 1993, 217,700 children were moderately or severely harmed as a result of sexual abuse. Finkelhor (1994) reviewed 21 international population studies of child sexual abuse, primarily from English-speaking and northern European countries. The prevalence rates of child sexual abuse in these studies ranged from 7 per cent to 36 per cent for women and from 3 per cent to 29 per cent for men. Sidebotham and colleagues (2000) in the United Kingdom reported that of 14,238 children enrolled in the Avon Longitudinal Study of Pregnancy and Childhood, 389 had family situations that were investigated as possible child abuse and 163 of these were placed on child protection over the period of the study. Of these cases, 10.9 per cent were considered to be childhood sexual abuse. Also in the United Kingdom, Plant and colleagues (2004) found that of 1,052 women and 975 men in a general population survey, 12.5 per cent of the women and 11.7 per cent of the men indicated that they had experienced sexual abuse before the age of 16. Peake (2003), an English educational psychologist, suggests that incidence estimates are greatly affected by who the respondents are to questions about child abuse, and who is asking the questions. Despite the differences in numbers, research suggests that a significant portion of adults have experienced some form of sexual abuse as children.

Long-term effects

Just as the prevalence of childhood sexual abuse was denied, the long-term effects of sexual abuse have historically been minimized. Some have maintained that sexual activity between a child and an adult is harmless. Ramsey (1979), for example, suggested that incest could have beneficial results if it were not for society's negative reactions to it. Research has revealed, however, that a history of child sexual abuse is associated with numerous and varied long-term psychological, behavioural, interpersonal, and physical effects.

Psychological effects of childhood sexual trauma have been identified in several comprehensive reviews of research on the long-term consequences of child sexual abuse (Beitchman et al., 1992; Browne and Finkelhor, 1986; Finkelhor, 1990; Polusny and Follette, 1995). Studies have shown that child sexual abuse is associated with an increased level of general psychological distress, depression, anxiety (phobias, panic disorder, obsessive symptoms) and long-term post-traumatic effects (Bifulco et al., 1991; Fromuth and Burkhart, 1989; Pribor and Dinwiddie, 1992; Roland et al., 1989; Saunders et al., 1992; Stein et al., 1988). Studies in Great Britain indicate that in British samples, childhood sexual abuse is associated with adult depression (Hill et al., 2000), childhood-onset depression (Hill et al., 2004), low self-esteem (Kuyken and Brewin, 1999), and anxiety (Roberts et al., 2004).

Associations between a history of child sexual abuse and behavioural or relationship effects that may pose health risks have been documented. Women who were sexually abused as children are more likely to report a lifetime prevalence of alcohol abuse/dependence and drug abuse/dependence than women who were not abused (Stein et al., 1988). Certain types of eating disorders, including obesity, have been associated with child sexual abuse (Bushnell et al., 1992; Calam and Slade, 1987, 1989; Smolak et al., 1990; Springs and Friedrich, 1992). A sexual abuse history is relatively rare in restrictive anorexia, more common in anorexia of the bulimic subtype, and most common in bulimia without a history of anorexia (Waller, 1991, 1992a, 1992b). Researchers in the United Kingdom have reported similar findings with histories of childhood sexual abuse found to be linked to adult sequelae of alcohol abuse (Moncrieff et al., 1996) and use of illicit drugs (Plant et al., 2004).

Women with a history of child sexual abuse also report more adult sexual behaviours associated with health risk, including an earlier age at first intercourse, a greater number of sexual partners, and a higher rate of unintended and aborted pregnancies (Springs and Friedrich, 1992; Stein et al., 1988; Wyatt et al., 1992; Zierler et al., 1991). One study demonstrated that when sexual abuse is accompanied by other forms of abuse (e.g. physical abuse), it may be associated with HIV-risk behaviours, such as not using condoms, engaging in prostitution, and using injectable drugs (Cunningham et al., 1994). Accumulated data from numerous studies suggest a significant relationship between childhood sexual abuse and experiences of victimization in adulthood, including adult sexual assault and partner physical violence (Chu and Dill, 1990; Elliott and Briere, 1993; Wyatt et al., 1992).

A history of child sexual abuse has been associated with a number of medical problems in adult women (Laws, 1993). While research findings implicating child sexual abuse in the development of specific diseases have been equivocal, associations between a history of sexual abuse and self-report of a variety of medical problems and concerns have been reported (Friedman and Schnurr, 1995; Fry, 1993). For example, there is a high prevalence of child sexual abuse histories in women who report chronic pelvic pain, backaches, headaches, and functional gastrointestinal disorders (Drossman et al., 1990; Felitti, 1991; Harrop-Griffiths et al., 1988; McCauley et al., 1997; Pecukonis, 1996; Reiter and Gambone, 1990; Reiter et al., 1991; Walker et al., 1988). Compared with women who were not abused, women who were sexually abused as children have reported more hospitalizations for illness, a greater number of physical and psychological problems, and lower ratings of overall health (Moeller et al., 1993); more medical problems and somatization (Springs and Friedrich, 1992); and poorer health perceptions, more functional limitations, more chronic disease, and a greater number of somatic symptoms (Golding, 1994).

In their review of the initial and long-term effects of childhood sexual abuse on boys, Urquiza and Capra (1990) cited several effects that were similar to those experienced by women and girls (e.g. self-concept disturbance, somatic complaints), but identified two effects that 'stood out' for males: disturbances of conduct and acting out of compulsive sexual behaviours. The authors suggested that these effects are related to gender-based differences in coping with trauma – most specifically, the use of externalizing behaviours by males. Little research has been conducted on medical problems in adult men who are sexually abused as children. Coxell and colleagues (2000) conducted a study examining the prevalence of sexual molestation in a sample of males attending a genitourinary medicine service and reported that 12 per cent had experienced CSA.

Abuse situation characteristics

Researchers have attempted to determine whether certain characteristics of the sexual abuse situation or the aftermath are associated with long-term outcomes. Although the relationship between some characteristics (age at onset, duration) and severity of negative effects is unclear, sexual abuse that includes threats, force, or violence; involvement of a father or father figure; or invasive sexual activities (genital contact, vaginal or anal intercourse) seems to be particularly noxious (Beitchman et al., 1992; Browne and Finkelhor, 1986; Finkelhor, 1997). Ussher and Dewberry (1995) reported similar findings in a study of 775 women survivors in Great Britain. Other British researchers (Farrell and Taylor, 2000) have noted that sexual abuse by clergy seems to have unique characteristics that are associated with particular long-term consequences. Bagley and Mallick (2000) studied the relationship between childhood abuse and other factors on emotional difficulties in late adolescent Canadian females. Lengthy duration of sexual abuse, multiple types of abuse, family dysfunction and poverty, and lower cognitive function were associated with impaired emotional functioning in the women at age 17.

Child sexual abuse and other forms of maltreatment

Childhood sexual abuse is often accompanied by other forms of childhood maltreatment. For example, psychological abuse (acts that are rejecting, isolating, terrorizing, ignoring, and corrupting) and physical abuse (hitting, kicking, punching, beating, and threatening to use or using a weapon) often accompany child sexual abuse (Briere, 1992; Garbarino et al., 1986). Also, child sexual abuse typically occurs in the context of general family dysfunction. Women who were sexually abused are more likely to report that their families of origin were emotionally distant (lacking in cohesiveness, devoid of intimacy), rigid (controlling, governed by rules and traditional roles, exhibiting low adaptability), and conflicted than are women who were not abused (Carson et al., 1990; Edwards and Alexander, 1992; Jackson et al., 1990; Yama et al., 1993). Because these differences tend to appear whether the abuse occurred within or outside of the family, it seems that even when a family member does not perpetrate the abuse, there may be an association between its occurrence and certain family interactional patterns (Yama et al., 1993).

Researchers who have investigated several types of childhood abuse (psychological, physical, and sexual), family-of-origin characteristics, and later outcomes report a complex relationship between childhood maltreatment and adult functioning. In some studies, researchers have found that sexual abuse experiences were related to later negative effects even when variables of general family functioning were controlled by various statistical procedures (Briere and Elliott, 1993; Greenwald et al., 1990). Other researchers have found that the relationships between experiences of sexual abuse and adult outcomes are mostly non-significant when family variables are controlled (Nash et al., 1993; Parker and Parker, 1991; Yama et al., 1992). Several studies have found that physical, psychological, and sexual abuse are associated with specific long-term effects beyond the effects they have in common (Briere and Runtz, 1990; Hall et al., 1993; Wind and Silvern, 1992). In a study of college women, for example, a history of psychological abuse was specifically related to low self-esteem; physical abuse was specifically related to aggression toward others; and sexual abuse was specifically related to maladaptive sexual behaviour (Briere and Runtz, 1990). Cumulative evidence from a review of all the studies suggests that: (a) family-of-origin dynamics and all forms of maltreatment are important in understanding adult outcomes; (b) the severity of the abuse and the presence of two or more types of abuse play a role in producing adult vulnerability to disturbance; and (c) sexual abuse experiences contribute to specific symptomatology in adulthood (Draucker, 1996).

Mediating factors

A few studies have begun to examine factors that might mediate the effects of abuse on long-term adjustment. Survivors who attribute negative events to internal, global, and stable factors (depressive attributions) are unable to find meaning in their abusive experiences or to regain a sense of mastery, or continue to blame themselves for the abuse, or show poorer adjustment (Draucker, 1989, 1995; Gold, 1986; Silver et al., 1983; Wyatt and Newcomb, 1990). British researchers have reported that shame served as a mediator between childhood abuse and post-traumatic stress disorder (PTSD) symptoms in victims of violent crime (Andrews et al., 2000) and between intrafamilial sexual abuse and bulimic attitudes (Murray and Walker, 2002). Other British researchers have indicated that level of dissociation was a mediator between childhood trauma and deliberate self-harm in adults (Low et al., 2000). This line of research suggests that there are certain cognitive processes that might exacerbate *or* reduce the harmful effects of childhood sexual abuse.

Summary

Principles of counselling adult survivors are, therefore, based on research which suggests that childhood sexual abuse is prevalent in the population and in the histories of those who seek counselling, and that it often results in varied long-term effects. While certain characteristics of the abuse situation are related to long-term effects, these relationships can be mediated by certain psychological processes employed by survivors. As Herman stated, 'To be sexually exploited by a known and trusted adult is a central and formative experience in the lives of countless women' (1981: 7). It is now also believed that the same could be said about the lives of countless men (Urquiza and Keating, 1990).

Theories of abuse effects

Several theories have been proposed to explain the relationship between childhood sexual abuse and negative outcomes in adulthood. Two theories that have been widely discussed and a framework that deals with the long-term effects of male survivors are presented here.

Disguised presentation of undisclosed incest

Gelinas was one of the first experts to organize the varied and commonly reported symptoms of incest survivors into a 'coherent, explanatory, and heuristic framework' (1983: 312). She identified three underlying negative effects: chronic traumatic neurosis; continued relational imbalances; and increased intergenerational risk of incest.

The intense affect and vivid memories experienced by survivors following disclosure and discussion of the incest are referred to as *chronic traumatic neurosis*. Phases of denial or repression alternate with intrusive experiences of trauma repetition (e.g. nightmares, pseudo-hallucinations, obsessions, emotional repetitions, behavioural re-enactments). Symptoms such as depression, anxiety, and substance abuse are secondary elaborations related to the hidden and untreated traumatic neurosis.

The *relational imbalances* exhibited by survivors are considered to be a result of the family dynamics that produced and maintained the secret of the incest. Gelinas (1983) discussed a scenario that typifies the development of incestuous family dynamics. Parentification occurs when a child, often an eldest daughter, assumes responsibility for parental functions. The child learns to protect and nurture her parents, thereby developing a caretaking identity. She becomes skillful in meeting the needs of others, but denies her own needs. She chooses as a partner a man who requires caretaking, typically one who is needy, narcissistic, or insecure. As she might still be meeting the needs of her family of origin, she soon becomes emotionally depleted. When she and her husband have children, maternal caretaking is added to her responsibilities. She is then less able to attend to her husband's needs, and might attempt to enlist his support. He feels both threatened and abandoned and becomes increasingly unavailable to her. She might then attempt to get emotional support from her child, often her eldest daughter, and this daughter then begins to experience parentification. The husband, if unable to meet his needs outside the family, may do so through his daughter. Sexual abuse is most likely to occur if the father is narcissistic, exhibits poor impulse control, and uses alcohol.

The daughter, now an incest survivor, becomes an adult who is also very skillful at caretaking, but who has a poor self-concept and lacks the social skills needed to meet her own needs (e.g. assertiveness). She is unable to establish mutually supportive relationships with others and becomes isolated or abused and exploited in the relationships she does establish. As she also remains emotionally depleted, she will experience parenting difficulties, and another generation of parentification may begin.

The *intergenerational risk* of incest is due to the establishment of the relational imbalances discussed above. The incest survivor's daughter becomes at risk for incest as the processes of parentification and marital estrangement are repeated. The survivor, experiencing an untreated traumatic neurosis, will avoid stimuli that provoke memories of her own abuse and is therefore less likely to detect or attend to the sexual abuse of her daughter. Gelinas (1983) stressed that this does not suggest that the mother is to blame for the incest. Although each parent is responsible for the incestuous family dynamics, the offender alone is responsible for the sexual contact.

The profile of an incest survivor thus often includes a presenting problem of chronic depression with complications that stem from the affective disorder (e.g. substance abuse, suicidality), atypical dissociative elements (e.g. nightmares, depersonalization), impulsive behaviours (e.g. impulsive eating, drinking, spending, child abuse), and a history of parentification (e.g. premature responsibilities in childhood).

A self-trauma model

More recently, Briere (1996) posited a theoretical model of symptom development for adults severely abused as children. Briere suggested that three self-functions and capacities are affected by childhood abuse and neglect, accounting for the myriad difficulties exhibited by survivors later in life. These functions are identity (a consistent sense of personal existence), boundary (an awareness of the demarcation between self and others), and affect regulation, which consists of both affect modulation (the ability to engage in internal activities to reduce negative affect states) and affect tolerance (the ability to maintain negative affect without resorting to avoiding, soothing, or distracting external activities). Childhood maltreatment interferes with the development of those skills by disrupting parent–child attachment and psychosocial learning. The child's development of a sense of self-efficacy, social skills, and ability to manage affect are affected.

The psychological distress stemming from maltreatment produces avoidance responses, including dissociation and tension-reducing activities. Due to impairment in self-functioning, the individual is easily overwhelmed by trauma-related affects, resulting in further avoidance and disruption in the development of self-capacities. The re-experiencing of fragments of the trauma through intrusive symptomatology are attempts to accommodate the trauma. Due to dissociation, however, the individual does not experience the exposure to the traumatic material needed for desensitization and resolution of chronic symptomatology. Briere concluded:

> This process may lead the abuse survivor in therapy to present as chronically dissociated, besieged by overwhelming yet unending intrusive symptomatology, and as having 'characterological' difficulties associated with identity, boundary, and affect regulation difficulties. (1996: 145)

Gender

Many of the empirical studies and much of the clinical literature on childhood sexual abuse has focused on girls and women. Because of this, gender differences in responses to the experience of childhood victimization have not been extensively explored. However, many experts call for consideration of the influence of gender role socialization on men and women's experiences of victimization when developing treatment models. Gender role socialization is the process by which men and women are conditioned to respond in ways consistent with culturally determined norms of masculinity and femininity (Krause et al., 2002). Women are generally expected to have lower power positions, to do more family caretaking, express more affiliative emotions, and exhibit less aggression, whereas men are expected to have higher power positions, maintain greater personal independence, be family providers, and express fewer emotions associated with vulnerability (Krause et al., 2002). In the area of sexuality, women are expected to restrict their sexual activities and set limits on the sexuality activities of men, while men are expected to have a greater sexual drive and to have more sexual experiences (Krause et al., 2002).

Due to gender socialization related to sexuality and emotional expression, gender issues need to be addressed to understand male and female sexual victimization. Krause et al. reviewed a number of case studies and narrative investigations of trauma themes for male and female survivors of interpersonal violence and identified a number of 'subtle, but meaningful' (2002: 351) gender differences in how the trauma is experienced and how survivors attempt recovery. For example, while female survivors of abuse often blame themselves for provoking the abuse, male survivors are more likely to blame themselves for not being 'man enough' to stop it. Women who endorse rigid gender roles may attempt to regain control of their bodies following sexual victimization through verbal aggression, self-victimization, or sex with powerful men, whereas men who endorse rigid gender roles might attempt to regain control through physical or sexual violence. Following experiences of trauma, women may be more likely to suppress anger and aggressive impulses, whereas men may experience anger as their 'sole emotional outlet' (2002: 373). Lisak (1994) analysed interviews with adult male survivors of childhood sexual abuse and found that they expressed a feeling of damage to their sense of masculinity, had a dread of homosexuality, and experienced conflicts related to sexual orientation and a number of sexual difficulties.

Issues related to gender, therefore, need to be considered when working with adult survivors of childhood sexual abuse. Krause and colleagues (2002) suggest that counsellors help clients identify and confront the gender norms that influence their healing. They recommend that counsellors discuss issues related to gender, provide psychoeducational materials on gender stereotyping, and help clients to formulate a flexible attitude toward identity and sexuality.

Counselling issues

When discussing the counselling of adult survivors of childhood sexual abuse, several basic issues or questions arise. Although there are no definitive answers to these questions, each will be addressed in turn.

Counsellor qualifications

Many counsellors ask whether the unique needs of the adult survivor require that he or she be seen by a sexual abuse 'specialist', a professional who works with adult survivors as a primary clinical focus. If we continue to find that a large percentage of individuals who seek counselling have had some experience of childhood sexual victimization, it is unlikely that all of these clients can be seen by a 'specialist'. Although it is important for counsellors to recognize that survivors' needs are unique and complex, to suggest that they need to see a 'specialist' might convey the message that their needs are extremely complicated or unusual, thereby increasing their sense of isolation and their view of themselves as being different. In fact, in a study conducted in England, respondents who had been sexually abused as children indicated a preference for a counsellor who had personal experience as a survivor of childhood sexual abuse (Gray et al., 1997).

Counsellors do need to develop skills and competencies to meet the needs of survivors effectively. For example, the development of self-awareness regarding one's attitudes and beliefs related to the issue of childhood sexual abuse is essential. As mentioned earlier, helping professionals come from a tradition of denial of the reality and prevalence of childhood sexual abuse. This reflects deeper societal values regarding gender roles, power issues, and the rights of children. Counsellors need to examine their own values and attitudes that could interfere with effective counselling (e.g. denial, disgust, blaming the victim). They must also question whether they accept any myths that research and clinical experience have consistently disproved. Hall and Lloyd (1989) have outlined several commonly accepted myths related to sexual abuse. These myths include the following: sexual abuse occurs only in certain subgroups of the population (e.g. poor, isolated families); if a child does nothing to stop the abuse he or she must therefore have welcomed it; and mothers often 'collude' with the abuser and so share responsibility for the abuse.

In addition to evaluating their beliefs and attitudes, counsellors need training and supervision in counselling adult survivors. A counsellor who is inexperienced in dealing with this clinical issue needs to develop and maintain competencies just as one would when faced with any special clinical concern (e.g. treating substance abuse or counselling individuals from varied cultural backgrounds). Training can include classroom or workshop instruction and supervised clinical experience. Because counselling survivors is an intensely emotional experience that can provoke numerous personal issues, supervision or professional consultation is recommended even for counsellors who are experienced in this area. Etherington (2000) writes from the personal perspective as a supervisor of counsellors of survivors of childhood sexual abuse in the United Kingdom and indicates that supervision should be conducted from a trauma perspective. Counsellors themselves respond to listening to trauma stories with trauma-coping strategies. Supervision should be focused on the relationship between counsellor and client rather than on the client.

The counsellor's gender

Another question that frequently arises is whether counsellors should be of the same gender as the survivors with whom they are working. Some clinicians have concluded that, at least initially, a female counsellor is preferable for female survivors. Faria and Belohlavek (1984) suggested that while a male therapist would allow survivors to learn to develop healthy relationships with men, a female counsellor is preferable as she can serve as a role model. Blake-White and Kline (1985) argued that female therapists are more effective as leaders of incest therapy groups because it is usually easier for survivors to trust women. These authors also suggested that introducing a male co-therapist at a later point could benefit the group by providing the survivors with an opportunity to explore their attitudes toward men. While Hall and Lloyd (1989) identified the advantages of a female counsellor, they also acknowledged that a male counsellor provides survivors with an opportunity to establish a healthy relationship with a male. Others have maintained that the gender of the counsellor is not a significant issue. For example, Westerlund (1983) emphasized that counselling style is more influential than the gender of the counsellor in determining how issues of power are handled within the relationship.

Less has been written regarding the gender of counsellors working with male survivors. Bruckner and Johnson (1987) recommended the use of mixed-gender co-leaders for male survivor groups because having a female present can facilitate the discussion of issues and feelings. Evans, who discussed the treatment of male sexual assault survivors and Vietnam veterans, stated that 'The key issue in gender identification with the client . . . is not the gender of the client and the survivor but the gender attitudes' (1990: 71). The ability of counsellors to examine their own gender-related issues, and the ways in which power issues are handled within the counselling relationship, therefore, may ultimately be more important than the gender mix between counsellor and client.

Male survivors

As mentioned above, we recommend that gender issues be addressed for both male and female clients. A commonly raised question is how the counselling needs of males differ from those of females. Because many female and male responses to childhood sexual abuse are similar (e.g. guilt, shame, anger), many counselling processes and techniques discussed in this book are applicable to both genders. Because the socialization of males and females differs, however, it can be expected that males will be confronted with different sexist biases, exhibit gender-specific presentations of symptoms, and have specific treatment needs (Draucker and Petrovic, 1996, 1997; Hunter and Gerber, 1990).

Struve (1990: 38) has identified nine factors that may have an impact on the presentation of the male survivor. These nine factors are:

1   Reluctance to seek treatment due to the beliefs that men are not victims and, if they are, that they are less traumatized by the victimizing experience than are females.
2   Minimization of the experience of victimization due to the belief that sexual activity with an older woman is a privilege and that victimization by a male reflects one's own sexual orientation.
3   Shame-based personality dynamics based on one's perceived failure to protect oneself or to achieve appropriate revenge against the offender.
4   Exaggerated efforts to reassert masculine identity in an attempt to compensate for the failure to protect oneself.
5   Difficulties with male identity resulting in the avoidance of any behaviours perceived as feminine, including emotional intimacy with other males.
6   Confusion about sexual identity due to one's perceived passivity or sexual arousal experienced during same-sex abuse.
7   Behaviour patterns with power/control dynamics due to attempts to overcompensate for the powerlessness experienced during the abuse.
8   Externalization of feelings due to social prescriptions that males can act on, but not express, their feelings.
9   Vulnerability to compulsive behaviours due to attempts to deny feelings by excessive involvement with 'product- and task-oriented activities'.

The needs of the male survivor related to the abuse 'may be unresponsive to, or further precipitated by, a programme model that assumes universality when it comes to sexual victimization' (Sepler, 1990: 76). By failing to acknowledge the male's view and by working from a model of victimization based primarily on women's experiences, counsellors could increase the male survivor's sense of isolation and alienation (Draucker and Petrovic, 1996, 1997).

Several specific treatment models for men who have experienced childhood sexual abuse have been presented (Bolton et al., 1989; Gonsiorek et al., 1994; Hunter, 1995; Spiegel, 2003). We recommend that counsellors become familiar with some of these models. When applicable, we will integrate salient principles drawn from these models in this book.

Abuse by members of the same sex

A closely related issue is that of same-sex versus opposite-sex abuse. Whereas girls are most frequently victimized by men, boys are most frequently abused by other males. In addition to addressing the impact of socialization on males' responses to victimization, the issue of same-sex abuse is pertinent. The most frequently discussed specific effect arising from the experience of male-to-male abuse is confusion related to sexual identity. Struve (1990) pointed out that if the abused boy perceives himself as experiencing pleasure or sexual arousal, which are normal physiological responses to stimulation, he may interpret those reactions as latent homosexual feelings; this can later lead to identity confusion. The male survivor often directs anger towards himself for not protecting himself from another male, and therefore views himself as unmanly (Struve, 1990). His attempts to overcompensate for this failure may result in exaggerated 'macho behaviours', homophobia, sexually aggressive behaviours, and, in some cases, sexual offending.

Abuse by females

Little is known about abuse of both males and females by female offenders. Kasl (1990) suggested that the prevalence of childhood sexual abuse by female offenders is higher than originally believed. Finkelhor and Russell (1984) estimated that approximately 24 per cent of male victims and 13 per cent of female victims are abused by females. These females were often acting in conjunction with another offender. The under-reporting of abuse by females, especially in intra-familial situations, might be due to society's tendency to view males as aggressors and females as victims, or to possible differences in the types of offence committed by female offenders (Hetherton, 1999). Offences by female offenders may be less overt and embedded in typical parenting behaviours (e.g. caressing the child while bathing him or her, becoming sexual with a child while 'cuddling' in bed) (Hetherton, 1999).

Because so little is known about abuse by female offenders, it is premature to identify any specific counselling needs of survivors. In many situations, however, it is believed that abuse by females is male-coerced and often accompanied by sexual and emotional abuse by both parents (Matthews et al., 1990). It is likely that the counselling needs of these survivors are quite complex. Some researchers have examined men who were abused by their mothers (Etherington, 1997) and report that these men may feel particularly ashamed and confused about their sexuality. In addition, they may have particular concerns about their own parenting.

Another scenario of abuse by females involves the extra-familial abuse of a younger male by an older woman, such as that between teacher and student. Often each party considers this to be a 'love affair'. Due to cultural influences, the male might not consider his experience abusive, but may experience long-term effects that he does not understand. Denial would be a significant counselling issue in this instance.

Structure of book

This book will first address counselling implications of the false memory debate and review outcomes of research on abuse-focused psychotherapeutic approaches.

This book will then discuss the counselling of adult survivors of childhood sexual abuse by identifying significant healing processes thought to be necessary for recovery. These processes include disclosing the abuse, focusing on the abuse experience, reinterpreting the abuse from an adult perspective, addressing issues related to the context of the abuse, making desired life changes, and dealing with abuse resolution issues. As each of these processes is discussed, counselling interventions that facilitate resolution will be outlined. Common dynamics and difficulties in therapeutic relationships with survivors are addressed.

The book will not discuss specific issues and interventions that are applicable to varied types of childhood sexual abuse (e.g. same-sex and specific opposite-sex abuse, abuse of males and females). An effort will be made, however, to avoid the assumption of 'universality' (Sepler, 1990) by addressing significant differences between abuse experiences, when applicable.

Specific relationship combinations of offenders and survivors (e.g. father–daughter, brother–sister, stranger–child) will not be addressed separately. Although the impact of the relationship between the victim and the offender is significant, relationship variables are complex; factors other than the formal relationship between the two may be important, including the emotional closeness or amount of authority possessed by the offender. Most survivors who seek treatment as adults are dealing with abuse that occurred in the context of their intimate social world and this will be the primary focus of the book.

In most instances, case examples described and interventions recommended are drawn from the authors' clinical and research experiences with survivors. To ensure anonymity of individual clients and research participants, all names are changed and identifying facts are disguised. To protect confidentiality further, some clinical examples are actually composites of several cases.

When the client referred to is an adult who was abused as a child, the term 'survivor' will be used to avoid the connotations associated with the label of 'victim'. When the client is a child who is experiencing abuse, the term 'victim' will be used to emphasize his or her inability to consent to the sexual activity. In all cases, clients who are dealing with childhood sexual abuse are considered individuals who have shared a common traumatic experience, but who have unique needs, desires, and strengths.

In addition to presenting a counselling model based on essential healing processes, several future directions and trends in counselling adult survivors are addressed. Discussions of advances in understanding the neurobiology of trauma, principles of multicultural counselling, and complementary treatment approaches are included in the final chapter.

2 The False Memory Debate: Counselling Implications

Counsellors who work with adult survivors of childhood sexual abuse will undoubtedly confront issues raised by the controversy related to the phenomenon of recovered memories, i.e. the recall of traumatic events not previously remembered. Courtois has suggested that three issues comprise the false memory debate: 'whether trauma can be forgotten and then remembered, the accuracy and credibility of memories of CSA [childhood sexual abuse], and the role of therapist influence on memory' (1999: 81). One cadre of experts maintains that recovered memories are confabulations that are typically iatrogenic in nature; that is, they are induced by questionable therapeutic practices or the self-help literature. This view is endorsed by the False Memory Syndrome Foundation (FMSF) in the United States and the British False Memory Society (BFMS) in the United Kingdom. Both of these organizations are well-funded coalitions of parents accused of abuse by their adult children and professionals who question the phenomenon of recovered memories (Sinason, 1998). Opponents maintain that recovered memories are typically accurate and should not be met with scepticism by clinicians. The counselling implications of the controversy will be discussed.

Trauma theory

Theories regarding the nature of traumatic memories are the basis for many counselling processes used with adult survivors of childhood sexual abuse, and are at the root of the false memory debate. Traumatologists argue that memories of traumatic experiences, defined as overwhelming events outside of the realm of normal experience, are encoded, stored, and retrieved differently than are memories for ordinary events (Horowitz, 1976; Janet, 1925/1976; van der Kolk and van der Hart, 1991). Because traumatic memories do not fit existing cognitive schemata, they may not be integrated with ordinary verbal autobiographical memory or incorporated in one's conscious self-representation (Brown et al., 1998).

Traumatic memory loss is best understood as one type of defensive dissociation. Braun (1988) identified four parameters of experience: behaviour, affect, somatic sensation, and knowledge. When an individual experiences a traumatic event, these parameters of experience can become disconnected (dissociated) as a defence against overwhelming affect. Defensive dissociation may include numbing (separation of feelings from awareness of current events), derealization (sense of detachment from surroundings), depersonalization (sense of detachment from one's body), and dissociative amnesia (inability to recall events or periods of time). Dissociative identity disorder (DID) involves a sense of internal fragmentation of the self (Chu, 1998). Post-traumatic stress disorder (PTSD) involves a numbing phase (the dissociation of traumatic events from cognitive awareness) that alternates with an intrusive phase (the return of awareness of traumatic events through thoughts, dreams, and flashbacks). The severity of the dissociative symptoms seems to be associated with the severity of the early trauma (Chu, 1998). Repression, the involuntary, selective forgetting of material that causes pain (Holmes, 1990), is therefore only one manifestation of dissociation associated with traumatic experiences.

Most trauma experts believe that traumatic memories are less malleable than ordinary memories because they are not subjected to the same processing mechanisms, such as transformations, deletions, and insertions. Dissociated traumatic memories can nonetheless implicitly influence consciousness and return intrusively as fragmentary sensory or motor experiences (Brown et al., 1998). Because the storage of traumatic memories is state- or context-dependent, memories can be triggered by situations reminiscent of the original trauma (contextual cues) or by emotional and physiological arousal or sensory stimulation associated with the trauma (state cues). Retrieved traumatic memories are often accompanied by intense physiological arousal and affective distress. Recovery from trauma involves the transformation of traumatic memories into narrative language and the integration of such memories into existing mental schemata. Brown et al. concluded that: 'to the extent that traumatic memory remains dissociated, the basic assumption guiding treatment is the integration of dissociated memory components' (1998: 440).

The false memory perspective

False memory proponents question the basic tenets of trauma theory – most specifically, the concept of repression. They often cite a critical review of the research literature by Holmes (1990), who concluded that there is little scientific validation of the existence of repression, and challenge clinical reports indicating that a large percentage of survivors of childhood trauma suffer from some degree of amnesia. Much of the false memory argument is based on laboratory research that demonstrates the malleability of human memory (Lindsay and Read, 1994).

One line of research has investigated the misleading information effect. In a typical experimental paradigm, subjects are asked to witness pictures, slides, or videotapes of an event in a laboratory setting, are given misleading suggestions or questions regarding some details of the event, and are tested on their memories of the event. In many experiments, subjects report events or details consistent with the misleading information (Lindsay, 1990, 1994; Weingardt et al., 1994). Some subjects express confidence in their illusory memories and provide vivid and detailed descriptions of inaccurate details.

Researchers have demonstrated that memory suggestibility for misleading post-event information is increased by several factors: delay between the event and attempts at recall; the perceived authority of the source of misleading information; repetition of false statements; plausible rather than implausible suggestions; and the use of lax memory-monitoring criteria, such as being asked to respond only with a 'yes' or a 'no' to memory items or being encouraged to guess

(Lindsay and Read, 1994). In a similar paradigm, children are interrogated by adult interviewers about an event they have witnessed (Ceci and Bruck, 1993; Ceci et al., 1994). After repeated, misleading questioning, some children report events that never occurred. As the interrogation continues, they often provide increasing detail about the fictitious events.

Another line of research has demonstrated that individuals can be led to experience pseudo-memories of fabricated childhood events in the laboratory setting (Hyman et al., 1995; Hyman and Pentland, 1996). In several experiments by Hyman and colleagues, investigators interviewed parents of college students to gather data on the students' childhood experiences. The students were asked to recall several real life events and a fictitious event, having been told that information regarding all the events had been supplied by parents or close relatives. When the students were repeatedly interviewed about all events, about 25 per cent eventually recalled the fictitious event. Susceptibility to false recall was increased by the plausibility of the event, suggestions by the investigator that mental practice (imagining, reflection) would improve recall, repeated trials of remembering, and by certain cognitive and personality variables.

An often-cited example of confabulation of real life events is drawn from a study involving a 14-year-old boy named Chris (Loftus, 1993). In a laboratory experiment, Jim, Chris' older brother, helped construct a fabricated childhood story that he then told to Chris. Chris was told that at the age of five he had been separated from his family at a shopping mall and was later found crying in the presence of an older man, who said that he was trying to help Chris find his parents. In addition to recalling the incident, on subsequent days Chris began to describe it more vividly, expanding on details originally provided by Jim. When told about the deception, Chris had difficulty believing that the event never occurred.

Research has also demonstrated that individuals may mistake memories of imagined events for real events, especially when the memories were formed during childhood (Lindsay and Read, 1994). Mentally rehearsing such events makes recollections more vivid and detailed. Individual differences may affect memory distortions. Individuals who are field dependent (rely heavily on environmental cues for perceptual judgements), depressed, or hypnotizable may be especially vulnerable to memory distortion (Lindsay and Read, 1994).

Drawing on these experimental data, false memory proponents suggest that certain therapeutic techniques aimed at memory recovery and self-help strategies for survivors of childhood trauma run the risk of implanting false memories in vulnerable individuals. Lindsay and Read, for example, suggested that:

> For present purposes, the important point is that many of the factors that memory researchers have found contribute to the likelihood of illusory memories (e.g. perceived authority of the source of suggestions, repetition of suggestions, communication of information that heightens the plausibility of the suggestions, encouragement to form images of suggested events and to reduce criteria for the acceptance of current mental experiences as memories) are typical of memory recovery therapies. (1994: 294)

Therapists and authors of self-help literature who suggest to individuals that they are 'likely' to have been sexually abused on the basis of suggestive histories and/or symptom profiles have been challenged by false memory proponents (Loftus, 1993). The incest book industry was heavily criticized, especially the popular book *The Courage to Heal* (Bass and Davis, 1994). Loftus questioned 'suggestions to readers that they were likely abused even if there are no memories, that repressed memories of abuse undoubtedly underlie one's troubles, or that benefits derive from uncovering repressed memories and believing them' (1993: 525). Loftus also criticized therapists who use intrusive probing to assess for a history of childhood sexual abuse or who persist in interrogating a client after the client indicates that he or she was not abused in childhood.

Specific therapeutic techniques, such as hypnosis, that are used to provoke or enhance repressed memories of childhood sexual abuse are the most suspect. Observers argue that individuals who experience vague or weak images under hypnosis are likely to report them as actual memories and, when in a waking state, they feel confident that these memories are accurate (Lindsay and Read, 1994). Similarly, procedures using guided imagery may place a client at risk of mistaking imagined events for actual occurrences. Proponents of the false memory perspective also object to therapeutic strategies that use uncritical free association, instructions to guess about past events, interpretation of suggestive dreams as unconscious messages about childhood sexual abuse, and interpretations of physical symptoms as 'body memories' of childhood sexual abuse (Lindsay and Read, 1994; Loftus, 1993). Survivor groups for individuals who have no abuse memories are criticized because such groups often reinforce the telling of abuse narratives and encourage members to assume the 'survivor' role. Madden (1998) warned that the following techniques have been associated with the creation of false memories in legal proceedings: guided imagery, age regression, journalling, dream work and interpretation, eye movement desensitization and reprocessing (EMDR), art therapy, feelings/emotional release work, group therapy, and bibliotherapy.

The rebuttal

The false memory perspective has been criticized on several grounds. Conte (1999) challenged the argument that there is no scientific evidence for the existence of repression. He argued that Holmes' (1990) review focused only on laboratory research and pointed out that Holmes himself stressed that the lack of empirical evidence for regression should not be interpreted as suggesting that repression does not exist, only that it has not been proven in the laboratory. Based on the results of several clinical studies (Briere and Conte, 1993; Cameron, 1994; Gold et al., 1994; Herman and Schatzow, 1987), several experts have argued that some degree of amnesia is relatively common among adult survivors of childhood trauma (Chu, 1998; Harvey, 1999). In a study conducted by Williams (1994), for example, 38 per cent of 129 women who had childhood abuse experiences that were documented by medical and social service records did not recall these events during an interview 17 years later.

Conte (1999) critiqued laboratory research findings related to the misinformation effect. He argued that much of this research involves subjects who have no personal investment in events to be remembered, provides no data indicating how much effort is needed to produce what effect or whether misinformation effects are resistant to change, and does not address what intrapersonal factors (IQ, stress level, emotional state) increase susceptibility to the effect. Conte also pointed out that the rate of error in these experiments tends to be low (less than 20 per cent). He recommended that future memory researchers focus on events more similar to actual abuse and trauma incidents and involve individuals more similar to those likely to be affected by memory issues, for example, those seeking psychotherapy for help with anxiety, depression, or other troubling emotions.

Research findings related to the creation of pseudo-memories have also been questioned because the responses of the subjects in these experiments are likely to be influenced by the expectations of the investigator (Conte, 1999). Additionally, subjects are given information supposedly provided by individuals who should have the most accurate knowledge about their childhood, i.e. their own parents and close relatives.

Finally, Conte challenged the conclusions of false memory proponents that certain therapy techniques create false memories. He cautioned that there is no research evidence to support criticisms that guided imagery, journalling, dream interpretation, and survivor groups produce false memories of childhood sexual abuse.

Professional response

Professional organizations in the United States and Great Britain have responded to the controversy by forming work groups to investigate the state of the science related to memory retrieval and to propose recommendations for practitioners. In 1998, the American Psychological Association (APA) Working Group on Investigation of Memories of Child Abuse presented their final conclusions, including points of agreement and disagreement and implications for clinical practice. After an extensive review of literature related to memories of child abuse, the Working Group outlined areas of agreement:

1　Controversies regarding adult recollections should not be allowed to obscure the fact that child sexual abuse is a complex and pervasive problem in America that has historically gone unacknowledged.
2　Most people who were sexually abused as children remember all or part of what happened to them.
3　It is possible for memories of abuse that have been forgotten for a long time to be remembered.
4　It is also possible to construct convincing pseudomemories for events that never occurred.
5　There are gaps in our knowledge about the processes that lead to accurate and inaccurate recollections of childhood abuse. (APA Working Group, 1998: 933)

The Working Group also acknowledged an inability to reach consensus in a number of areas due to the 'profound epistemological differences' (1998: 934) between the psychological scientists and the psychological practitioners in the group. Areas of dispute included the accuracy with which events can be remembered over time, the mechanisms that underlie delayed remembering, the uniqueness of memories for traumatic events, the frequency with which pseudomemories can be created by suggestion, and the ease with which real memories and pseudomemories can be distinguished without outside corroboration (APA, 1998).

Despite these differences, the group presented several implications for practice. They recommend that therapists should be well versed in developmental psychology, cognitive psychology, particularly the study of memory, and research on trauma. They also recommended that 'care, caution, and consistency' (1998: 935) should be used with all clients, especially those who experience what is believed to be a recovered memory of trauma. Therapists should provide clients with information about a variety of possible treatment strategies, the opportunity to provide informed consent for treatment, and a comprehensive assessment that addresses a range of risk factors. When clients experience what they believe to be memories of previously unrecalled events, therapists should reduce the risk of creation of false memories and avoid endorsing these retrievals as either clearly factual or clearly confabulated. Clients should be informed that hypnosis is not recommended for the purpose of retrieving or confirming memories of trauma.

Similarly, the Professional Affairs group of the British Psychological Society (BPS) set up a working party to develop guidelines for practitioners working with those likely to be at risk for false memory. They presented a draft of the Guidelines to their membership in 1999 (Frankland and Cohen, 1999). Like the APA report, this group stressed that practitioners should have up-to-date knowledge regarding theory and research concerning memory. The Guidelines state that CSA is a serious social problem and that at least some recovered memories of CSA reflect historical events. However, the Guidelines caution that some psychological interventions may foster false beliefs and lead to illusory memories. The guidelines include a recommendation that psychologists remain open to the emergence of previously unrecalled memories of trauma, but avoid drawing conclusions prematurely about the historical truth of the memory. Psychologists are cautioned that the issue of whether traumatic memories are processed differently than normal memories is not yet determined, and they must tolerate the uncertainty of memories of early experiences. The Guidelines state, 'Psychologists should be alert to a range of possibilities, for example, that a recovered memory may be literally/historically true or false, or may be partly true, thematically true, or metaphorically true or may derive from fantasy or dream material' (1999: 83). Psychologists are cautioned not to diagnose CSA on the basis of a symptom checklist and to avoid the use of techniques such as hypnosis for the primary purpose of memory retrieval. The Guidelines also stress that psychologists should be aware of the impact of their work on clients' families and social networks.

Guidelines put forth by professional organizations have been critiqued. Madill and Holch, for example, argue that guidelines such as those proposed by the BPS 'are notoriously difficult to implement and are open to interpretation' (2004: 306) and suggest that researcher–clinician collaboration is needed to develop ecologically valid research paradigms.

Brown (2004) reviewed scientific developments related to the phenomenon of delayed recall that have occurred since the APA and BPS reports. One area of research that has been advanced since the publication of the reports is investigations of the somatosensory modalities of processing information. Brown reviewed the results of van der Kolk's (1996) research using active imagining technology during trauma recall:

> Brains of traumatized individuals were highly activated in the limbic system, particularly the amygdala, and in sensory areas, particularly the visual context. However, in these same brains, Broca's area, from which verbal language and speech are derived, was deactivated, as was the prefrontal cortex. These findings strongly suggest that memory for trauma is, in general, stored as sensory and raw affective data that is not yet integrated into the cognitive, verbal form taken by memories for everyday events. (Brown, 2004: 193)

Such research supports the belief that traumatic memories are processed differently than are memories for ordinary events.

Another scientific advancement discussed by Brown (2004) is the betrayal trauma (BT) model, a sociocognitive model developed by Freyd and colleagues (2001) to explain the forgetting and later recall of childhood sexual abuse. The model argues that children have an evolutionary mandate to maintain an attachment to their caretakers as well as to detect betrayal, because both functions are necessary for survival. If a child is betrayed by a primary caretaker, the need for attachment takes precedence over the need to detect betrayal. When a child is sexually abused, therefore, he or she develops cognitive mechanisms to maintain the attachment and ward off recognition of the betrayal. When the attachment is no longer necessary for survival, knowledge of the betrayal can be accessed. Research by Freyd and colleagues (2001) provide support for this model by demonstrating that less persistent memories for childhood sexual abuse are more strongly associated with betrayal by a caretaker than by typically implicated factors such as severity and intensity of the abuse, even when the child's age at the time of the abuse and the duration of the abuse are considered.

Another line of cognitive research that explains the phenomenon of delayed recall of CSA is the inhibitory memory model (Brown, 2004). This model suggests that 'attention to one thing that is paired with a stimulus cue will actively inhibit retrieval of other things paired with that stimulus cue. Rehearsal of the first pair will inhibit other pairs' (2004: 202). Anderson (1998) applied these principles to memory for CSA, arguing that if the perpetrator is coded in the child's memory in ways other than as abusive, the memory for the abuse will be inhibited by the more frequently rehearsed construction of that individual. If the cue 'grandfather', for example, is paired with the social construction of 'good and loving', that pairing will crowd out the less frequent pairing of 'grandfather' and 'abusive'. The pairing of 'grandfather' and 'abusive' will be stored, but will be less available for retrieval and therefore experienced as forgotten.

Implications for counsellors

Experts generally call for a reasoned, balanced perspective that is informed by emerging information on the complex topic of traumatic memory (Brown et al., 1998; Chu, 1998; Courtois, 1999). Recommendations for counsellors who work with clients who have sustained trauma, especially regarding memory issues, have been proposed. There is general consensus that counsellors should operate from a broad knowledge base and maintain an 'open, reflective and neutral' (Courtois, 1999: 271) stance regarding memory issues, recognizing that memory is fluid, malleable, and reconstructive. Counsellors who work with trauma survivors must stay current with the rapid proliferation of knowledge related to trauma and memory, and ongoing supervision, consultation, and periodic review of treatment plans are crucial.

Brown et al. (1998) argued that the term 'memory recovery therapy' is a misnomer for contemporary trauma treatment in so far as the primary goal of treatment is rarely memory retrieval. Trauma therapy typically has a number of treatment foci. Memory enhancement may be one component of treatment and is used only when indicated (as discussed in Chapter 5). Memory work should always serve the purpose of integration; that is, trauma-related symptoms and behavioural re-enactments are translated into a coherent narrative for the purpose of finding meaning in one's history and gaining mastery of the trauma (Brown et al., 1998). Counsellors should always conduct a comprehensive assessment that focuses on a multitude of life issues and should develop a comprehensive and integrated treatment plan addressing all issues, not just those related to abuse.

An assessment for risk of false memory production is indicated before beginning any memory work (Brown et al., 1998; Courtois, 1999). The following client characteristics may indicate susceptibility: high level of hypnotizability or interrogatory suggestibility, certain personality factors (immaturity, dependence, external locus of control) or disorders (hysteria, borderline, antisocial), depression, and dissociative states. Counsellors should ascertain what memories clients have of childhood trauma when treatment begins to provide a baseline for any later recovery of trauma memories.

Counsellors should neither unequivocally validate nor automatically disbelieve recovered or continuous trauma memories presented by clients in therapy. Free narrative recall, in which clients are encouraged to discuss thoughts, feelings, and experiences in response to open-ended, non-suggestive questioning, often yields significant information about past events without increasing the risk of memory error (Brown et al., 1998). Often, even in instances of full or partial amnesia, no special memory enhancement techniques are required. Gold and Brown stated: 'when clients are allowed to develop sufficient coping abilities and trust in therapy relationships, recall of previously traumatic material will occur relatively spontaneously, without leading or prodding' (1997: 186). Client-driven recall fosters a sense of control and mastery.

Counsellors, therefore, should avoid leading or close-ended questions, premature conclusions, and uncritical acceptance of memories as historical truths. Regressive techniques and the use of hypnosis for memory retrieval are generally discouraged (Brown et al., 1998; Courtois, 1999).

Informed consent is an important aspect of trauma work, especially when memory issues are involved. Each client should be provided with information alerting him or her to the general office policies and procedures (e.g. payment for services, the limits of confidentiality, interactions with third-party payers). The basic elements, parameters, and risks and benefits of counselling in general should be discussed (Madden, 1998). If memory integration may be a component of treatment, accurate and detailed information regarding the nature of memory and memory retrieval should be provided. Brown et al. (1998) recommend that clients be informed that memories contain a blend of accurate and inaccurate information and that even memories that are emotionally compelling may be inaccurate with respect to historical truth. Common errors in memory, such as detail reconstruction, source misattribution, and confabulation, should be discussed. If any specialized memory enhancement interventions are used, specific information should be provided regarding the anticipated duration and cost, the advantages and disadvantages, and available alternatives. Possible risks should be clearly delineated.

The impact of counselling on third parties has also received closer scrutiny due to the false memory controversy. Trauma clinicians are advised to refrain from recommending that clients separate from family members who have abused or wronged them. If a current family relationship presents a danger, the counsellor may assist the client in determining the steps needed to ensure safety (Courtois, 1999). If a family member is invited to a treatment session, counsellors should be aware that this might imply a professional treatment relationship – and, therefore, a duty owed – to that person (Brown et al., 1998). Several experts have also stressed that it is inappropriate for a counsellor to recommend litigation (Brown et al., 1998; Courtois, 1999). If clients opt to instigate a lawsuit, the counsellor should help them explore their thoughts and feelings related to this choice and gather pertinent information regarding the legal process in their local area. Brown et al. argued that 'therapists should caution adult patients against impulsive actions of any kind based on information uncovered in psychotherapy or hypnotherapy, encouraging them to evaluate thoughtfully and critically this material for a substantial period of time, as well as consider potential negative consequences of confrontation or disclosure of this information' (1998: 503).

Thorough documentation of clinical work with trauma survivors is critical (Brown et al., 1998; Courtois, 1999). Counsellors' records should reflect that they have discussed the dynamics of memory, including issues of adequacy and completeness, with clients for whom abuse memories may be a pertinent issue. All notes should reflect a neutral and objective stance regarding the accuracy of recovered memories. For example, the records should indicate that the counsellor avoided suggestive influence, critically evaluated memories retrieved in therapy, and refrained from encouraging impulsive actions that might be injurious to third parties. When techniques with a high risk of suggestibility are used, detailed documentation should accompany each procedure.

Case example

The following case vignette highlights problems resulting from clinical errors related to memory retrieval. Jason, a 32-year-old maintenance worker at a local industry, sought counseling following an arrest for driving under the influence of alcohol. On intake, he revealed a number of life concerns, including alcohol abuse, an inability to maintain a long-term relationship with a woman, sexual dysfunction, and sleep difficulties, including frequent nightmares.

(Continued)

(Continued)

He reported that his family of origin was 'pretty normal'. He revealed that his father was a strict disciplinarian, who often punished him and his two older brothers by beating them with a belt. He said he was very close to his mother, who would often hug and comfort him after each beating. He also indicated that he had a sense that she would 'tend to his wounds' after each beating, but said he did not remember much more about the beatings. He described his mother as desperately unhappy in her marriage and believed that she might have been hospitalized several times for depression. He stated that he was a 'loner, geek' in school and would not have survived his childhood had it not been for her support.

Jason lived by himself and had been at his current job for ten years. He continued to enjoy a good relationship with his mother, despite her becoming increasingly needy due to her failing health. His brothers often teased Jason that he was a 'mama's boy' because he spent a good deal of time with her. Jason had few other social contacts apart from two 'drinking buddies'.

After several sessions, he stated that he thought maybe 'something happened' between him and his mother that wasn't quite right.

Jason:	I am thinking that maybe something went on that wasn't really right, if you know what I mean. Maybe we were too close and affectionate.
Counsellor:	Do you mean in a sexual way?
Jason:	I don't know if it was sexual, just sort of weird. What do you mean by sexual?
Counsellor:	Well, you said your mother tended to your wounds after your father beat you. Were the wounds on your buttocks or private parts?
Jason:	I guess. I don't really remember very much. You think I might have been sexually abused?
Counsellor:	Well, your discomfort and feeling that 'something happened' might suggest that.
Jason:	My mother was very good to me. She was a little odd, but that doesn't mean … I sure don't remember anything happening, but, well, I do remember my brothers making fun of how much she 'loved' me.
Counsellor:	I think it is important that we explore this further. Often, individuals forget sexual abuse because it is traumatic. Some of your symptoms, especially your problems relating to women, might be due to abuse by your mother.

As the counselling relationship progressed, the counsellor continued to focus on the relationship Jason had with his mother, suggesting this might be the 'root' of his problems. Jason revealed that after talking about his mother so much in counselling, he began to have dreams of her in her 'nightgown'. When he shared this with the counsellor, she gave him feedback that he was becoming stronger because he was remembering events that were most likely painful. She recommended that they spend a session focusing on remembering as much as he could about what happened when his mother was in the nightgown. Jason initially lamented that he had a sense that 'something' happened, but had no clear memory. His counsellor reassured him that this was normal, that clearer memories would come to him as they continued their work together. She then had Jason relax, close his eyes, and visualize his mother as a younger woman wearing the nightgown that appeared in his dreams.

(Continued)

(Continued)

After several sessions using this technique, Jason began to remember more and more about his mother 'tending to his wounds' and had a 'breakthrough' memory of her fondling him in the bathtub. Jason was distraught at this memory, but the counsellor assured him that it was necessary for his healing.

Jason decided to cut off contact with his mother, who was alarmed by the sudden change in Jason's attitude toward her. Jason claimed that he felt better because he now had an understanding 'of what had been wrong all those years'. However, his drinking increased. When he was reprimanded by his supervisor for missing too much work in a manner he felt to be degrading, he lashed out at her, stating 'All you women are alike. You just want to control us. Go to hell.' He was suspended for two weeks without pay. The counsellor lauded Jason's actions because he had been 'assertive' with a woman for the first time.

In this case, the counsellor made several errors related to memory retrieval. When Jason indicated that he experienced that something was 'not quite right' between him and his mother, the counsellor did not encourage him to explore the meaning of 'not quite right', but suggested that his mother was sexually abusive. Her questions and comments were leading and suggestive. She further implied that the symptoms he experienced as an adult, especially his problems with women, were likely to stem from early sexual abuse and abandoned discussion of other problematic early experiences, including the clearly remembered severe physical abuse by his father. By encouraging Jason to focus on as many details as he could related to seeing his mother in her nightgown, using a guided imagery technique to retrieve memories, and praising Jason when he began to 'recover' memories of early abuse, she may have contributed to Jason retrieving memories that were unreliable but of which he eventually became more confident. The counsellor failed to maintain an open and objective stance regarding Jason's memories and immediately validated them as objective, historical truth.

The appropriate response to Jason's unease that something was 'not right' in his relationship with his mother would have been to explore his experiences in an open-ended, non-leading manner using free-recall techniques. The counsellor should have facilitated Jason in achieving his own sense of what was credible, avoided the creation of pseudomemories by using suggestive techniques such as guided imagery, and focused on a range of historical and contemporaneous experiences that might be associated with Jason's current troubles. Jason would have benefited from a discussion of the multiple possibilities regarding retrieved material, ranging from 'reasonably accurate memory of real events' to 'a form of self-suggestion emerging from the client's internal suggestive mechanisms' (APA, 1998: 936). As Jason's drinking increased and he began to experience outbursts that interfered with his current work situation, the focus of the counselling should have been on stabilization rather than on memory retrieval. The impact of Jason's retrieved memories on his relationship with his mother, which had been primarily positive, should have been considered.

Phase-oriented treatment

The controversy has prompted trauma clinicians to develop a standard of care for trauma treatment and to identify acceptable practice parameters (Madden, 1998). Numerous experts agree that a phase-oriented treatment is the most acceptable

Table 2.1 Phase-oriented treatment models for adult survivors of childhood sexual abuse

Author	Phase		
	I	II	III
Courtois (1999)	Early phase ■ establishment of treatment parameters ■ development of therapeutic relationship and working alliance ■ maintenance of personal safety and relative life stability ■ development of additional sources of support ■ attention to self-functions and symptom management skills	Middle phase ■ deconditioning (graduated and controlled exposure to traumatic material) ■ mourning ■ resolution and integration of trauma	Late phase ■ self and relational development ■ life reconsolidation and restructuring
Herman (1992)	Establishing safety ■ naming the problem through diagnostic evaluation ■ restoring control of body ■ establishing a safe environment	Remembrance and mourning ■ reconstructing the story ■ transforming traumatic memory ■ mourning traumatic loss	Reconnection ■ learning to fight (taking power in real life situations) ■ reconciling with oneself ■ reconnecting with others ■ finding a survivor mission ■ resolving the trauma
Chu (1998)	Early-stage treatment ■ self-care ■ symptom control ■ acknowledgment of trauma ■ functioning ■ expression of affect ■ establishing mutual and collaborative relationships	Middle-stage treatment (abreaction) ■ increased symptomatology ■ intense internal conflict ■ acceptance and mourning ■ mobilization and empowerment	Late-stage treatment ■ consolidation of gains ■ increasing skills in creating healthy interactions with outside world

approach for working with trauma victims, including adult survivors of child-hood sexual abuse. Phase-oriented treatment 'divides the overall treatment into discrete phases or stages of treatment, each with its own treatment objectives or goals' (Brown et al., 1998: 437). There is much consensus in the literature regarding the stages, nature, and goals of treatment. Several authors describe an early phase of treatment that focuses on stabilization and mastery, including building the therapeutic relationship, attenuation and containment of stress-related symptomatology, establishing safety, and coping with current life problems. The second phase typically involves the integration of traumatic memories. A final phase often focuses on self-development, relational development, or adaptation to daily life. Three examples of phase-oriented treatment models applicable to adult survivors of childhood sexual abuse are presented in Table 2.1.

3 Outcomes Research on Abuse-focused Psychotherapy Approaches

Outcomes research

The selection of one psychotherapeutic approach over another should be based on empirical evidence that the selected approach is the one that works best in reducing psychological distress, enhancing interpersonal relationships, and/or improving physical health for a particular population (Speer, 1998). Outcomes research needs to be conducted on the abuse-focused psychotherapy approaches used in clinical practice.

Outcomes research in mental health is a growing field (Speer, 1998). The literature related to various psychotherapy approaches for some populations is quite large and allows general conclusions to be drawn about the efficacy of an approach. Most studies examine the efficacy of an approach in reducing symptoms for a particular *Diagnostic and Statistical Manual* (DSMIV) (American Psychiatric Association, 1994) diagnostic category, e.g. major depressive disorder. Conclusions about treatment efficacy are based on changes in client outcomes and are categorized as:

- empirically supported (numerous independent research studies with similar findings);
- efficacious (similar findings from two independent research sites); and
- possibly efficacious (supportive findings from one study).

(Kendall et al., 2004)

Psychotherapeutic approaches that have been 'shown to be efficacious in randomized clinical research trials with given populations' (Kendall et al., 2004: 17) are termed 'empirically-supported' therapies.

The key characteristics of an empirically-supported therapy are:

- The therapy has been compared with a no-treatment control group, alternative treatment group, or placebo.
- The comparison occurred in a randomized clinical trial, controlled single-case experiment, or equivalent time-samples design.
- The therapy was shown to be significantly more effective than no treatment, alternative treatment, or placebo.
- The treatment is documented in a treatment manual or similar guiding document.
- The treatment was examined in a very specific population and inclusion criteria were strictly applied.
- Outcome measures were reliable and valid, and measured appropriate outcomes for the population.
- Data analysis was well conducted.

Outcomes research on psychotherapy for survivors

No treatments for adult survivors of childhood sexual abuse have been deemed empirically supported. Because these survivors often do not have symptoms specific to any one DSMIV category, outcomes research based on reduction of a primary symptom is problematic. Research does indicate, however, that many survivors experience a similar constellation of symptoms, and research on approaches that are effective and efficacious for this population is highly warranted.

An exhaustive search of CINAHL, Medline, and PsychINFO databases yielded 29 outcome studies related to adult survivors of childhood sexual abuse. In each of these studies, the researchers described the use of at least one abuse-focused psychotherapeutic approach, and quantitative methods were used to measure outcomes considered target behaviours or symptoms addressed by the therapy. Because the first study was conducted in 1986, this area of inquiry is in its early stages. Only five studies met the criteria for a randomized study. The remaining studies used pre-test/post-test (12 studies) or quasi-experimental (12 studies) designs. Pre-test/post-test studies typically measure target behaviours or symptoms before the subjects engage in the psychotherapeutic approach and again at the completion of therapy. Before-treatment and after-treatment measurements are compared, but these studies lack a control group against which to make comparisons. Quasi-experimental studies typically measure target behaviours or symptoms before and after a group of subjects engage in the psychotherapeutic approach. A control group or comparison group consists of those who received an alternative treatment or who want to receive treatment. Quasi-experimental studies differ from randomized clinical studies in that subjects in quasi-experimental studies are not randomly assigned to groups (Powers and Knapp, 1995).

Randomized outcomes studies

The five studies in which participants were randomly assigned to treatment, no-treatment, or alternative treatment groups examined five different treatment approaches. The five approaches were: an affect-management group (Zlotnick et al., 1997); a feminist theory-based group and individual therapy (Stalker and Fry, 1999); eye movement desensitization and reprocessing (Edmond et al., 1999); an interpersonal transaction group and a process group (Alexander et al., 1989); and a symbolic confrontation group (Apolinsky and Wilcoxon, 1991). Table 3.1 summarizes the key characteristics of these studies according to: type of treatment; type of comparison group; use of a manual; target outcome; validity and reliability of measures, inclusion criteria; type of data analysis; and results.

A review of Table 3.1 suggests that no abuse-focused psychotherapeutic approach for adult survivors of childhood sexual abuse has been determined to be an empirically-supported treatment. Each of the five approaches was shown to be efficacious when compared to an alternative or non-treatment condition, and can therefore be classified as 'possibly efficacious'. Furthermore, sample sizes were relatively small, thereby limiting the generalizations that can be made. An additional challenge with this group of studies is that the target outcomes varied. Depression, as measured by the Beck Depression Inventory (Beck and Steer, 1993),

Table 3.1 Randomized studies

Researchers	Type of treatment	Comparison group	Used manual?	Target outcome	Validity and reliability of outcome measures	Inclusion criteria	Data analysis	Results
Alexander et al. (1989)	10-week interpersonal transaction group	10-week process group wait-list control	Uncertain. Groups were described briefly; no discussion of a written manual.	Depression	Beck Depression Inventory – no validity or reliability discussion.	1. Woman 2. Abused by father or step-father. 3. > 18 years 4. Not in concurrent individual therapy (6 participants were abused by brother or uncle).	Repeated-measures multivariate analysis of variance at pre-treatment and post-treatment across the treatment and two comparison groups.	Treatment groups showed greater improvement on measures of depression and psychological distress than wait-list group; changes were maintained at 6 months.
				Social adjustment	Social Adjustment Scale – originally normed on 40 depressed and 40 normal women; interrater reliability in this study 0.90.			
				Psychological distress	SCL-90-R – internal consistency 0.77–0.90; test/retest 0.78–0.90.			
				Fears of rape victims	Modified Fear Survey – shown to be successful			

(Continued)

Table 3.1 (Continued)

Researchers	Type of treatment	Comparison group	Used manual?	Target outcome	Validity and reliability of outcome measures	Inclusion criteria	Data analysis	Results
Edmond et al. (1999)	6 individual sessions of eye movement desensitization and reprocessing (N = 20)	6-session routine individual treatment (N = 20) Delayed treatment (N = 19)	Description of the treatment indicates that specific protocols exist for each of 8 phases of treatment. It is implied that this protocol was used.	State anxiety	State–Trait Anxiety Inventory – construct validity reported; concurrent validity with 2 other scales; internal consistency 0.90; test/retest is low.	1. Adult female survivor 2. No previous EMDR exposure 3. No contraindications for EMDR (e.g. ocular problems) 4. Not receiving concurrent therapy.	Multivariate analysis of variance	EMDR group showed greater improvement on measures of trauma-specific anxiety, depression, trauma-specific post-traumatic stress, and negative beliefs. Improvements in anxiety and depression were maintained at 3-month follow-up.
				Post-traumatic stress symptoms	Impact of Events Scale – internal consistency 0.79–0.92.			
				Depression	Beck Depression Inventory – internal consistency 0.78–0.93; test/retest 0.48–0.74.			

(Continued)

Table 3.1 (Continued)

Researchers	Type of treatment	Comparison group	Used manual?	Target outcome	Validity and reliability of outcome measures	Inclusion criteria	Data analysis	Results
					in discriminating rape from non-rape victims; internal consistency 0.98; test–retest 0.73			
Apolinsky and Wilcoxon (1991)	10-week eclectic group with symbolic confrontation (N = 15)	10-week eclectic group without symbolic confrontation (N = 15)	A manual is implied. Both groups followed the same weekly procedures, except that weeks 8 and 9 for the treatment group included the use of symbolic confrontation.	Depression Perception of self-worth and adequacy	Beck Depression Inventory – internal consistency of 0.79–0.90. Adult Self-perception Profile – reported internal consistency 0.61–0.91; factor analysis subscale loadings 0.65–0.89; concurrent validity between two groups (p<.05).	1. Over age 18 2. Female survivor 3. Able and willing to talk about abuse experiences. 4. Motivation for group participation.	Chi square analyses of pre-treatment scores; chi square analyses of post-treatment scores; paired t-tests on pre- and post-treatment scores.	Symbolic confrontation group had significant improvement in depression and self-concept. No change in the comparison group.

(Continued)

Table 3.1 (Continued)

Researchers	Type of treatment	Comparison group	Used manual?	Target outcome	Validity and reliability of outcome measures	Inclusion criteria	Data analysis	Results
				Distorted beliefs	Belief Inventory – test/retest 0.93. Concurrent validity 0.55.			
Stalker and Fry (1999)	10 sessions of group therapy (N = 33)	10 sessions of individual therapy (N = 32)	No manual. Early sessions had general topics to be covered.	Psychological symptoms	SCL-90-R – stated that the validity and reliability is well established.	1. Clear memory of at least one incident of sexual abuse under age 18.	Repeated measures analysis of variance. T-tests.	Both treatment groups showed significant improvement in psychiatric symptomatology and psychosocial functioning at post-therapy and at 6- and 12-month follow-up. Neither treatment modality was superior.
		Wait-list control	Later sessions were less structured.	Frequency of dissociative symptoms	Dissociative Experiences Scale – valid for discriminating persons with and without dissociative identity disorder; test/retest 0.84.	2. Abuse included physical contact. 3. Previously known perpetrator. 4. Touch was unwanted if during adolescence.		
				PTSD Symptoms	Post-Traumatic Stress Scale – split-half reliability 0.91. Validity established in two studies.	5. Consent to be randomly assigned to group or individual therapy.		

(Continued)

Table 3.1 (Continued)

Researchers	Type of treatment	Comparison group	Used manual?	Target outcome	Validity and reliability of outcome measures	Inclusion criteria	Data analysis	Results
				Traumatic Impact	Trauma Symptom Checklist – discriminates between sexually abused and non-abused individuals; reliability ranges 0.89–0.90.			
Zlotnick et al. (1997)	15-week affect management group (N = 17)	Wait-list control (N = 16)	Standardized manual outlines each session of the affect management group in detail.	PTSD symptoms	Clinician-administered PTSD Scale – states that it has sound psychometrics.	1. Female with history of sexual abuse before age 17. 2. Met criteria for PTSD. 3. In concurrent individual therapy.	Analysis of covariance	Treatment group showed significantly greater improvement in PTSD and dissociative symptoms than the comparison group.
				Frequency and severity of PTSD symptoms	Davidson Trauma Scale – states that scale has convergent and discriminant			

(Continued)

Table 3.1 (Continued)

Researchers	Type of treatment	Comparison group	Used manual?	Target outcome	Validity and reliability of outcome measures	Inclusion criteria	Data analysis	Results
					validity, internal consistency, and test/retest reliability SCL-90-R.			
				PTSD symptoms	Crime-related Post-traumatic Stress Scale – states that have high internal consistency and specificity for PTSD.			
				Dissociative experiences	Dissociative Experiences Scale – states that scale has adequate test/retest reliability and good split-half reliability and good clinical validity.			

and psychological distress, measured by the Symptom Checklist-90-R (Derogatis, 1992), were examined in several, but not all, studies. Additionally, researchers either did not use a treatment manual or implied the use of a manual through a description of the treatment sessions. Only one study (Zlotnik et al., 1997) included an explicit statement that a manual had been used.

Despite these limitations, research in the area of abuse-focused psychotherapy for adult survivors shows promise. Each of the five approaches discussed above was shown to be efficacious in a randomized study when compared to an alternative; in follow-up, most positive outcomes were maintained.

Pre-test/post-test outcomes studies

Twelve studies using a pre-test/post-test design examined individual approaches (Clarke and Llewelyn, 1994; Jehu et al., 1986; Paivio and Patterson, 1997), group approaches (Carver et al., 1989; Hall and King, 1997; Kreidler et al., 1999; Longstreth et al., 1998; Lubin et al., 1998; Roberts and Lie, 1989; Sultan and Long, 1988), a combination of individual and group (Chard et al., 1997), and partial hospital and inpatient therapies (Smith et al., 1995). While no two studies examined identical treatments, the approaches did cluster into cognitive, emotion-focused, process-focused, family, eclectic, and use of partial hospital/inpatient special care units. Treatment length varied from 10 to 50 sessions, with six studies examining approaches that lasted for 16 to 24 sessions. Sample size in the 12 studies ranged from 11 to 95, with only five studies examining samples of more than 50 participants (Carver et al., 1989; Hall and King, 1997; Kreidler et al., 1999; Roberts and Lie, 1989; Smith et al., 1995). Participants in all 12 studies showed significant improvements on outcome measures at the conclusion of the therapy.

Of the three pre-test/post-test studies that examined individual therapies, Jehu and colleagues (1986) recommended the most sessions (approximately 24). After participation in cognitive restructuring therapy, participants showed significant improvement on measures of distorted beliefs and depression. Clarke and Llewelyn (1994) examined the use of 16 weeks of a cognitive analytic therapy. The seven women in the study showed significant improvement in levels of depression, self-esteem, distorted beliefs, and general psychological distress. Paivio and Patterson (1997) investigated the effects of 20 weeks of emotion-focused individual therapy for 33 adults who had experienced childhood emotional, physical, and sexual abuse. Participants showed significant improvements in psychological distress and trauma symptoms.

Six studies used pre-test/post-test formats to examine the effects of group therapies for women who had experienced childhood sexual abuse. Sultan and Long (1988) enrolled 15 women who had been incarcerated into a 16-week psychodidactic support group. Participants showed significant improvements in self-esteem, trust in others, alienation, and perceived control. Carver and colleagues (1989) used an eclectic approach for female incest survivors. The 95 participants in the study were placed into one of three 10-week groups or one of seven 15-week groups. In general, the participants showed significant improvements on measures of psychiatric symptomatology, depression, and self-esteem. Hall and King (1997) used an open analytic group approach for 94 women survivors. Group members were expected to stay in the group for at least six months. The researchers were able to contact 79 of these women after they had completed the group, and 54 participants responded to questionnaires to determine levels of depression and overall satisfaction with the group. Participants who found the group to be most helpful were those whose depression scores had improved the most over the pre-test scores. A 16-week process-oriented group was studied by Longstreth and colleagues (1998). Nineteen women showed significant improvements on measures of psychiatric symptomatology at the conclusion of the group. Except for levels of hostility, these changes persisted after one year. Lubin and associates (1998) examined a 16-week, trauma-focused, cognitive-behavioural group therapy for multiply traumatized women diagnosed with chronic post-traumatic stress disorder (PTSD). Participants showed significant improvements on measures of PTSD and depression; these improvements were maintained at six-month follow-up. Kreidler and colleagues (1999) provided a 50-week group therapy using a family systems model for 72 female survivors. Some of the participants were considered severely and persistently mentally ill. Participants showed significant improvement on measures of self-esteem, depression, and psychiatric symptoms.

Two pre-test/post-test studies examined combination therapies or specialized therapy units. Chard and colleagues (1997) studied 15 women with a history of childhood sexual abuse who were being treated in a community mental health centre. Participants engaged in a 17-week, 26-session cognitive processing therapy in both individual and group formats. Participants showed significant improvement in PTSD symptoms and depression. A specialized unit offering care, therapy, and support was examined by Smith and colleagues (1995). Fifty-nine women with a history of childhood sexual abuse completed a battery of self-report questionnaires at the start and end of therapy. Participants showed significant improvement in measures of social activities, general health, delusions, and psychiatric symptoms.

Quasi-experimental outcomes studies

Twelve quasi-experimental studies examined various psychotherapeutic approaches for adult survivors, including individual (Clarke, 1993; Paivio and Nieuwenhuis, 2001), group (Bagley and Ramsey, 1986; Bagley and Young, 1998; Cloitre and Koenen, 2001; Morgan and Cummings, 1999; Morrison and Treliving, 2002; Richter et al., 1997; Saxe and Johnson, 1999; Wallis, 2002; Westbury and Tutty, 1999), and partial hospital and inpatient treatments (Talbot et al., 1999). The parameters of the approaches varied. Treatment length lasted from 8 to 20 sessions. One study examined long-term group therapy that lasted at least six months (Morrision and Treliving, 2002). Sample sizes ranged from 9 to 115, with only two samples of more than 50 participants (Richter et al., 1997; Wallis, 2002). In comparison to the wait-list control or alternative treatment groups, participants in the treatment groups in all 12 studies showed significant improvements on outcome measures at the conclusion of the therapy. Outcome measures differed greatly across studies; the outcome measure used most frequently was the Beck Depression Inventory (Beck and Steer, 1993), which was used in five studies

(Cloitre and Koenen, 2001; Morgan and Cummings, 1999; Richter et al., 1997; Saxe and Johnson, 1999; Westbury and Tutty, 1999).

Two quasi-experimental studies investigated individual therapies. Clarke (1993) compared an eight-week integrative constructivist form of individual therapy to an eight-week cognitive restructuring individual therapy. Each approach was used with a sample of nine women. Those women who experienced the individual constructivist therapy showed greater meaning resolution than those who had experienced the cognitive restructuring therapy. There was no significant difference between the two groups on self-esteem. Paivio and Nieuwenhuis (2001) compared 22 adult survivors of childhood abuse treated with a 20-week emotion-focused therapy with 24 participants in a wait-list control group. Participants who received the emotion-focused therapy showed significant improvements on measures of general psychological distress, interpersonal problems, and trauma symptoms.

Eight studies used quasi-experimental formats to examine the effects of group therapies for women who had experienced childhood sexual abuse; in most cases, these groups were compared to wait-list control groups. A ninth study examined the effects of a group for male survivors (Morrison and Treliving, 2002). Bagley and Ramsey (1986) worked with women survivors who were participating in a longitudinal study of at-risk children and their parents. Thirty-four women were entered into a 15-week multi-modal group therapy, focused on how survivors cope with their own mothering tasks, how their negative childhood experiences affect current functioning, how to demonstrate warmth and empathy in current relationships, and how to reduce social isolation. The therapy group showed significantly greater improvement on measures of depression, self-esteem, and reported number of supportive friends than the wait-list controls. Bagley and Young (1998) determined that women who had been in group counselling generally maintained the psychosocial gains.

Richter and colleagues compared a 15-week group process group to a wait-list control condition. One hundred and fifteen women were entered into the process groups in cohorts of approximately nine women. The treatment group members showed improvement on measures of depression and self-esteem, and showed maintained positive effects at six-month follow-up. Morgan and Cummings (1999) examined a 20-week feminist empowerment group and compared it to a no-treatment control group. The treatment group showed greater improvements on measures of depression, social maladjustment, self-blame, and post-traumatic stress response. Saxe and Johnson (1999) compared outcomes of 32 women in an eclectic survivors group and 32 women in a wait-list control group. The treatment group showed greater improvement on measures of interpersonal symptomatology, and these changes were maintained at six-month follow-up. Westbury and Tutty (1999) entered 22 women (in groups of six to eight) into a 10- to 12-week integrative body psychotherapy group based on a feminist model. The treatment group was compared to a wait-list control group of 22 women and showed greater improvement on measures of depression and anxiety. Cloitre and Koenen (2001) recruited women with PTSD related to childhood sexual abuse to participate in a study of a 12-week interpersonal process group. Participants in the groups in which there were no members diagnosed with borderline personality disorder showed significant improvement on measures of anger and PTSD symptoms.

Participants in the groups with at least one member diagnosed with borderline personality disorder and wait-list groups did not show any significant improvements. Wallis (2002) explored the use of a 12-week psychoeducational group for adults with histories of child abuse and neglect. Fifty-six participants were entered into the psychoeducational groups, and 17 participants were in a wait-list control group. The treatment group showed significant improvement on measures of trauma symptomatology, while the control group did not experience a reduction in trauma symptoms.

Morrison and Treliving (2002) examined an open, long-term, dynamically-oriented group for male survivors of childhood sexual abuse. Using a quasi-experimental design, a group of 13 men in group therapy for more than six months was compared to a group of men in the same group therapy for less than six months. The participants who engaged in therapy for more than six months showed significant improvements on measures of general psychological distress, depression, and interpersonal sensitivity.

The use of an integrated inpatient and partial hospitalization unit for women with a history of childhood sexual abuse was examined by Talbot and associates (1999). Forty-eight women were entered into the Women's Safety in Recovery Group, which met three times each week for three weeks. The group focused on psychoeducation, problem solving, and skill building. The treatment group, who were compared to 38 women who received usual care, showed greater improvements on measures of psychiatric symptoms, both at discharge and at six-month follow-up.

Summary

Outcomes research on abuse-focused psychotherapeutic approaches for adult survivors of childhood sexual abuse began as early as 1986, with much of the work being conducted in the mid to late 1990s. Although this line of inquiry has been explored for almost 20 years, there is no one empirically-supported treatment for this population. Only a few randomized studies have been conducted, and no treatment approaches have been found to be efficacious in numerous, independently conducted studies. Furthermore, sample sizes have been quite small, usually under 50 participants. Many of the studies, regardless of design, have been shown to reduce depression and general psychological distress. Because target outcomes and outcome measures have varied across studies, it is difficult to compare the expected clinical effects of the various interventions. Additionally, very few of the studies utilized a treatment manual. So, it is difficult to transport the interventions into clinical practice. Several variables have not yet been investigated: maintenance of therapeutic gains for more than one year; therapist factors, such as ability to develop a therapeutic alliance; client factors, such as education, race, socioeconomic class, length of the abuse, severity of pre-treatment symptoms; group factors, such as the impact of group composition.

Prevalence rates of childhood sexual abuse are high worldwide. The long-term effects of this abuse are evidenced by decreased physical, psychological, and interpersonal health among survivors (see Chapter 1). These sequelae are expensive in terms of healthcare costs, lost work days and human loss. Individuals, private health insurers, and governmental agencies that purchase healthcare are demanding evidence that certain treatments are more efficacious than alternative treatments or no treatment (Hall and Mullee, 2000). The 29 studies reviewed in this chapter demonstrate that abuse-focused psychotherapeutic approaches are helpful in improving psychological and interpersonal function of adult survivors of childhood sexual abuse. Continued research in this area is critical in order to validate empirically-supported treatments.

Researchers need to develop networks and conduct multi-site trials. The 29 studies reviewed here indicate that research in this area has a strong international focus. While the majority of outcome studies were conducted in the United States, several were conducted in the United Kingdom (Clarke and Llewelyn, 1994; Hall and King, 1997; Morrison and Treliving, 2002; Smith et al., 1995), several in Canada (Bagley and Young, 1998; Carver et al., 1989; Clarke, 1993; Jehu et al., 1986; Morgan and Cummings, 1999; Paivio and Nieuwenhuis, 2001; Saxe and Johnson, 1999; Stalker and Fry, 1999; Westbury and Tutty, 1999), and one in Australia (Wallis, 2002). Utilizing this international pool of researchers could contribute to the development of empirically-supported treatments for adult survivors of childhood sexual abuse.

4 Disclosing an Experience of Child Sexual Abuse

Inquiry about childhood sexual abuse

Inquiry about early trauma, including childhood sexual abuse, should occur in the context of an ongoing, comprehensive assessment. Such an assessment should include: discussion of the presenting problem(s); identification of clinical signs, symptoms, and diagnostic indicators; a social, personal, treatment, legal, and financial history; and evaluation of personality factors, including strengths and assets, that may influence the course of treatment (Courtois, 1999).

Some counsellors may hesitate to ask about childhood sexual abuse during an initial assessment due to fear of creating unnecessary distress for the client ('opening a can of worms') or concern that such questioning may be too suggestive. Most experts agree, however, that routine inquiry about childhood sexual abuse, as well as other experiences of current and past violence, should be conducted in an open-ended, non-judgemental, and straightforward manner. Ratna and Mukergee (1998) from the Department of Psychiatry at Barnet General Hospital in the United Kingdom suggest that clients should be asked a mixture of questions about childhood sexual abuse that are either non-specific ('What is your best or worst childhood memory'), indirect ('As a child, were you ever touched in a way that felt uncomfortable/embarrassing, frightening to you?'), or direct ('As a child, did anyone ever ask you to do something sexual, such as ...?', 'As a child, did anyone hurt you or use you in a sexual way?'). Courtois (1999) recommended asking about childhood sexual abuse in terms that are descriptive and behavioural. It may not be helpful, for example, to ask clients if they ever experienced 'sexual abuse' because individuals differ as to what they consider sexual or abusive.

These questions may be coupled with a more traditional psychosexual history (e.g. 'Tell me about your first sexual experience'; 'How did you learn about sex?'). Discussion of clients' retrospective views of their childhood sexual experiences will determine whether they considered these experiences harmful, even if they do not label them as sexual abuse. In addition to asking when the client's first sexual experience occurred, for example, it is helpful to ask how he or she felt about this and subsequent sexual experiences.

Josephson and Fong-Beyette (1987) researched factors associated with disclosure of incest in counselling. They interviewed 37 female incest survivors who had been to a counsellor; those survivors who had disclosed their sexual abuse to the counsellor indicated that they did so because they believed that they would feel better, because a media piece or others encouraged them to do so, or because the counsellor had directly inquired about the incest. Those who did not disclose the sexual abuse to their counsellor reported that they were not thinking about the incest, did not believe it was related to their present concerns, or considered their present concerns to be more important. In addition, they reported that their counsellors did not ask about childhood sexual abuse. These authors recommended that counsellors can elicit disclosure by directly questioning clients about childhood sexual, emotional, and physical abuse, along with more general questioning related to the quality of childhood experiences and family relationships (e.g. the client's best and worst childhood experiences).

Standardized assessment

Briere (1997) reviewed five standardized instruments used to assess childhood abuse histories. These instruments are:

- the Assessing Environments III (AEIII), Form SD (Rausch and Knutson, 1991);
- the Childhood Trauma Questionnaire (CTQ) (Bernstein et al., 1994);
- the Child Maltreatment Interview Schedule (CMIS) (Briere, 1992);
- the Childhood Maltreatment Questionnaire (CMQ) (Demaré, 1993); and
- the Traumatic Events Scale (TES) (Elliot, 1992).

In addition, several instruments have been developed to measure symptoms related to childhood abuse. These instruments are:

- the Impact of Event Scale (IES) (Horowitz et al., 1979);
- the Dissociative Experiences Scale (DES) (Berstein and Putnam, 1986);
- the Los Angeles Symptom Checklist (LASC) (Foy et al., 1984);
- the Trauma Symptom Checklist-40 (TSC-40) (Elliott and Briere, 1992); and
- the Trauma Symptom Inventory (TSI) (Briere, 1995; Elliott and Briere, 1995).

Briere cautioned, however, that these instruments have been primarily used in research and need further development and testing prior to widespread clinical application. Because the long-term effects of childhood sexual abuse are so variable, a symptom checklist alone is not sufficient to make a definite determination of abuse.

Traditional personality inventories (e.g. the Minnesota Multiphasic Personality Inventory Manual (MMPI), Hathaway and McKinley, 1967; the Millon Clinical Multi-axial Inventory III (MCMI-III), Millon, 1994) are often used in the assessment of survivors who present for treatment. Although these instruments may be used to assess personality characteristics (e.g. impulsiveness) or acute clinical states (e.g. suicidality), they cannot detect a history of childhood sexual abuse. For example, certain MMPI profiles and the endorsement of certain critical items have been frequently reported in clinical samples of sexual abuse survivors, but the same patterns have also been found in non-survivor samples (Briere, 1989). At this point, there is no specific profile for sexual abuse that has been identified for any standardized personality instrument.

Factors such as suggestibility and hypnotizability, which are associated with risk of pseudomemory production, should be evaluated, especially if memory work is likely (Brown et al., 1998; Courtois, 1999). The use of standardized instruments, for example the Hypnotic Induction Profile (Speigel and Speigel, 1987) and the Gudjonsson Suggestibility Scale (Gudjonsson, 1984), is recommended for this purpose.

Undisclosed sexual abuse histories

Despite a comprehensive assessment, many individuals with a history of childhood sexual abuse do not disclose these experiences to the counsellor. In some cases, survivors may recall their abuse experiences and recognize their significance, but choose not to talk about the experiences because they do not yet trust the counsellor. Other survivors with memories of childhood sexual abuse may not disclose their experiences because they do not believe that the abuse played a significant role in their lives. These individuals often claim that they did not bring up the abuse initially because they believed it was 'in the past' or 'no big deal'. Such minimization may be especially pronounced in male survivors, as gender socialization often inhibits males from viewing themselves as victims. Clients may not disclose their abuse experiences because they do not have clear memories of them.

Counsellors should not make assumptions regarding lack of disclosure; it may simply mean that no abuse occurred. Under certain conditions, however, counsellors need to consider that the client may have experienced childhood trauma, including childhood sexual abuse. Courtois suggested:

> When the individual's symptom picture is acute and/or has a strong resemblance to complex dissociative PTSD . . . or when the therapist observes certain behavioral and response patterns commonly associated with trauma (such as dissociation in the session or a high degree of personal risk-taking, substance abuse, chronic self-harm and suicidality, and/or a history of re-victimization), the possibility of undisclosed or unrecognized abuse or other trauma or forms of abuse that often go unrecognized (extreme neglect, attachment abuse, or emotional abuse) should be considered. (1999: 229)

When a sexual abuse history is not disclosed, counsellors should not 'diagnose' repressed memory or undetected sexual abuse; they may, however, formulate an 'index of suspicion'. Brown et al. stated:

> Our confidence level in suspecting genuine abuse is raised when the patient presents with: signs and symptoms consistent with abuse; five or greater family history risk factors associated with abuse; clear evidence of dissociation; and no evidence of being in the high range of hypnotic or memory suggestibility. (1998: 508)

Even when abuse is strongly suspected, but not known, the counsellor should neither speculate about nor confirm past sexual abuse when responding to the client. The counsellor should refrain from attributing all the client's problems and concerns to any single aetiology, including childhood sexual abuse (Brown et al., 1998; Courtois, 1999). If the counsellor has a high index of suspicion and believes it is in the client's best interest to communicate this, he or she should do so tentatively, exploring other aetiological possibilities as well.

Counsellor's responses to disclosure

The counsellor's initial response to the client's disclosure of childhood sexual abuse is extremely important. If disclosure is not handled skilfully by the counsellor, it can have deleterious effects. If clients perceive the counsellor's response to disclosure as non-supportive, they may leave counselling, resist further discussion of the abuse issue, or minimize the impact of their abuse experience (Josephson and Fong-Beyette, 1987). Non-supportive responses may include: not believing clients who reveal a history of childhood abuse; blaming the client for the abuse; asking intrusive or voyeuristic questions related to the abuse; or minimizing the importance of the abuse.

In a qualitative study of the healing process of incest survivors (Draucker, 1992b), several participants reported that one of the most destructive counsellor responses to disclosure is that of shock, termed by the survivors as 'Oh, my God' or 'jaw-drop' responses. Although counsellors may perceive such intense reactions to be empathic or genuine, given the client's history, such responses may exacerbate the clients' feelings of stigma and isolation. One survivor in this study stated:

> A lot of what happens for an incest survivor is very threatening to people who haven't been through it, and any kind of disbelief or shock or 'Oh, my God' you know, that kind of judgement is very damaging to me. One of the things that my first counsellor did at our first meeting was she just, her mouth dropped open and she just said, 'Oh, my God!' and I have just been telling her the basic things in my life.

Examples of non-helpful counsellor responses to disclosure may include:

- 'Oh, my God. I can't believe anyone could actually do anything that horrible to a child. What your father did was disgusting' (Shock response.)
- 'It sounds like you believe your father did these things to you. You were so young, it is hard to know what really happened' (Disbelief.)
- 'Why did you agree to have sex with him? Why did you not tell your mother? Why did it go on for so long?' (Blaming.)
- 'You say that this experience is in the past and that you've coped with it. Why don't we move on then to the concerns you have today?' (Minimization.)
- 'Tell me exactly what he did to you sexually' (Voyeuristic response.)

Counsellors who reacted calmly but with 'appropriate concern' were perceived by the women in the incest healing study (Draucker, 1992b) to be both empathic and yet 'strong enough' to deal with the abuse issues. Supportive responses may include: acknowledging the difficult step of disclosing; offering support and indicating one's availability after the session during which the client disclosed; inviting the client to discuss the abuse at his or her own pace; and evaluating the client's mental status and determining any immediate safety concerns (e.g. suicidal thoughts).

Examples of helpful counsellor responses to disclosure may include:

- 'I would like to hear more about that experience. Sexual abuse can be very painful for children and can continue to have an impact on one's life as an adult' (Showing calm concern.)

- 'I can imagine it was hard for you to share that experience with me. I respect your courage for being able to do so' (Acknowledging difficulty of disclosure.)
- 'It can be important to discuss your sexual abuse experience, as it may be related to your current concerns. However, we can do this at a pace that feels right to you' (Reinforcing client's control of disclosure process.)
- 'For some women (men), sharing an abuse experience for the first time (with a counsellor) can result in some very strong (confusing, distressing) feelings. How are you feeling now? ... Do you feel unsafe in any way?' (Acknowledging feelings, assessing safety.)

Case example

The following case description exemplifies the process of an initial disclosure in counselling. Jean, a 34-year-old woman, was seen in a mental health centre following a family crisis in which her husband Jack, aged 42, was charged with physically abusing the couple's 16-year-old son, Bill. Bruises on Bill's arm had been noticed by a teacher and reported to the child protection agency, who referred the family for counselling. A family evaluation revealed that Jack had beaten Bill following an altercation regarding Bill's desire to leave school. The incident closely followed Jack's being fired from his job after a disagreement with his boss. Jack admitted to frequently using physical discipline (i.e. spanking) on his sons, but indicated that the most recent beating of Bill was the most serious. He stated that he lost control because of his drinking. The couple also had another son, Tom, aged 14, and a daughter, Sally, aged 12. All family members stated that Sally was never abused; they claimed she was always the 'good girl' who never did anything wrong and never needed any discipline.

Following the family evaluation, Jean was referred for individual therapy as she had revealed some vague suicidal ideation during the course of the meeting. She claimed that she was 'too tired' to deal with any more family problems, especially the fighting between Jack and Bill, and wished she 'never had to get out of bed again'. Jean was the oldest of eight children in her family. Her father was an alcoholic with a 'mean' temper who had worked at a local factory until his death several years earlier. He was physically abusive of his sons but had never hit Jean, who was always 'well behaved'. She described her mother as being a kind and gentle woman who was always sickly, but who 'waited on my father hand and foot'.

Jean married Jack when she was 17 because she saw marriage as a way of escaping her extensive responsibilities of caring for the younger children in the family. Also, Jack was 'pushing' her to marry shortly after high school graduation. Soon after they were married, Bill was born. Jean described the first year of Bill's life as the happiest time in her life. When she became pregnant with Tom, however, Jack began drinking heavily and would sometimes 'shove her around'. She explained that her husband demanded much of her attention. The drinking continued over the years, but Jack's abuse of her subsided. Jean stated that she never enjoyed their sex life. She eventually tried to avoid sex, although Jack would often demand it when he had been drinking.

Jean revealed that she had 'given up' on the boys. She would attempt to discipline them in a non-physical manner (e.g. by 'grounding them'), but they would not listen to her. Although Jean stated she was not close to either boy, she indicated that she was very close to Sally. She and Sally would often go shopping together and Sally would listen to her problems. Jean worked as a sales clerk at a local mall. She had started

(Continued)

(Continued)

working on a college degree at a local community college on several occasions but stopped because of 'family responsibilities'. Shortly after Sally was born, Jean went to a psychiatrist and was treated for 'postpartum depression'. She was given antidepressant medication at that time.

Records revealed that Jack and Jean had been to the clinic for marriage counselling several years prior to the current crisis. A school guidance counsellor had recommended they seek help after Bill had got into several scrapes with the law for petty theft and Tom, at age 11, had failed the fifth grade. It was recommended at that time that Jack attend Alcoholics Anonymous. Jean was diagnosed as having a dysthymic disorder and a dependent personality disorder. The couple discontinued counselling after three sessions, but Jean saw the counsellor individually for several more sessions. These sessions focused on her troubled marriage and on the behavioural problems of her sons.

Jean told her current counsellor that she was feeling depressed and admitted to feeling 'somewhat' suicidal at times. She said that she was spending every morning in bed. When the current crisis of Bill's beating occurred, she considered taking an overdose of some of her mother's 'nerve' pills but was 'too chicken' to do so. She stated she had lost over ten pounds in two weeks. She denied any substance abuse herself. Her main complaint was: 'I'm just tired of it all and I want some peace.'

Assessment of Jean's presenting problem and history revealed that she exhibited several of the long-term effects frequently seen in adult survivors of abuse, including: depression; low self-esteem and self-efficacy; general sexual dissatisfaction; an unsatisfactory marital relationship involving physical abuse and the alcoholism of her husband; and parenting difficulties. A history of parentification, as described by Gelinas (1983), was evident. As the oldest of eight children, she had assumed many family responsibilities. Her father was a dependent, needy man who abused alcohol. Jean married a man with similar traits. She was unable to meet her own needs and began to show symptoms of depression after the birth of her third child, although she indicated that she was 'worn out' long before that time. Although there was no evidence that her daughter Sally had been sexually abused, Sally was experiencing parentification: at the age of 12, she had assumed the role of the responsible child and had become her mother's confidante.

Because of Jean's background and presenting symptoms, an assessment of a history of abuse was particularly important. Jean probably would not have revealed her abuse experiences to the counsellor unless directly asked. The following dialogue reflects the interaction between Jean and the counsellor that led to the disclosure that Jean had been sexually abused by her father. The disclosure occurred when the counsellor was inquiring about Jean's childhood experiences, and followed Jean's denial that she had been physically abused by her father.

> *Counsellor*: You describe some difficult times in your childhood. Did anyone hurt you or use you in a sexual way?
>
> *Jean*: Well, yes, I guess you could say so. I really don't like to talk about it. It's kind of embarrassing. It was my father and it was sexual. I guess it doesn't matter much now.
>
> *Counsellor*: I realize this can be difficult to talk about. Oftentimes, sexual experiences in childhood are hurtful and can continue to influence women as adults. Therefore, it could be helpful for us to discuss it further. Would you be willing to do so?

(Continued)

(Continued)

Jean:	Ya, I guess so. It happened so long ago, though. It wasn't like we really had sex or anything.
Counsellor:	What did happen?
Jean:	It would usually happen when he was drunk, which was not all the time. Maybe once a month or so. He would come into my room and feel me up – mostly my breasts, sometimes my private parts. It happened mostly when I was in junior high. [*Jean begins to cry.*] He would sometimes pass out in my bed but he always found his way back to his own by morning. I was afraid my mother would find out. It would have killed her. He stopped when I started to get interested in boys, I think. I really can't talk more about this any more. It's really my Billy that I'm concerned about.
Counsellor:	I can sense it was hard for you to tell me about this. These are clearly painful memories. How are you feeling now?
Jean:	Weird. I've never talked about it before. I guess I figured it is best to leave it dead and buried. It is so embarrassing, you know. I don't know, I feel kind of sad. I'll be OK, though. I do not think I can talk about my feelings any more. I'm not sure what they are. I have enough to deal with. Can we stop now?
Counsellor:	Yes. Women often experience many different, and sometimes strong, feelings after sharing an experience such as yours. You may continue to experience these feelings when you leave here. Please feel free to contact me before we meet again if you are troubled by these feelings and want to talk. I also know you have been having some thoughts related to suicide …
Jean:	Yes, but like I said, I won't do anything.
Counsellor:	If the thoughts get stronger or if you feel unsafe in any way, will you call me?
Jean:	Yes. Will we talk about my father again next time? I don't think it will help with my problems with Jack or Bill, but I don't know.
Counsellor:	Although it can be very difficult to deal with, I do recommend we discuss it further when you feel ready. Many of the things you are experiencing now, including your relationships with Bill and Tom, could be influenced by things you have experienced earlier in your life, including what happened with your father. We can explore these issues at a pace that feels right for you so that it will not seem so overwhelming. We would focus on how the abuse relates to your current problems, as it is these problems that trouble you now.
Jean:	Maybe it is important. I've seen some movies about this kind of thing. I'll think some about it.

The counsellor initially intervened by acknowledging the difficulty of disclosure, validating the significance of the abuse, and inviting Jean to discuss it further. Counselling interventions were aimed at acknowledging the courage it took for Jean to discuss this experience, exploring her feelings, assessing her safety needs, and stressing the counsellor's availability. The counsellor also proposed a connection between this experience and Jean's current concerns and suggested that they explore the issue further at a pace that Jean controlled.

5 Focusing on the Abuse Experience

Following disclosure, the counsellor and the client may decide to explore the sexual abuse as a significant counselling issue. The current standard of care in trauma treatment, the phase-oriented approach to therapy discussed in Chapter 2, calls for a preparatory or stabilization phase that precedes the exploration of traumatic memories. Depending on the client's initial presentation, this phase may involve a focus on symptom management, affect modulation and tolerance, cessation of self-injurious behaviours, control of addictions and compulsions, general self-care, and the formation of healthy relationships. The second phase of treatment involves exploring the abuse experience for the purpose of resolution and integration of the trauma. Both these phases are addressed in this chapter.

Preparing for exploration of childhood sexual abuse

Clients who present with severe, pervasive, and persistent symptoms may need considerable work in this initial phase; clients with well-developed self-capacities and support systems may start exploratory work relatively soon after beginning counselling. Adequate coping skills and psychosocial resources are crucial to the success of abuse-focused treatment. The task of developing coping and self-care techniques should be approached 'collaboratively and incrementally' (Gold and Brown, 1997: 187).

Chu (1998) stressed that although intensive exploration of abuse is contraindicated before stabilization is achieved, it is important to acknowledge the abuse at this stage. If early in treatment the counsellor does not acknowledge the influence of childhood trauma on the client's life, the client's denial may be exacerbated. Counsellors should, therefore, state that they consider the abuse a significant life experience but explain that it cannot be explored in greater depth until the client has certain resources and supports in place.

Managing trauma symptomatology

Many survivors of childhood sexual abuse are troubled by trauma-related symptoms (e.g. flashbacks, nightmares, perceptual disturbances) that may increase once the client begins to focus on the abuse experience. A temporary increase in trauma symptoms may be a necessary and therapeutic part of the healing process, representing the loosening of defences. As Sgroi has pointed out, the goal of treatment is 'not to suppress flashbacks or disturbing memories but rather to experience them and process them as a necessary step in coming to terms with and moving beyond the entire victimization experience' (1989: 116). It is advisable, however, to help the client develop skills to manage the symptoms prior to exploratory work, so that these symptoms do not become overwhelming.

Counsellors should explore the nature of the client's flashbacks, nightmares, and intrusive thoughts; acknowledge how frightening these symptoms can be; and assist clients in gaining control over them. Clients may be taught to identify circumstances that trigger intrusive symptomatology. Some clients experience certain prodromal experiences or emotional 'markers' (e.g. a sudden onset of depression) that precede the onset of intrusive symptomatology (Gold and Brown, 1997). If clients can identify these internal cues, they can develop responsive coping strategies. Such strategies may include contacting a supportive other or going to a physically safe place.

When clients re-experience past trauma, grounding techniques, i.e. strategies used to focus on current reality, can be useful (Blake-White and Kline, 1985; Cole and Barney, 1987; Meichenbaum, 1994). These strategies include physical methods (e.g. planting one's feet firmly on the ground or grasping the arms of one's chair during a flashback), or cognitive techniques (e.g. repeating one's name, age, and current location), to reinforce that one is not actually in the childhood situation. Clients may use an associational cue, an object that reminds them of safety and comfort, to maintain an awareness of current reality. They may also learn to find a 'safe space', either in actuality (e.g. the home of a trusted friend) or through imagery, to cope with intrusive symptoms (Meichenbaum, 1994). In a similar fashion, some clients can also learn to control the course of their nightmares. They may tell themselves before going to sleep, for example, that if they dream they are being chased by an intruder, they will stop and turn and order the intruder to leave – and he or she will do so.

Clients should be given the opportunity to discuss, process, and understand the aetiology and function of trauma symptoms (Meichenbaum, 1994). Examining the messages about the trauma that are encoded in flashbacks or frightening dreams, for example, can help the client make sense of his or her symptoms. Meichenbaum stated, 'The client is encouraged to write, talk about, and even draw the experience so it shifts from a "seemingly random, senseless reliving of the past" to a more meaningful controllable portion of one's biographical narrative' (1994: 370).

Affect modulation and tolerance

In addition to post-traumatic symptomatology, clients often experience intense affect, including anxiety, fear, depression, shame, hopelessness, and rage. When they begin to focus on their traumatic experiences, these feelings may intensify. One survivor in the incest healing study (Draucker, 1992b) discussed her response when she first began to connect her current experiences with her childhood abuse:

> It was really scary in one sense because my feelings became real and wasn't – I couldn't sleep – I couldn't stay by myself and it was like the worst thing, of going into therapy or counselling. Everything just became so real. And it became such a controlling force in my life at that time.

Counselling interventions for such affective responses include helping the client to identify and label his or her feelings, to understand the relationship between these feelings and the trauma that they experienced, and to experience feelings without evaluating or rejecting them. In this phase of counselling, clients often need to learn to express feelings verbally or through other means, such as writing, art, and music (Chu, 1998). Counselling interventions at this stage are aimed at the healthy expression of emotion in general, rather than the evocation of trauma-related affect. If clients gain a sense of control over their emotional responses prior to the exploration of abuse, they will be better equipped to tolerate distressing affect when such exploration begins. Additionally, if clients are informed about how emotional responses are related to healing, and are assured of the counsellor's support and availability, they may feel less overwhelmed by their reactions when they begin exploratory work.

Self-injurious behaviours

Clients may present with self-destructive behaviours (e.g. suicide attempts, non-lethal self-mutilation) that may exacerbate as they begin to focus on their sexual abuse experiences. A thorough assessment of suicidal and parasuicidal (self-mutilation) potential may be indicated. Self-destructive behaviours often represent long-standing coping mechanisms in response to overwhelming affect. Self-cutting, for example, may serve to reduce tension or may reflect a sense of self-hate stemming from the abuse (Chu, 1998). Potential for self-harm must be addressed early in treatment; safety planning should be an active, ongoing, and collaborative process (Courtois, 1999). The following counsellor response may be helpful for clients whom the counsellor has assessed as being at risk of suicidal or self-injurious behaviours:

> Working on childhood sexual abuse can be difficult and painful. You've shared with me that at times when you experience painful emotions, you do things to deal with the pain that may be hurtful to you. Therefore, we need to find ways you can keep yourself safe before we start exploring your abuse experience.

Clients and counsellors can devise an action plan specifying what the client will do if he or she becomes at risk for engaging in self-harm. For example, non-suicide contracts detailing actions to be taken in the event of suicidal ideation can be helpful. Action plans may include self-control techniques (e.g. becoming involved in some activity), calling the counsellor or a hotline, or going to the emergency room of a hospital in the event of imminent danger. Designing such explicit agreements demonstrates the counsellor's concern for the client's safety while giving the client responsibility for his or her actions by devising specific guidelines for managing self-destructive urges. Crowe and Bunclark (2000) describe the use of a specialized inpatient unit in Great Britain for individuals who engage in frequent self-harming behaviour. Participants in this treatment programme are taught that self-harm is often a quick response to distressing thoughts and they learn alternative behavioural reactions such as the use of art or verbal expression of feelings. Postponing the self-injurious behaviour by doing something like taking a walk is also suggested. Cognitive-behavioural approaches for dealing with continuing suicidal ideation and self-mutilation, such as those outlined by Meichenbaum (1994), Beck (1994), and Linehan (1993), may be indicated.

Aggression against others

Counsellors may help clients anticipate and prepare for aggressive impulses that might arise when they begin to explore abuse issues. Aggression may be a special concern for male survivors. Bruckner and Johnson (1987), who conduct group therapy with male survivors, reported that group members have often expressed intense anger following disclosure. This anger was sometimes accompanied by plans for retribution, including physical assault on offenders. Counsellors need to assess the potential of harm to others, while validating the client's angry feelings. A helpful counsellor response to a survivor who threatens or implies intent to harm another might be:

> The rage you feel toward [the offender] is understandable given what he did. You have every right to feel anger that intensely. However, I am concerned that you are considering harming him, which you may later regret. Let's discuss your plans.

Anger management training, in which clients are taught to express anger verbally and constructively, may be indicated for some clients. Meichenbaum (1994) described a stress inoculation training programme for anger control and conflict management that includes: increasing the client's awareness of his or her anger; education regarding the components and function of anger; learning time-out procedures and relaxation and visual coping skills; cognitive restructuring; the use of humour; and skill building (communication skills, assertiveness training).

Addictions and compulsions

Clients may present with a variety of addictive behaviours, including substance abuse, eating disorders, and sexual compulsivity; these behaviours may also represent long-standing coping mechanisms used to deal with intolerable affect related to earlier trauma and must be addressed prior to exploratory work. Some counsellors may have the training and expertise to deal with such problems in their own practices; others may refer the client to self-help groups, specialized treatment programmes, or practitioners who specialize in these issues. Structured treatment manuals and therapy guidelines that address chemical dependency (Brower et al., 1989; Brown and Fromm, 1986; Meichenbaum, 1994), eating disorders (Friedman and Brownell, 1996; Garner and Garfinkel, 1997), and sexual compulsivity (Schwartz and Masters, 1993) are available.

Sexual abuse survivors may be particularly resistant to involvement in self-help groups such as Alcoholics Anonymous. Several counselling interventions are recommended to deal with this resistance (Skorina and Kovach, 1986). The first step of an AA programme is the admission of powerlessness over alcohol and life, a terrifying prospect for survivors of sexual abuse. Counsellors may discuss the difference between being powerless over a substance and being powerless over one's body or psyche, stressing that admission of powerlessness over a substance is actually a way of gaining control. Because another block to survivors' participation in an AA programme is lack of trust, counsellors can recommend finding home groups and sponsors (i.e. peers from AA with a history of sobriety who provide personal support) who are sensitive to abuse issues. If the survivor is a woman, the choice of an all-female group and a female sponsor may be helpful. Further, the invitation to 'tell one's story' in an AA meeting may be experienced as intrusive by the survivor; counsellors may help the survivor prepare for this in advance.

Trotter expressed concern that 'over focusing either on rigid sobriety while ignoring post-trauma symptoms or on issues secondary to serious addiction can create for the recovering person the potential for relapse' (1995: 100). She proposed a developmental model for recovery for the chemically dependent trauma survivor, based in part on Gorski's (1992) recovery-from-addiction model. In the five stages of the model (transition, stabilization, early recovery, middle recovery, and ongoing recovery) issues related to dynamics of trauma, the nature of addiction, and the relationship between trauma and addiction are addressed. For example, during the stabilization phase, the symptoms of post-acute withdrawal from alcohol (e.g. inability to think clearly, memory problems, emotional reactions or numbness, sleep disturbances) can mimic the symptoms of PTSD; clinicians are advised, therefore, to refrain from making a psychological diagnosis until the chemical withdrawal is completed. In the model, the 12 steps of Alcoholics Anonymous are interwoven with the stages of trauma recovery. Special attention is paid to relapse prevention by identifying and managing warning signs.

General self-care

Survivors who are not self-destructive in one of the ways discussed above may have a tendency to neglect their general self-care needs (e.g. poor eating habits, neglect of healthcare, lack of pleasurable activities). This neglect may be due to feelings of low self-worth that stem from the early abuse. One of the participants in the incest healing study (Draucker, 1992b), for example, described how she learned to attend to her personal needs:

> I also learned to do little things that make me feel better about myself, like – really small things but before I go to bed at night maybe I'll fall into bed and I'll think – 'Well, wait, you forgot to brush your teeth and wash your face. Get up and do it!' Whereas before I'd lie in bed and say 'Well, so what?' You'll get a cavity; so maybe your face will break out.

Constructing a self-care plan may be something as simple as agreeing to treat oneself to a desired article of clothing or to take a warm bubble bath after a particularly difficult session; it may be as comprehensive as a nutrition and exercise plan to accompany the counselling process. Clients may need a medical evaluation if they have neglected their healthcare needs. Providing for self-care typically becomes easier when survivors are further along in the healing process. Making a commitment to a reasonable plan early in treatment, however, suggests to clients that they can take action to tolerate the painful aspects of the counselling process.

Relationship issues

Clients may present with disturbed interpersonal relationships that must be addressed prior to beginning exploratory work. They may be isolated and without social support, or may be involved in relationships that are stormy and abusive. Courtois stated that: 'Much therapeutic time must be spent identifying and unlearning the "relational rules of abuse and victimization" and replacing them with skills and attitudes necessary for healthy, interdependent connections with supportive others' (1999: 200).

For some clients, social skills training may be indicated so they can begin to seek out sustaining social activities and relationships. Structured educational groups may be useful for this purpose. If the client is currently involved in an abusive relationship, this must be addressed in this phase of counselling.

Because the client may attempt to re-enact old relational patterns with the therapist, the formation of a therapeutic alliance that is mutual and collaborative is necessary. Chu stated, 'The therapy helps to introduce mutuality and collaboration in relationships, rather than control, aggression, abandonment, and betrayal that formed the core experiences of the patient's early life' (1998: 85).

Exploring childhood sexual abuse

The goal of exploratory work
The middle stage of treatment involves exploration of the childhood sexual abuse experience(s). Courtois stated:

> The primary goal of trauma resolution and integration is for the patient to gradually face and make sense of the abuse/trauma and to experience associated emotions at a pace that is safe, manageable, and not overwhelming. (1999: 203)

The solicitation of memories or the intense re-experiencing of early trauma is not the goal of this stage of treatment. As Gold and Brown argued, 'Neither the clinical nor the research literature on CSA [childhood sexual abuse] and its treatment suggest that *remembering* is the crux or culmination of effective therapy for this population' (1997: 184). The purpose of recounting abuse experiences is to allow for the processing, desensitization, and integration of traumatic memories that return as fragmentary intrusive experiences. Dissociated memories are translated into a coherent narrative. Traumatic material is 'told and retold' until it becomes an integrated aspect of the self and takes on new meaning 'as part of a socially shared autobiographical history' (Brown et al., 1998: 481). According to Brown et al., 'Recovery of memories is not about gathering information about the past. It is about mastery over what has been unclear or avoided in memory, making meaning out of one's personal history, and achieving integration' (1998: 481).

The emotional expression (e.g. crying) that accompanies exposure to trauma-related material contributes to desensitization (Briere, 1996). The positive emotional experience of the discharge of emotions in the context of a supportive relationship serves to inhibit and counter-condition the fear associated with the trauma. Catharsis pairs the positive experience of emotional discharge with trauma stimuli, thereby counter-conditioning traumatic stress.

The counselling agreement
Counsellors should discuss the rationale for this phase of treatment in terms that clients can understand and appreciate. Abuse survivors have often had the experience of describing their experiences to others, only to have them respond

with disbelief or excessive interest based on curiosity rather than concern. Clients should, therefore, be active participants in the decision to pursue this phase of treatment, and should explicitly agree to engage in exploratory work.

Pacing exploratory work

The pacing of exploratory work is crucial for therapeutic success. The counsellor should proceed at a pace consistent with the clients' ability to tolerate painful affect. Briere discussed the concept of the therapeutic window, a heuristic used to guide exploratory work. The therapeutic window is:

> that psychological place during treatment wherein appropriate therapeutic interventions are cast. Such interventions are neither so nondemanding as to be useless nor so evocative or powerful that the client's delicate balance between trauma and avoidance is tipped toward the former. (1996: 146)

Counsellors 'undershoot' the therapeutic window if they avoid exploration of childhood trauma or provide only support and validation for clients who have the capacity to engage in exploratory work (Briere, 1996). The trauma is not processed and the client continues to employ avoidance or dissociative defences. On the other hand, interventions that 'overshoot' the therapeutic window are too intense or fast-paced to allow for adequate processing of traumatic material. The client will become overwhelmed with affect and experience increased defensive dissociation. In some instances, counsellors inaccurately label this dissociation as 'resistance'. If the client's defences are not adequate, he or she may become overwhelmed by intrusive symptomatology and resort to soothing, but self-destructive, behaviours, such as self-mutilation or substance abuse. Other clients may flee treatment. Maintaining the therapeutic window, therefore, involves titrating discussion of traumatic material so that clients experience the exposure necessary for desensitization without provoking unwanted avoidance.

Cole and Barney addressed the concept of the therapeutic window, which they believe is characterized by moderate distress and manageable symptomatology. They claimed that the counsellor's task is to 'judge carefully the amount and exposure to ... memories and affects the survivors can tolerate. That is, the therapist should monitor the "dosage" of intensity and duration so that it is of therapeutically manageable proportions' (1987: 603).

It may be helpful to discuss the concept of the therapeutic window with clients. The counsellor may explain:

> Although painful feelings are necessary for healing, we can discuss the abuse material at a pace that does not feel overwhelming for you. If you feel our discussions are too stressful or emotional to be helpful, we'll slow down. If you start to feel stuck or don't feel anything, we'll begin to explore the abuse in more depth. It's this middle ground where the most productive work gets done.

Once clients understand the concept of the therapeutic window, the counsellor may periodically 'check in' with them to see if they believe they are working within the window.

Working within the therapeutic window requires a balance between interventions of exploration and interventions of consolidation (Briere, 1996). Exploratory interventions involve an examination of traumatic material, both cognitively and affectively. Consolidation interventions focus on safety, support, and stability. Effective therapy requires a balance between these types of intervention, based on the counsellor's ongoing assessment of the client's changing internal state. Clients who are emotionally overwhelmed or functioning poorly will benefit from a greater focus on consolidation; clients who are emotionally stable will profit from a focus on exploration.

Counsellors also need to control the intensity of affect provoked within each session (Briere, 1996). Exploratory work should begin gradually. The intensity of affect should peak in the middle of the session, and time should be left for clients to regain a sense of control and composure before they leave the counsellor's office.

Exploratory work involves a gradual re-exposure to the affect and stimuli associated with traumatic material within the context of a well-established therapeutic relationship. Exploratory work is a form of systematic desensitization in which less upsetting memories are discussed and desensitized before moving on to more painful ones (Briere, 1996). Kluft (1996) recommended processing traumatic material 'from the top down'. The client is asked to describe consciously available material first. Unavailable material will often emerge naturally in the course of these discussions.

Because abuse memories are coded both verbally and through the sensorimotor system, exposure and desensitization must include both of these systems. Factual, verbal memories are generally processed first, as they tend to be less overwhelming than sensory memories (physical sensations and affects). Clients are asked first about 'facts' of the abuse (the who, what, when, where) and later about associated affective and perceptual experiences.

Dealing with affect

The constricted affective lives of many survivors can be attributed to defensive processes stemming from the abuse, as well as from growing up in family systems where feelings were not respected. Many survivors will initially appear emotionless when describing their abuse experience (Hall and Lloyd, 1989). When asked, these individuals are often unable to identify or express their feelings.

Male survivors may have special difficulty expressing, naming, and understanding feelings. As Johanek (1988: 112) states, 'Most men with whom we deal have learned to avoid experiencing and displaying emotions at all costs. They tend to describe events and their reactions to those events without using emotional terms.' Men may feel especially threatened when asked to explore their feelings in counselling.

Clients may experience different feelings at varying degrees of intensity when exploring the sexual abuse. Sgroi (1989), for example, suggested that fear, anger, and perception of loss of control are primary responses that occur when survivors begin to acknowledge the reality of the abuse. Survivors learn that these responses are painful but tolerable. Secondary responses such as guilt, shame, and a sense of damage are subjected to what Sgroi (1989) refers to as contemporary denial, i.e. the denial of current responses to the abuse experience. Although survivors have acknowledged the reality of the abuse, they minimize its importance in order to block the pain of these secondary responses.

Blake-White and Kline (1985) also differentiated the varied feelings experienced by survivors of childhood sexual abuse. They suggested that feelings of guilt and shame are often acknowledged by survivors spontaneously; anger and sadness are often just under the surface and discussion of these feelings can be facilitated by the counsellor. The stronger emotions of terror, despair, abandonment, fear of pain, and fear of being alone may continue to be denied.

Counsellors should first validate expressed emotions so that survivors can learn to trust and accept their feeling states and then work toward increasing the survivors' awareness of deeper, less available emotions. There are several interventions that can be used to facilitate this process. First, counsellors may ask clients to name and describe feelings. The following interaction exemplifies a possible counsellor response when a client describes an event, but does not connect it with an affect.

Client: I remember being so all alone. I was only five, for goodness sake. My mother and father were separating so I spent lots of time with him [an abusive babysitter]. I knew I was losing my father, and my mother in some ways too. She was so depressed.

Counsellor: As you describe this experience, what are you feeling?

Client: Sad, incredibly sad. I was only five. I was losing everyone.

When survivors do respond with feeling statements, counsellors can acknowledge the feelings with empathic responses:

Client: The devastation I felt when my mother found out was tremendous. Even now, years later when I see her I want to fall through the floor; just want to be invisible. I was her perfect angel and I was sleeping with her husband. I would have rather died than let her know what a slut I was.

Counsellor: As a child you experienced great shame. It is a feeling that's stayed with you all these years, still causing you pain.

Third, when working with clients whose families, or society, discouraged the expression of feelings, counsellors may address this dynamic. The following interaction is with a male survivor:

Client: He was my own brother. I looked up to him. When I realized what he did … [*starts to cry*]. See, I'm still a wimp today.

Counsellor: It sounds like you've gotten the message that 'real men don't cry'. That message prevents you from allowing yourself to feel sad about a sad thing that happened to you. Where did that message come from?

Retrieving repressed memories

As mentioned previously, most trauma experts have suggested that repressed memories, or otherwise unavailable material, will emerge gradually throughout the course of treatment as the client's capacities to tolerate painful material increase and defensive dissociation decreases. The use of specialized memory recovery techniques is generally unnecessary.

Brown et al. argued, however, that there are some cases where memory retrieval techniques may be appropriate: 'Specialized memory recovery techniques are sometimes indicated when ... the patient is suffering from a more pervasive or extreme amnesia for trauma ... that has not been reversed by the previous methods designed to minimize memory accuracy errors, such as free narrative recall' (1998: 483–4).

These authors recommended that if it is necessary to use specific interventions to facilitate memory retrieval, a step-wise approach be used. Techniques with the lowest likelihood of causing memory errors, such as free narrative recall, are used first. If these approaches do not reverse the amnesia, techniques that involve a mild increase in memory error rates, such as transference interpretations and context reinstatement combined with free recall (having the client focus on a period of time in which the abuse probably occurred) should be tried. If these are not successful, state-dependent recall techniques (focusing on trauma-associated affect or using techniques to amplify affect), which are associated with a mild to moderate increase in memory error rates, might be considered. A modest increase in memory error rates is associated with specialized memory recovery techniques such as hypnosis or age regression; these techniques should be used with extreme caution and only by counsellors who are well trained in their use. A high increase in memory error rates is associated with interrogatory and coercive interviewing, including the supplying of false or misleading information; these methods are always ill-advised.

Mourning

Exploring the abuse experience often provokes a period of grief and mourning as survivors come to terms with the reality of the abuse and the losses and missed opportunities associated with it (Chu, 1998; Courtois, 1999; Herman, 1992). Survivors may mourn the loss of their childhood; their psychological and, in some cases, physical integrity; and the capacity to trust others:

> The telling of the trauma story thus inevitably plunges the survivor into profound grief. Since so many of the losses are invisible or unrecognized, the customary rituals of mourning provide little consolation. The descent into mourning is at once the most necessary and the most dreaded task of this stage of recovery. (Herman, 1992: 188)

Herman suggested that resistance to mourning may take the form of fantasies of revenge, forgiveness, or compensation. During this time, the survivor may be at increased risk of suicide. Positive memories of caring others in the survivor's life, or the survivor's own capacity for compassion, may serve as 'a lifeline during the descent into mourning' (1992: 194).

Case example

The following case exemplifies the process of exploring an experience of childhood sexual abuse. Susan, a 40-year-old woman, sought counselling because she was distressed about the 'direction' her current relationship with her partner Ray, aged 52, had taken. Susan had dated Ray steadily for four years and had hoped to marry him, but he never proposed. She reported that their sex life was 'OK', although she had always been inorgasmic. Ray was not interested in a 'commitment' such as marriage. He claimed his prior marriage had been 'hell' and he was still supporting his two teenage sons. Susan stated that she had accepted this, but was very upset to learn recently that Ray had been dating another woman.

Susan had worked for 21 years as a secretary and a bookkeeper for a small local industry. She indicated that she did very well at her job, but sometimes felt 'pushed around' by her boss. Describing herself as a 'shrinking violet', she reported that she had only two close female friends. She had little contact with her elderly parents, who lived approximately one and a half hours' drive away.

Susan had never been married but had been in two long-term relationships prior to meeting Ray. She claimed both men were 'losers', both were alcoholic, and one had been physically abusive to her. She reported being very grateful that Ray was 'different' from these men. Susan denied using alcohol or drugs, but she did discuss a significant weight problem and admitted to occasional binging in the past. She had sought counselling on several prior occasions and reported feeling somewhat better about herself after each attempt at counselling. She denied any significant trauma symptomatology, self-destructive behaviour, or anxiety or depression.

During the initial interview, Susan was asked about sexual abuse. She readily revealed that she had been molested by an uncle on several occasions over three summers, from the ages of 9 to 11. Her uncle had a farm that she and her younger brother visited during school vacations. She stated that her uncle had 'taught' her to perform oral intercourse on him and told her she would need to know how to do this to boys when she got older. She reported being 'disgusted' by the experience but preferred the freedom she experienced on the farm to the strict rules (e.g. early bedtime, many 'chores', frequent church attendance) of her parents, who were 'strict fundamentalists'. Susan described her parents, who were neither physically nor sexually abusive, as 'good people' who worked hard but who did not show any emotion.

After one summer when the abuse was particularly bad, she and her brother never returned to the farm and did not have much further contact with this uncle. Susan always wondered if this was because her mother found out what had happened, and recalled being very worried that this was the case. Nothing was ever said, however, about the visits to the farm. Susan stated that she had put the abuse behind her and had forgiven her uncle because he was 'sick'.

Susan had not discussed the sexual abuse in her prior counselling situations because she had not been asked about it. She readily disclosed the abuse on inquiry, but minimized the impact that both the abuse and the family dynamics surrounding the abuse had on her life. The following interaction between Susan and her counsellor illustrates this dynamic:

Counsellor: What was the experience with your uncle like for you?
Susan: I felt like a tramp, sort of. Mostly I hoped my mother would not find out. It was so long ago though. He was probably sick. I do not think he meant to hurt me. I'm sure I'm over it. In fact, to be perfectly truthful, I really don't like to talk about it.

(Continued)

(Continued)

Counsellor:	Yes, these experiences can be hard to discuss. Initially, talking about them can feel like you are digging up the past for no reason. Could the experiences you had with your uncle and other childhood experiences be related in some way to the concerns you have today?
Susan:	Well, my experience with my uncle could I suppose have something to do with my sexual problem, and maybe even with my track record with men. Every so often – actually, quite often – I think about it. But it is Christian to forgive. Maybe I am too forgiving. How many times have I forgiven Ray? Mostly I think I just wanted to have fun on the farm. I could not really be a kid anywhere.

Because Susan was functioning relatively well without significant psychiatric symptomatology, the preparatory phase of counselling was brief. The counsellor did address Susan's history of binging, but Susan felt this was not a current problem. Susan enlisted the support of her closest friend, Connie, as she began to discuss painful issues in counselling. The exploration of the sexual abuse began with the following interaction:

Counsellor:	Describing this experience with your uncle helps me to appreciate and understand what you went through as a little girl, and helps you begin to sort through what happened and make sense of it. However, we can go at your pace and stop whenever you feel the need to. Are you feeling ready to start telling me what happened?
Susan:	Yes, I am ready. I just do not really know where to begin.
Counsellor:	Why don't you start with the first incident you remember.
Susan:	I think I was 9 – maybe 10. I had been at the farm only a day. I was really happy to be there. Uncle Bob treated me real nice. He had bought me some new dresses. Anyway, I was in the barn. He came out and told me how pretty I was. No one ever said that to me. Come to think of it, no one does now either. [*Laughs*] Even though I was skinny then I was pretty homely. Anyway, he told me he was going to teach me how to kiss boys as they would be wanting to kiss me because I am pretty. Then he said I needed to learn about petting. That's when he began to fondle my breasts.

Susan began to describe her experiences in great detail and began to remember more invasive sexual activities. Over the next several sessions, she began to recall some sadistic aspects to the abuse (e.g. being tied up, being whipped). After a particularly difficult session, during which Susan described her rage at her mother because Susan was not able to talk to her about the abuse, Susan reported a serious binging episode. Shortly after, she left counselling at Ray's request. He told Susan she need not 'dig up the past'. Repeated phone calls from the counsellor went unanswered.

Four months later, Susan returned to counselling. She informed the counsellor that Ray had left her for another woman and that she had started to think more and more about her relationship with her uncle and her 'poor choice of men'. She had experienced nightmares related to some especially violent episodes. She also reported a dramatic increase in her food consumption, although she denied further binging. She and her counsellor worked on a self-care contract, which included her

(Continued)

(Continued)

participation in a Weight Watchers' group, a short daily walk, and a 'no binge' agreement. They also discussed some techniques she might use to manage her nightmares. At this point, Susan and her counsellor agreed to continue their work on her childhood experiences and to explore the connections between these experiences and her current problems, but at a slower pace.

Susan described more abuse incidents, which had involved progressively more invasive and physically violent sexual activities; techniques used by her uncle to continue to engage Susan in the abuse; her memories of her childhood reactions to the abuse; her relationship with her parents at the time of the abuse; and the circumstances in which the abuse stopped. Although Susan had initially denied being distressed by the abuse experience, she slowly began to describe her feelings in depth. She remembered feeling like a 'dirty girl'. She experienced much guilt because she hated the sexual activity, but enjoyed the attention from her uncle. Mostly, she reported fearing her parents would discover what had happened. She imagined they would completely reject her or bring her 'sins' to the attention of their minister. She experienced terror at being discovered and abandoned. Betrayal, by both her parents and her trusted uncle, emerged as a key issue for her.

With the support of the counsellor, Susan would take frequent breaks from what she called 'heavy stuff'. She would discuss more day-to-day problems before returning to discussion of the abuse and the issues surrounding it. Susan continued to connect her past experiences with her current distress. She recognized that as a child she could not express her needs for attention or protection. She considered herself to be 'bad' and, therefore, not worthy of having either of these needs met. She began to see her choice of men as being related to her belief that she did not deserve better, and her sexual dysfunction as related to her belief that she did not deserve sexual pleasure. After approximately one year of counselling, she began to feel better about herself. She had lost a considerable amount of weight. Her nightmares subsided. She did become involved with a man, Bob, who had been introduced to her by Connie. Bob was 'not always as considerate' as she would like, but was not abusive. She chose not to become sexually intimate with Bob, although he sometimes pressured her for a sexual relationship. Susan decided to stop counselling because, 'I know I have more to work on but I just want to enjoy feeling better for a while.'

Discussion

Abuse-focused work was indicated for Susan as her childhood experiences, both the abuse by her uncle and her parents' lack of emotional support, seemed to be related to her current difficulties, including her problematic relationships with men, her sexual dysfunction, and her self-image. Because the exploration phase began too quickly and intensely, Susan engaged in problematic coping responses and fled from treatment. When she returned, the counsellor addressed Susan's need for stabilization and paid increased attention to her 'therapeutic window'. At a slower pace, Susan was able to share many abuse experiences with her counsellor and addressed multiple family issues that had caused her pain. Memories that had been dissociated were integrated into Susan's narrative. No specialized memory recovery techniques were needed. She was able to connect her current distress with aspects of her abuse history and began to make some desired changes in her life. The counsellor respected Susan's choice to take a break from counselling and invited her to return if she wanted to continue her work at a later point.

6 Reinterpreting the Sexual Abuse Experience from an Adult Perspective

Describing sexual abuse experiences allows clients to begin to interpret them from an adult perspective. Because dissociative processes begin at a time when the child's cognitive skills are still developing, survivors retain a 'child's concept of the event' (Blake-White and Kline, 1985: 398). Individuals who were maltreated as children often judge their behaviour by attributing to themselves, as children, the adult resources of freedom of choice, social support, and the power of reasoning. They believe, therefore, that they were to blame for the abuse, enjoyed it, or could have stopped it and did not. These beliefs often remain unchallenged because the survivor has not shared them with others. In many cases, important others in the survivor's life reinforced his or her sense of blame and responsibility. In counselling, survivors may reinterpret their childhood experiences using an adult understanding of their stage of development and the dynamics of their family at the time of the abuse. The issues that are important for survivors to reframe in this way and counselling procedures that can facilitate this are discussed in this chapter.

Issues to reframe from an adult perspective

Attribution of blame

Survivors' self-blame for the abuse is a key therapeutic issue (Chu, 1998; Courtois, 1999). Herman suggested that, for women, self-blame reflects the attitudes of society that blame the daughter, or at times the mother, for sexual abuse that occurs in the family. She described this myth: 'Ensnared by the charms of a small temptress, or driven to her arms by a frigid, unloving wife, Poor Father can hardly help himself, or so his defenders would have us believe' (1981: 36). Herman argued that the concept of the 'Seductive Daughter' is culturally embedded in religious traditions (e.g. the biblical story of Lot and his daughters), popular literature (e.g. the story of Lolita), and even some clinical literature. Westerlund (1983) listed three attitudes of society that contribute to the self-blame of the female survivor: females incite male sexual behaviours; 'boys will be boys'; and it is the responsibility of females to control male sexuality. One participant in the incest healing study (Draucker, 1992b) stated:

> Your parents teach you that you are responsible if you get pregnant or if you have sex with a boy. You are the one that's responsible, you're the one that's in control of the situation and, you know, if your dad's taking advantage of you, you are responsible.

Offenders often tell child victims that they are to blame for the abuse. Children may also receive blaming messages from significant others; many survivors believe the sexual abuse was punishment for being 'naughty'. Undoubtedly, incestuous family dynamics, as outlined by Gelinas (1983), also reinforce self-blame. Due to the process of parentification, incest survivors learn to assume responsibility for the feelings, needs, and behaviours of others.

Male survivors often blame themselves for failing to protect themselves against the offender (Draucker and Petrovic, 1996, 1997; Struve, 1990). This may result in internalized anger or compensatory behaviours to regain control (e.g. aggression, exaggerated masculine behaviours). Boys are taught that males are not victims and should be powerful enough to protect themselves from the intrusion and aggression of others.

Reframing the attribution of blame from an adult perspective entails acceptance of the fact that the offender, not the survivor, is always responsible for the abusive sexual activity. This is true regardless of the 'engagement strategies' (e.g. threat, bribery, force, 'brainwashing') employed by the offender (Sgroi and Bunk, 1988). By virtue of their stage of psychosocial and cognitive development and their dependent position within the family structure, children are unable to make a free choice regarding involvement in sexual activity. It is the responsibility of the adult, or the more powerful other, to resist engaging in exploitative sexual activities with the child.

Childhood sexual responsiveness

Because survivors remember experiencing physical pleasure or arousal during the abuse experience, they conclude that they enjoyed and sought the experience. Males, who are often the victims of same-sex abuse, may believe that such responses represent latent homosexual desires (Struve, 1990). Reframing the issue of sexual responsiveness from an adult perspective involves realizing that sensations experienced by children are natural physiological reactions to sexual stimulation. Such responses differ from sexual arousal in adulthood, when mature emotional and cognitive responses determine one's enjoyment of a sexual experience. Arousal in childhood does not indicate that the child either sought out or enjoyed the sexual experience.

Issues of attention and affection

Many survivors enjoyed the attention or affection associated with their abuse, and concluded that as children, they instigated the sexual activity. Given the dysfunctional nature of their family, the attention or affection they received from the offender may well have been the only emotional nurturance they received. Because the abused child's life is often devoid of caring from others, special attention is frequently used as an engagement strategy (Sgroi and Bunk, 1988). Survivors should consider that the need for attention and affection from a significant adult is basic to all children, and that children will naturally try to meet this need in any ways that are open to them. Children may desire the emotional nurturance that accompanies the abuse, but not the sexual activity.

Why me?

Survivors often believe that they were singled out for abuse because of inherent characteristics they possessed as children. This belief is especially prevalent among those who were the only victim within their family. Some survivors assume they were basically bad or 'naughty', and some assume they were especially 'sexy' – although often in an evil way (Herman, 1981). Reframing the 'Why me?' issue from an adult perspective allows survivors to appreciate that they were chosen as victims, not because of any inherent personality defects, but because of factors related to the offender's motives or to the family dynamics. The offender often seeks a child who is parentified, vulnerable, or at an age consistent with the offender's emotional or sexual needs. When survivors consider their 'level of sexual knowledge and awareness before the start of the abuse' (Hall and Lloyd, 1989: 112), they realize they did not have the capacity for sexual seductiveness as a child. Seductive behaviours are not the cause of the abuse; they are typically learned as a result of it.

Having kept the secret

Many survivors experience self-blame because they never told anyone of the abuse and, therefore, did not 'stop' it. This concern is especially salient if the abuse went on for a long time, the child was older when the abuse started, the offender's engagement strategies did not include the use of force, and the child had no role in stopping the abuse. Reframing 'secret keeping' from an adult perspective involves having survivors consider what they believed as children would be the consequences of disclosure (e.g. punishment, family break-up, disbelief by significant others, rejection by the offender). It is also important for survivors to consider that telling others, a proactive behaviour, is outside the behavioural repertoire of some children. Disclosure would also have required the availability of receptive significant others, something many survivors did not have. As one survivor in the incest healing study (Draucker, 1992b) stated:

> Even at the time it never occurred to me to tell anybody. I didn't know who to tell, I didn't know how to tell, I didn't know what the consequences of telling would have been, I just wanted it to stop. But it never occurred to me to tell. That given the way I was raised in the household, no, I wouldn't have told. I just wouldn't have. Again, that's me being a normal little kid if you will.

Counselling procedures for reframing

There are several counselling procedures that can facilitate the reinterpretation of the sexual abuse experience from an adult perspective. These procedures include cognitive restructuring, techniques encouraging survivors to view themselves as children at the time of the abuse, and the experiential reinforcement of new beliefs.

Challenging beliefs

A cognitive challenge is a response by a counsellor that disputes the survivor's problematic belief with logical reasoning (Sgroi and Bunk, 1988). Cognitive challenges are exemplified in the following counsellor interventions. The first intervention challenges the belief that a survivor caused the abuse because she was flirtatious.

Harriet:	I think I was a flirt even when I was that young. If I had said something he would have stopped. I do think I must have been at least partly to blame. Why else would I feel like such a slut?
Counsellor:	A five-year-old child cannot really flirt as we think of flirting because at that age she does not understand adult sexual behaviours enough to know how to flirt. Also, as a five-year-old child, you could not be responsible for what happened. You were totally dependent on your father and were unable to say no to his requests. As an adult, it was his responsibility to protect you, not to exploit you to meet his needs.

This next intervention challenges the belief that a survivor enjoyed the abuse because he was sexually stimulated.

Jonathon:	When I talked to him [the offender] about it [the abuse], he had a good point. In some ways, it felt good to me, the sex I mean. I mean I knew it was wrong and I was scared, but it felt good. I don't know how to say this — but at times I ended up, you know, responding when he touched my private parts. He's right, I must have liked it somewhat.
Counsellor:	The response you felt when your brother touched your genitals was a normal physiological response to stimulation, not an indication that you sought or desired the sexual activity.

Cognitive challenges can also be in the form of questions. The following client–counsellor interaction involves questioning aimed at addressing a survivor's belief that she was responsible for the abuse because she never told anyone that it was occurring.

Mary:	The abuse went on for almost four years. I was eight when it first started — but about 12 when it stopped. I was almost a teenager, for heaven's sake. I could have done something, you'd think, to stop it, if had really wanted to.
Counsellor:	What might have you done to stop it?
Mary:	Tell him, 'Stop it or I'll tell the rest of the world.'
Counsellor:	What might he have done if you had done that?
Mary:	Deny it. Everyone would have believed him. Famous attorney that he was. What a joke! Do you know he was president of the Lions Club [a local civics organization]?
Counsellor:	As a child you realized that telling him to stop or you would tell others would not have been successful in stopping the abuse?
Mary:	Also remember he had a violent temper. I was afraid of him. He would beat us for forgetting to bring in the garbage. What would he do if I blew the whistle?
Counsellor:	So you believed that, if you told, not only would no one believe you, but you would probably have been beaten. What else do you think you could have done to stop it?
Mary:	Telling my mother would have been a joke. She couldn't stop him from beating her. She certainly couldn't stop him from coming on to me. I suppose if I really wanted out, I could have run away.
Counsellor:	Where would you have gone?
Mary:	Probably to the streets. I'd be a hooker now. Lots of us turn out that way, you know.

Counsellor: So even though the abuse went on for four years, until you were 12, as a kid you had no real options for stopping what was happening to you. If you told, no one would have believed you or you would have been beaten. Your mother was no help and you really had no place to go if you did run away. That's a hard situation for a 12-year-old, isn't it?

Mary: Ya, I guess it is.

Cognitive restructuring

Jehu et al. (1986) recommended cognitive restructuring as an approach to address distorted beliefs associated with abuse. The counsellor begins by explaining the process of cognitive restructuring to the client. Cognitive restructuring is based on the principle that beliefs influence feelings; if beliefs are distorted, the resulting feelings can lead to behavioural or emotional problems. Jehu et al. advised giving the client an 'everyday' example of how beliefs lead to feelings that lead to behavioural responses. The counsellor might say:

> If Joe concludes that he was turned down for a job because of basic incompetence, he will feel depressed, and it is unlikely that he will apply for another similar job. If, on the other hand, Joe believes he was turned down due to unusually stiff competition, he will feel mildly discouraged, but is likely to keep trying for other similar positions.

The next stage in cognitive restructuring is assisting clients to identify beliefs, which are often automatic or unconscious, that accompany their distress. Techniques to facilitate this include: reviewing the sequence of events leading to the distressing affect; re-enacting a distressing event in a role play; using relaxation and imagery to re-experience the event; responding to questionnaires that outline distorted beliefs commonly experienced by survivors; and keeping a journal to record one's thoughts.

In the following interaction, the client, a 20-year-old college student named Jane, and the counsellor work on identifying Jane's beliefs that result in depressed feelings whenever she visits her mother. One year prior to this interaction, Jane had told her mother how she was abused by her stepfather as a child.

Jane: Every time I go home I end up feeling awful. This time I cried for two days when I got back. I can't understand why. My mom has been great. She's supported me all the way. If I want to talk about it [the abuse], she will. If I don't, she won't mention it. I know from group that most other mothers are not that great. Why do I feel so sad when we are together?

Counsellor: During this visit, when did you notice yourself feeling sad?

Jane: I made note of it this time. It was Saturday night. I had a date with a high school boyfriend. When we said goodbye to my mom, she looked sad and lonely. I guess I started to feel bad then. Guilty, somehow.

Counsellor: What were you thinking at that point?

Jane: That I'm getting better, getting on with my life. She's all alone.

Counsellor: What thoughts did you have about her being alone?

Jane: That if I had not brought this all up, she would not be alone now.

Counsellor: The sadness results from your belief that your mom, whom you care about, is lonely. The guilt, and probably the depression you feel when you go home, results from the belief that you are responsible for that.

Jane: Yes, I guess I do believe that.

Assisting survivors to recognize distortions in their beliefs is the next step in the cognitive restructuring process. Survivors are taught commonly exhibited thought distortions (e.g. all-or-nothing thinking, over-generalization, mislabelling, emotional reasoning) and are assisted in identifying these distortions in their own thought processes. The authors (Jehu et al., 1986) gave an example of the negative belief that one was responsible for sexual abuse in childhood because it lasted a long time and was perpetrated without the use of force. They suggested that this belief is due to the common cognitive distortions of personalization (assuming responsibility for events for which one is not to blame) and arbitrary inference (drawing negative conclusions not supported by facts).

The next stage, exploring alternatives, involves assisting the client in replacing distorted beliefs with more accurate, realistic beliefs. This procedure can involve providing factual information (e.g. statistics on the prevalence of childhood sexual abuse, discussion of the dynamics of the incestuous family), encouraging analysis of evidence that supports or disproves the client's conclusions, shifting from the subjective to the objective perspective (e.g. asking the client to judge other survivors in their position), and assisting clients with the process of reattribution of responsibility for the abuse. Alternatives to the belief that one was responsible for the abuse because it lasted a long time would include the following beliefs: the survivor was indoctrinated to please adults; he or she needed the offender's attention; and telling others might lead to being disbelieved, ignored, or punished.

Jane and her counsellor focused on recognizing the distortion in her belief that she caused her mother to be lonely and on exploring alternative beliefs by 'analysing evidence'. After reading a list of the common distortions, Jane decided that her belief distortions included personalization and arbitrary inference. The following interaction involved a discussion of this.

Jane: I assumed my mother left my stepfather because of what I told her. When I read about 'arbitrary inference' I thought that might be applicable because I really do not know why she left him. We have never talked about that.

Counsellor: What evidence do you have that your disclosure was the reason for their separation?

Jane: Timing. It happened shortly, well about six months, after I told her. Why else?

Counsellor: Let's discuss the 'why else?' Are there other reasons why they may have separated?

Jane: Well, they really never got along. He was always away on business. She always stuck with him, though. She thought to leave him would make her a two-time loser. She never got over that my dad left her.

Counsellor: So leaving him was something she considered before your disclosure …

Jane: Yes, but she never did it. So I still have to think …

Counsellor: What might be some other possible reasons for her leaving him?

Jane: There must be others, I know. I just assumed it was me. You know, maybe I can ask her.

Jane did ask her mother why she had left her husband. Her mother revealed that Jane's disclosure had precipitated her action, but reassured Jane that it did not cause it. Jane's stepfather had been having a relationship with another woman; Jane's mother had known about this for several years. The 'other woman' had a five-year-old daughter. Jane's mother left her husband and then told this woman of her husband's abuse of Jane in order to protect the little girl. Jane's mother had done this with the support of her own therapist, with whom she had been working since Jane's disclosure. She did not tell Jane about the other woman because she believed Jane had 'been through enough'. Jane's mother was lonely, but felt she had taken a healthy step in leaving her husband.

For Jane, cognitive restructuring involved identifying the belief that led to her depressed feelings whenever she came home from college, determining the distortion in the belief, and challenging the belief by considering possible alternatives with her counsellor and by actually 'analysing the evidence' when talking with her mother. Jane was thus able to see that the separation was not caused by her disclosure per se, and that what she considered a negative experience in her mother's life was actually a positive, although painful, event.

Dealing with guilt

Sgroi and Bunk (1988) have pointed out that survivors' feelings of guilt are often resistant to cognitive challenges. They reported that while survivors may feel less ashamed about their role in the abuse situation in response to cognitive challenges, they continue to experience significant guilt. For these survivors, guilt may serve a protective function, preventing them from being overwhelmed by feelings of powerlessness. The assumption that the abuse occurred because they wanted it in some way may be less aversive initially than accepting that the abuse was completely out of their control. Being told by a counsellor that they are not to blame and 'should not feel guilty', therefore, can result in overwhelming anxiety. Counsellors can acknowledge the guilt and suggest that such recalcitrant feelings will begin to subside when survivors begin to feel better. This reinforces the idea that the survivors' feelings are under their control and can be abandoned only when they no longer need them (Sgroi and Bunk, 1988).

Sgroi and Bunk discussed a therapeutic technique to address the guilt experienced by survivors. In a survivor group, members are asked to list everything they have done since the beginning of their abuse about which they feel guilty. The survivors and the counsellor (or group therapy members) discuss which of those items constitute legitimate guilt (i.e. what most people would feel guilty about) and which constitute inappropriate guilt (i.e. what most people would not feel guilty about). Hurting a sibling at the time of the abuse would result in legitimate guilt; accepting responsibility for the break-up of the family following disclosure would result in inappropriate guilt. This activity helps survivors to identify specific aspects of their guilt rather than experiencing it as a pervasive, consuming affect, and allows them to receive feedback from others regarding the causes of their guilt. Often, survivors plan expiatory actions (e.g. asking for forgiveness, apologizing) for behaviours that have resulted in legitimate guilt. They also experience a gradual lessening of inappropriate guilt related to the sexual abuse experience.

Respecting survivors' loyalty to their families

Gelinas (1983) discussed another issue to consider in facilitating the reattribution of blame – the need for the counsellor to respect survivors' loyalty to their family of origin, including the offender. Survivors may continue to feel protective, and in some cases loving, toward those who were responsible for their abuse or to other family members who were present when the abuse occurred. If family loyalties are ignored by counsellors who prematurely encourage the expression of anger, survivors' resistance to the reattribution process will increase. Survivors must have the opportunity to express their positive feelings toward the offender and the family. If these feelings are accepted by the counsellor, survivors can then explore issues of responsibility without feeling the need to defend family members.

Encouraging survivors to see themselves as children at the time of the abuse

Many of the cognitive procedures discussed above can be reinforced by the use of techniques that allow the client to consider more experientially their 'childlikeness' at the time of the abuse. Hall and Lloyd refer to this process as 're-entering the world of the child' (1989: 169).

Viewing photographs of themselves at the time of the abuse and discussing their reactions to the photographs with a counsellor or in a group setting can reinforce survivors' perception that as children they were incapable of initiating or consenting to sexual activity (Cole and Barney, 1987; Hall and Lloyd, 1989). Family photographs allow clients to experience visually how small and dependent they were, and how large and powerful the offender was. Survivors can then often sympathize with the child in the photo, something they were unable to do for themselves as children.

Another technique that can serve a similar purpose is having survivors observe children who are close to the age they were at the time of the abuse (Gordy, 1983). Visiting a nursery school class, for example, can be a powerful experience for survivors, enabling them to get in touch with their childhood needs and limitations. Some clinicians (Gordy, 1983) have suggested supplementing such activities with discussion of the stages of normal growth and development (e.g. Erikson, 1968) to help survivors understand how the abuse interrupted their emotional growth as children.

Reinforcing reattribution of responsibility with other survivors

Bibliotherapy

Contact with other survivors is a way of reinforcing reattribution of blame. Learning how other survivors were engaged in the abuse, why they maintained their secret, and how they dealt with issues of responsibility can help clients more easily come to accept that they were not responsible for their own abuse. One way of learning about the experiences of other survivors is by reading about their lives. This can initially be less threatening than speaking personally with other survivors and is often done by survivors prior to entering group counselling. Books written about incest experiences include: *Daddy's Girl* by Allen (1980); *I Know Why the Caged Bird Sings* by Angelou (1971); *Kiss Daddy Goodnight* by Armstrong (1978);

I Never Told Anyone: Writings by women survivors of child sexual abuse, edited by Bass and Thornton (1983); *Father's Days* by Brady (1979); *Voices in the Night: Women speaking about incest*, edited by McNaron and Morgan (1982); *Inside Scars* by Sisk and Hoffman (1987); and *Men Surviving Incest* by Thomas (1989).

Group counselling

Involvement in groups with other survivors of childhood sexual abuse is another powerful way to reinforce new perceptions. In groups, survivors often find that the engagement and secrecy strategies used by their offenders and family were similar to those used in other families. Gordy (1983) reported that members in her group identified a 'central motif', which was that offenders frequently used brainwashing (e.g. convincing the child she had solicited the abuse) as a method of ensuring the child's silence and continued participation in the sexual abuse activities.

Discussing issues of responsibility, engagement processes, 'Why me?' issues, and secret keeping within the group setting can be especially useful. Survivors find they can appreciate the fact that their peers were not to blame, had reasons for keeping the secret, and were powerless to stop the abuse. Because it is easier to be 'objective' when evaluating the abuse situations of others, this process can reinforce survivors' developing beliefs about their own abuse.

Reaffirming new beliefs

Reframing the abuse experience, especially the reattribution of blame, can be reinforced with techniques involving vicarious or actual encounters with the offender or with significant others. These techniques include role playing, letter writing, and planned confrontations.

Role playing

After survivors have worked on reframing the abuse emotionally and cognitively from an adult perspective, it is helpful if they can assert their new beliefs experientially. When the survivor can vicariously verbalize a new belief to the offender or to important others, it can serve both to reaffirm the belief and to further integrate the affect associated with the belief. Role playing may be done by using the Gestalt empty-chair technique, in which the survivor is asked to imagine the offender or other person sitting before them. They can prepare a statement summarizing their new beliefs or discoveries, their feelings associated with these discoveries, and any questions they may have for the other individual before carrying out the role play. It is important for survivors to process their feelings and reactions to this experience as the role playing can be very powerful. Examples of role play scenarios may include:

- a female survivor telling her father that she now realizes that as a five-year-old child she was too young to initiate the abuse. Therefore, she was not a 'seductive little thing', as he had always called her;
- a male survivor telling his uncle, the perpetrator, that although he did experience sexual arousal during the abusive experiences, he did not enjoy or seek the sexual

activity. The survivor expresses his anger toward the offender, reaffirms his sexual preference, and then tells his uncle that he (the survivor) no longer needs to hide his feelings behind a 'macho' image; or

- a female survivor listing to her mother all the reasons she kept the abuse by her father secret for so many years. She expresses disappointment that her mother was not perceptive enough to see, or strong enough to admit, that the abuse was occurring.

The following client–counsellor interaction demonstrates how the counsellor may facilitate the role play described in the first example. An empty chair faces the client, Brenda. She has imagined that her father, whom she has not seen for many years, is in the chair. Brenda has made a list of things she would like to cover and has given this list to the counsellor to help prompt her.

Counsellor: What would you like to tell your father?
Brenda: What a jerk he is.
Counsellor: Why don't you tell him directly?
Brenda: OK, I think what you did to me when I was a little girl was horrible. It hurt me terribly. In fact, it really affected the rest of my life.
Counsellor: Would you like to tell him how it hurt you?
Brenda: Yes. I grew up thinking I was to blame. You told me it happened because I was seductive. It started when I was only five years old. Ever since then I've thought all I was good for was sex. I thought I was not good enough to have anyone love me.
Counsellor: I know you also wanted to tell your dad what the abuse was like for you when you were little.
Brenda: I was frightened to death. It hurt so much at first. I used to pretend I wasn't there, like it was a dream. Once Mom took me to the doctor for an infection. I felt so dirty. For years after I grew up I could never go to the doctor. I've had so many medical problems. Back then I prayed I would die. That's what you did to your little five-year-old girl. [Starts to cry]
Counsellor: You look at what happened differently now than you used to. Tell your father what you've come to believe.
Brenda: I now believe that it was not my fault. It was entirely your fault. You betrayed me. I did not know enough to be seductive at first. I learned that from you and then that was the only way I knew how to be with men. Now, I know I can be loved for me, as a person, not because I'm 'sexy'. That was a line you fed me to keep me involved with you.
Counsellor: What else would you like to say to your father now?
Brenda: I don't wish you harm but neither do I forgive you. Mostly I want you to know what you have done to me. You'll have to live with that.

The counsellor asked Brenda to take a few minutes at the end of the role play to gather her thoughts. She and the counsellor then discussed what the experience was like for her. Brenda stated that she began to feel very sad when discussing how she had felt as a five-year-old. At this point in the role play, she re-experienced the helplessness she had remembered from childhood. By telling her father her new beliefs, she was able to feel a sense of control. After the role play, Brenda identified her main feeling as sadness over the loss of her childhood, which her father had taken from her. The role play helped her to reinforce the conviction that the abuse was not her fault.

Letter writing

A similar technique to reaffirm new beliefs is the use of the unsent letter (Faria and Belohlavek, 1984; Hall and Lloyd, 1989; Joy, 1987). Survivors write a letter to the offender or to others with whom they wish to share their new beliefs regarding the abuse. This technique is effective for survivors who find the empty-chair technique too threatening or for survivors who find its dramatic aspects too awkward. The letter remains unsent, as this allows survivors to express their thoughts and feelings without concern for the other's reaction. As with the role play, it is important that the counsellor process the experience with survivors by exploring what it was like for them to write the letter and what feelings were associated with the experience. (Actually mailing the letter involves issues similar to confrontation, which is discussed below.) Survivors may wish to keep the letter in a safe place and add to it as they continue to develop new beliefs or experience new feelings.

Confrontation

Confronting the perpetrator can be a powerful opportunity for survivors to assert their new beliefs and perceptions of the abuse experience. Because confronting the perpetrator has many ramifications for the healing process of survivors, it should be discussed thoroughly in counselling before the confrontation occurs (Agosta and Loring, 1988; Hall and Lloyd, 1989; Swanson and Biaggio, 1985).

Agosta and Loring (1988) have stressed that the decision to confront the perpetrator must originate with survivors themselves, since it is imperative that the confrontation be their choice. It is also important for survivors to realize that a confrontation with the offender is not a prerequisite to healing; rather, it is an experience that can be very beneficial for some survivors. Confrontation is most successful when survivors use it to assert, rather than to test out, their new insights related to the sexual abuse. If survivors continue to struggle with denial, minimization, or self-blame, they are not ready to confront the offender, as the offender's response of denial, minimization, or blaming the survivor could be detrimental to the survivors' healing (Hall and Lloyd, 1989). Many survivors may harbour the hope, even without realizing it, that the offender will admit to the abuse, fully recognize the impact it has had, and ask for forgiveness. If survivors can verbalize this hope, they often realize it is unrealistic and re-evaluate their need for the confrontation.

It is also helpful for clients to consider what feelings the confrontation experience might provoke. Because a confrontation can evoke strong affective responses and at times a return of trauma symptomatology, survivors may need to provide for their self-care, safety, and self-nurturance.

One participant in the incest healing study (Draucker, 1992b) gives an example of an unplanned, unsuccessful confrontation with her brother during a family reunion:

> Out of the blue I just said, 'Do you remember when we were eight – or when I was eight and you were eleven', and described the first incident of incest. He's like 'Well, yeah, you know. I think I remember that.' And the way he was talking about it, it was like someone else had done it, not himself ... and I kept asking more and more questions – just to verify that yes, at least it happened and I'm not crazy, you know, it did happen. And then I said, 'How do you feel about that?' and he said, 'I don't feel responsible. My hormones were going crazy on me during adolescence and I had no control. I didn't know what I was doing.' ... I said, 'I want you to say you're sorry.' He said, 'No, I'm not going to say I'm sorry because it's not my fault. I couldn't help myself.' And that was the end of that confrontation and that plummeted me down because OK, he's not going to take the blame for it, then it must have been my fault. So I took the blame and hated myself. So all last year I was really hating myself. That's what led to my intense misery.

In addition to an awareness of the emotional risks of a confrontation to the survivor, counsellors, due in large part to the false memory controversy, have become increasingly sensitive to issues of harm to third parties. Courtois stressed that counsellors should not advise any action with the potential to harm others, such as confrontation, but should explore the advantages and disadvantages of such actions:

> I require as a condition of treatment that patients not make an impulsive and/or unplanned disclosure of abuse (whether known or suspected), especially to the alleged perpetrator or other family members. Any decisions to confront or disclose the abuse must be carefully discussed, decided upon, and planned, since it carries considerable risk potential to both the practitioner and the patient. If a patient does not abide by this agreement, I reserve the right to discontinue treatment and make a referral. (1999: 173)

Brown et al. express similar cautions:

> If a patient does decide to confront an alleged abuser, it is critically important for the therapist to clarify in writing that the confrontation does not create any type of therapeutic relationship between the therapist and alleged abuser. This should take the form of a written release by the patient that acknowledges that the confrontation may be emotionally distressing to both the alleged abuser and the patient. Informed consent documents should not be signed by the alleged abuser because that would create an appearance of a professional relationship. (1998: 503)

Counsellors may assist the client to prepare for a confrontation if he or she continues to express the desire for this after carefully considering all ramifications; has progressed significantly with issues of denial, minimization, and self-blame; and is not motivated by hope of the offender's contrition. Clients must first decide how they would like to confront the offender (face to face, over the phone, by sending a letter). The pros and cons of each of these approaches should be discussed. Sending a letter may be less threatening, but may leave the survivor wondering whether the letter was received and what the offender's response was. It is, nonetheless, often the method used when the survivor and the offender have been estranged for some time and the survivor does not desire personal contact. Confrontation over the phone can be less threatening than a face-to-face confrontation and is safer if violence by the offender is a concern. However, the survivor is not privy to the offender's non-verbal responses and the offender can easily choose to hang up the phone at any time.

The same survivor discussed above described a more successful confrontation with her brother approximately a year after she had been in treatment:

> I was finally able to say, 'You screwed me up – it's your fault.' And that was a big deal for me to say. And I said, 'Consequently, I don't want you touching me ever, ever again. I don't want you to hug me when I come home. I don't want you to kiss me. I don't want to be your sister any more. I'm not hanging out with you any more. Stay out of my way. I am going to get help because I like myself and I'm worth it ... You're the scumbag that did this to me and I'm going to reverse it if it takes the rest of my life. But you're not going to beat me.' I go, 'I'm surviving. I'm a survivor.' And he was crying, which was a big deal ... I don't care and I – it was a way of expressing myself and not really giving a s— what he had to say.
>
> (Draucker, 1992b)

Case example

The following case exemplifies the process of reframing an experience of childhood sexual abuse from an adult perspective.

Eleanor was a 42-year-old successful businesswoman who sought counselling to deal with her experience of childhood sexual abuse after she had viewed a TV movie that dealt with incest. From the ages of 8 to 13 she had been abused by her grandfather, who lived in her family's home. The abuse involved sexual fondling that usually occurred when Eleanor would come home from school and her parents were still at work. Although Eleanor described her adulthood as 'fairly normal', the movie caused her to wonder whether her avoidance of any intimate contact with men was related to her experience with her grandfather.

Eleanor made rapid progress in the early stages of counselling. She readily disclosed the abuse to her counsellor and was able to describe the experience in detail. However, after approximately six months in counselling, Eleanor described feeling 'stuck' and wondered whether she should discontinue treatment. When she introduced this concern, her counsellor asked her what she hoped would happen next in the healing process. Eleanor discussed her belief that she was the cause of the abuse, that her grandfather was really just a 'lonely, pathetic man', and that most of the fondling occurred because she would 'snuggle' next to him on the couch while they watched their afternoon TV shows. She claimed that she had hoped that counselling would decrease her feelings of guilt. The more she discussed her experiences, however, the more she realized she wanted and sought her grandfather's attention. The following interaction was aimed at reframing Eleanor's beliefs related to responsibility for the abuse:

Eleanor: I remember feeling miserable all day in school. I was lonely, didn't fit in with the other kids. Actually, I looked forward to coming home to be with Grandpa. He waited for me. I know this sounds stupid, but he always had milk and homemade cookies for me. We would have our afternoon shows. I would 'snuggle' with him on the couch and I liked that, so how can I say he abused me?

(Continued)

(Continued)

I really did seek him out. He was just a poor old man. I cannot blame him for what happened. If I had been out playing like normal kids, none of this would have happened.

Counsellor: Tell me more about the loneliness you felt as an eight-year-old.

Eleanor: Well, up until that time we moved a lot. My father did a residency in Chicago; then my mother did hers in Boston. Then back to Chicago, where my father did some research. You get the picture … Anyway, I was never in one place very long and my parents were always at the hospital or the lab. I spent a lot of time with relatives. I think my mother really resented Grandpa's needing to move in with us, because now she had two of us to take care of. I think she regretted having me. I interfered with her work, you know. No, I shouldn't say this. They were OK parents. Now my mother is kind of famous. She was just sort of cold and distant. I never remember either of them playing with me. It didn't help that I was so shy. I guess it's natural that Grandpa and I hooked up. God, I sound like a whiner, don't I?

Counsellor: No. You sound like someone describing a childhood during which you were uprooted a lot, you didn't feel wanted or attended to, and you experienced a lot of loneliness. You were missing the attention and the affection you needed. When your grandfather came along and provided those things for you, that naturally felt good.

Eleanor: Yes, it did feel good.

Counsellor: It sounds like, at that time in your life, your grandfather was the only one available to provide those things. All eight-year-olds need attention and affection.

Eleanor: Yes, so do forty-somethings. [*Laughs*]

Counsellor: How true!

Eleanor: Attention and affection were certainly things my parents did not provide. They gave me everything else. Everything else materialistic, that is. But I knew that the sex came along with the attention from my grandfather. I always knew that.

Counsellor: It sounds like you were needing your grandfather's attention and his affection when you 'sought him out'. Because you could not get those things from others in your life, you sought them from the only adult who was available. It was natural for you to do this as a child. *Other* lonely eight-year-olds would *likely* have done the same thing. Seeking attention and affection is very different than seeking, or being responsible for, sexual abuse.

Eleanor: Yes, I guess I really did need him for those other things.

Counsellor: As a child, everything probably seemed confusing to you. Although you needed your grandfather's affection, he also used you sexually. As an adult, you can appreciate that you were naturally seeking to meet your needs for attention and affection; you were not seeking the sexual abuse nor were you responsible for it.

Eleanor: Yes, that is true. The sex part I hated.

In this interaction, the counsellor explored with Eleanor what she had needed as an eight-year-old child and challenged the belief that because Eleanor was desperate for

(Continued)

(Continued)

her grandfather's affection, she also desired, and was therefore responsible for, the sexual abuse. The counsellor and Eleanor had several similar interactions to reinforce this belief as Eleanor had been convinced for many years that she had sought the sexual activity.

Eleanor was able to express anger and disappointment toward her 'absentee parents'. Actually attributing the blame for the abuse to her grandfather was very difficult and occurred only after the counsellor encouraged Eleanor to discuss the positive memories she had of him. When she could acknowledge that her grandfather was not a 'horrible monster', she could also acknowledge that he engaged in the sexual activity to meet his own needs. Eleanor struggled for some time before accepting the fact that she could be angry about the abuse without discounting the positive feelings she had toward her grandfather. In the following interaction between Eleanor and the counsellor, Eleanor began to accept her grandfather's responsibility for the abuse.

Eleanor:	He was really sweet and kind in many ways. Why he did what he did I will never know. He must not have known how much it hurt me.
Counsellor:	As children, we usually assume that adults are all good or all bad. Because your grandfather was kind and attentive, and because you really appreciated much of your time together, you assumed he was all good. Unfortunately, that led you to believe you were bad. As adults, we can appreciate that people have good and bad points and do good and bad things. Your grandfather is no exception. He was kind and gentle and attentive and he also used you as a little girl to meet his own needs.
Eleanor:	Yes, he did do that. And because of that I do feel betrayed by him. If he was sick, he should have gotten help. What he did has caused me grief my whole life. Sometimes I do feel angry about that. Yet, I still miss him. That does not make sense.
Counsellor:	Maybe it does. You loved him and would naturally miss him. But you can also feel angry and betrayed as well.

Eleanor also struggled with the fact that the abuse had lasted for a long time, past when she 'should have known better'. By considering her emotionally unmet needs, she was able to state that she needed attention and affection as much at the age of 13 as she did when she was eight. Eleanor was quite clear that she did not tell her parents of the abuse because they would have 'kicked' her grandfather out of the house, a prospect she could not tolerate.

Although she decided not to disclose the abuse to her parents, Eleanor identified the need to get some 'closure' on her relationship with her grandfather, who was now dead. She visited his grave, which was in another state, and told him how she had been hurt by the abuse. She explained to him that she could not forgive him, but that she was grateful for the non-sexual activities they had shared and for the attention he gave her. She told him that her sense of betrayal, rather than anger, was now paramount.

There were several aspects of Eleanor's abuse experience that made the reframing process challenging. Reattribution of blame was especially difficult because her grandfather had been her main source of emotional support as a child. For this

(Continued)

(Continued)

reason, it was especially important that the counsellor respected the loyalty that Eleanor felt toward her grandfather. Because she did not need to defend him, Eleanor could hold her grandfather, rather than herself, responsible for the abuse. A key issue that Eleanor needed to explore was the emotional void she experienced as a child. She could then see that although she would seek out her grandfather, it was because she craved his affection, a basic childhood need, not the sexual activity. Exploring what an average eight-year-old would know about sex might have further reinforced Eleanor's understanding that her needs were emotional, not sexual. She might also have realized that, as a child, she would have had trouble differentiating affectionate touches from sexual touches.

Although Eleanor responded well to cognitive challenges, the experiential part of her healing seemed to come when she visited her grandfather's grave. The counsellor's role in this was to assist Eleanor in planning what she wanted to say, in anticipating what her emotional response might be, and in planning ways to care for herself following the experience. Eleanor had several debriefing sessions with the counsellor following the graveside visit.

7 Addressing the Context of the Sexual Abuse

Because sexual abuse often occurs in the context of disturbed family functioning, exploration of other relevant issues that had an impact on childhood development can be important. This chapter will address the processes of exploring the context of the abuse, especially issues related to the client's family of origin. Such exploration can enhance the ongoing connection of developmental influences with current concerns.

Exploring the context of the abuse

Although focusing on the sexual abuse experience is important, it is essential to acknowledge that sexual abuse occurs within a larger context, often within a family system. Other significant factors that had an impact on the client's development, i.e. 'life context of the sexual abuse' (Sgroi and Bunk, 1988: 148), need to be addressed and explored. Addressing other experiences and relationships, both positive and negative, avoids the suggestion that the client's development was shaped entirely by abuse. As Davis has stated:

> For some survivors it [the sexual abuse] is by far the most pervasive influence. For others, growing up in a racist society, being adopted, living in poverty, or being the first child of five had an equal or greater impact. In assessing its effects on your life, it's important to put the abuse in perspective with the other forces that shaped you. (1990: 138–9)

One survivor in the incest healing study (Draucker, 1992b) stressed the importance of dealing with other contextual issues:

> I think what the incest survivors' group did for me was have a ... it was a forum for all of us to explore whatever those childhood issues were. It wasn't just the incest, but as soon as I say that, for me what comes up are the abandonment issues.

Significant childhood influences are, of course, numerous and varied. Important factors to explore include family composition (e.g. the loss of a parent through divorce, death, separation; the role of other significant caretakers; the survivor's birth order; the number of siblings in the family), social factors (e.g. ethnic origin, socioeconomic class, religious influences), other significant family pathology or stressors (e.g. parental alcoholism, emotional or physical abuse, mental illness, criminal behaviour), and extra-familial resources (e.g. relationships with teachers, sports activities, counselling involvement).

Family functioning

Recently, the concept of adult children of dysfunctional families has been applied to individuals from families with diverse problems (e.g. alcoholism, sexual abuse, physical abuse, emotional neglect), as these individuals often struggle with similar concerns. For example, there are significant parallels between Gelinas' (1983) description of the parentified child in the incestuous family and Wegscheider-Cruse's (1985) description of the family hero in the chemically dependent family (a family in which at least one member abuses drugs or alcohol). The family hero is the child who assumes responsibility for other family members and contributes to the family's public presentation of normality through his or her good behaviour and achievements. Both parentified children and family heroes assume adult responsibilities and learn to meet the needs of others while denying their own needs, often losing the opportunity for a normal childhood. Other roles identified by Wegscheider-Cruse (1985) include: the enabler, who supports the behaviour of the chemically dependent person by attempting to help or 'cover' for him or her; the family scapegoat, who draws attention away from the family's problems by getting into trouble (e.g. at school, with the law); the lost child, who quietly withdraws from the family; and the mascot, who draws attention away from the family's problems by providing humour and mischief.

Satir (1988) compared the closed system of 'troubled' families and the open system of 'nurturing' families. In a closed family system, communication is indirect, unclear, and non-specific; rules are inflexible and covert; and self-esteem among members is low. In an open family system, communication is direct, clear, and specific; rules are flexible and overt; and self-esteem among members is high. In a closed system, outside influences are discouraged; in an open system, free exchange with the environment is sought. Closed family systems are dysfunctional because they prohibit the growth potential of their members.

Farmer (1989: 18) has identified eight 'specific interactional elements' that are characteristic of abusive families. These elements are: denial; inconsistency and unpredictability; lack of empathy; lack of clear boundaries; role reversal; a closed family system; incongruent communication; and too much or too little conflict. Farmer has also identified the general effects exhibited by adults who have grown up in abusive families. These include: lack of trust, avoidance of feelings, low self-esteem, a sense of helplessness, and difficulty in relationships.

A concept that has emerged from the literature on adult children of dysfunctional families is that of 'healing the child within' (Whitfield, 1989). Whitfield defined the child within as 'the part of each of us which is ultimately alive, energetic, creative, and fulfilled; it is our Real Self – who we truly are' (1989: 1). Due to certain childhood experiences such as emotional neglect, alcoholism, or abuse, individuals learn to deny their child within. This results in passivity; self-criticism; orientation toward others; and inhibition of creativity, spontaneity, and joy in adulthood.

Counselling procedures have been developed on the basis of the concept of the child within, sometimes referred to as the inner child. Farmer (1989), for example, discussed techniques for reparenting the inner child using imagery. This involves first releasing one's original parents by recognizing that they are the products of their own fragmented, injurious childhoods (1989: 104) and accepting that one no longer requires anything from one's parents to survive. Creating new internal parents is accomplished by imaging a mother and father who possess the desired parental qualities, such as protectiveness, supportiveness, and sensitivity (i.e. a 'Good Mother' and a 'Good Father'). Finally, adopting one's inner child involves first imaging a time from one's childhood when one was hurt and then imaging a 'Good Mother' or a 'Good Father' showing concern and care for one's needs. Farmer suggests that this activity can teach one to provide nurturance for one's own inner child.

Healing is facilitated if survivors are able to place the sexual abuse experience in the larger perspective of their overall childhood development. For example, counsellors may ask clients to consider Farmer's eight elements of abusive families or the roles of a dysfunctional family as suggested by Wegscheider-Cruse. Clients then reflect on those issues that were salient in their own families of origin. Survivors may then consider how, for example, incongruent communication in their family of origin has had an impact on their current communication patterns or how their role as the family hero continues to be carried out in their present lives. It is also useful if survivors are encouraged to discuss the influence of positive intra-familial and extra-familial childhood experiences on their present development.

Case example

The following case vignette highlights the importance of exploring the context of the abuse in order for clients to be able to place their sexual abuse experience in a meaningful context. Heather, a 24-year-old graduate student, had been sexually abused by an uncle on several occasions when she was 12 years old. She had sought counselling originally to deal with frequent nightmares and several phobias (e.g. of being alone in the dark, or of taking showers when alone in her apartment). After focusing on the abuse experience, her symptoms essentially subsided. Yet Heather complained that she still felt that there were pieces of the experience with which she had not come to terms. After several sessions spent exploring what was 'missing', Heather decided to explore more closely the dynamics of her family of origin. She had claimed they were a normal, very close family. Her mother and father had maintained that the abusive uncle was truly a black sheep in an otherwise very respectable extended family. When Heather told her father that the uncle had molested her, her father banned him from any further contact with the family. After exploring her family's responses to the abuse more closely, and identifying some family dysfunction, Heather was better able to understand both her response to the abuse and her ways of coping with problems.

Heather:	It was weird. They [her parents] were very supportive. They told me it was not my fault, that I shouldn't worry about it. My father told my uncle never to see me or any of the family again. They even took me on a wonderful trip to help me get over it. In fact, at the time it brought us closer together.
Counsellor:	Looking back now, what about that seemed weird?
Heather:	Well, I guess that when we got back from the trip no more was said. I mean, they were still supportive. When I would dream

(Continued)

(Continued)

	about my uncle, my mother would come into my room, get me water, rub my back, generally calm me down. But she would never ask what the dream was about. I assumed she did not want to bring up bad memories.
Counsellor:	And what do you think now?
Heather:	Well now I realize I needed to talk about it. Also, I guess I wonder why they never brought charges against him or got me any professional help. In those days I guess people did not do that as much. But I still wonder why they didn't. What if he did the same thing to one of my cousins?
Counsellor:	What does their response tell you about your family?
Heather:	I think that they tried very hard to be the perfect family. We never fought, never got angry at each other. Appearance was important to the outside world. Because of this, I think, the abuse was denied, swept under the rug, maybe. They told me it was not my fault, for which I am really grateful, but we never talked any more about it again. They should have at least told my other uncles and aunts to watch out for their kids. I guess by not acknowledging it to the outside world, we could keep our image of the normal family. But, you know, it was not just the abuse. For example, my mother had breast cancer when I was young and never told anyone, not even me, until years later. She quit her job as a schoolteacher rather than tell anyone she had cancer.
Counsellor:	How did your family's way of handling the abuse affect your healing?
Heather:	It fed into my denial, I think. Made the abuse seem more unreal. Like it never happened. More importantly, I guess, I learned not to face things myself. Do you know, I've had a lump in my breast for six months and I've not had it checked out.

Exploring her family's functioning, both in response to the abuse and more generally, allowed Heather to gain insight into some of her present experiences. Although the trauma symptomatology did seem to result directly from her abuse, other issues she faced (such as her tendency to avoid problems) were also related to family and developmental influences. Until these issues were addressed, she had felt something was missing from her healing experiences.

Non-offending family members

Another context issue is the role of important non-offending family members. Survivors often struggle with their feelings toward other family members who were present when the abuse occurred but did not protect them. Because abuse often involves adult male offenders, often fathers or stepfathers, and female child victims, the non-offending family member most often addressed in the literature is the mother.

Mothers have often been blamed for the abuse that occurs in the family. In both popular and clinical literature, it has been suggested that the cold, sexually unavailable wife drove her husband to her daughter and at times colluded in the abuse to avoid her own sexual 'responsibilities'. The offender is therefore thought to hold no responsibility for the abuse. In reaction to this sexist attitude, some counsellors have discouraged survivors from exploring their feelings toward their mothers. Herman, for example, critiqued counselling approaches that prohibit 'mother-blaming' by survivors:

> Although fathers and not mothers are entirely to blame, victims must be permitted to express the depth of their anger at both parents. The victim who is not permitted to express her anger at her mother or her tender feelings for her father will not be able to transcend these feelings or to put them in a new perspective. (1981: 200)

In addressing reactions toward the non-offending family member, it is important for both counsellors and survivors to differentiate between responsibility for protecting the child and responsibility for the abuse itself (Hall and Lloyd, 1989). As Gelinas (1983) stated, the abuser is always responsible for the sexual contact, whereas all adult family members are responsible for the incestuous family dynamics. The non-offending family member could be any responsible older person or caretaker in the family when the abuse occurred. Because survivors usually struggle with issues related to a parent or parents who did not protect them, non-offending parents will be the focus of this discussion.

Inevitably, clients question the role of non-offending parents in the abuse. There are several possibilities regarding their role: they had no knowledge of the abuse; they suspected but did not acknowledge the abuse; they knew of the abuse but did not intervene; or they knew of the abuse and condoned it (Hall and Lloyd, 1989). Survivors may never definitely know which role a non-offending parent played. After exploring the possibilities and confronting their own denial and minimization, survivors usually come to some conclusion about this issue.

Some individuals state that it is easier to hate the offender than to be angry at the non-offending parent, whom they may still love and with whom they may have close, current contact. As one survivor in the incest healing study (Draucker, 1992b) stated:

> But my stepfather, I don't care about. I was more hurt by my mom staying with him. I couldn't care less. I don't care if I ever see him again. Just don't like him as a person but my mom hurt me more because I care about her more. Do you see that?

It is important, therefore, for counsellors to encourage survivors to express their feelings about non-offending parents. These feelings may range from disappointment that a parent was not strong enough to recognize the abuse to intense rage because a parent knew of the abuse and either ignored or condoned it.

Hall and Lloyd (1989) have suggested that it can be helpful if survivors explore the reasons for the actions or inactions of non-offending caretakers, and place their behaviour in the larger context of the family dynamics. This should not imply that survivors are not entitled to their angry feelings or that they should forgive the non-offending parent for his or her actions. Instead it may help survivors make sense of their own experience. For example, it could be helpful to understand the non-offending parent's family history, which may have included childhood abuse. Such information provides some explanation for the parent's inactivity and inability to protect the child.

Connecting present concerns with childhood experiences

Addressing abuse context issues will facilitate clients' ability to connect their childhood experiences with their current issues. Making these connections occurs throughout much of counselling. Clients gain insight into how certain responses that once served as a way to survive a harmful environment can now be relinquished in favour of alternative, healthy responses. Counselling involves a delicate balance between exploring childhood issues and addressing current functioning. One participant in the incest healing study (Draucker, 1992b) described this process in her own therapy:

> I think then probably what she [her therapist] did for me, or what we worked on together, was to talk about what had happened and for her to help me see how as a child, you start doing things to cope and to get by. And then what she did was bring it into the present day. It seemed like she had a very good ability to – you know, I would come in and start to talk about some problems that I was having today whether it was with my family or my boss or my husband, and in the next few sessions we would get back into the abuse time period and she would help me see how the way I reacted to that was affecting the way I react to people today.

Often, clients respond to the counsellor as they did to significant individuals from their past. They may expect the counsellor to hurt them through rejection, exploitation, or manipulation and respond to the counsellor with fear, mistrust, rage, or excessive dependency. It is important for clients to be given the opportunity to explore their current reactions to the counsellor in relation to reactions they have toward other significant individuals in their lives. To avoid repeating problematic interactional patterns that clients have experienced previously, counsellors should avoid an authoritarian approach, set clear and realistic limits, and reinforce clients' independence and self-acceptance (Briere and Runtz, 1988).

Case study

The following case shows the importance of addressing the context of a sexual abuse experience in counselling.

Jerry was a 36-year-old married male who worked with his father in a small family-owned machine shop. He sought counselling at a community mental health centre because he had a depression that he 'could not shake'. Jerry claimed that he was tired most of the time, could not concentrate on his work, and had lost all sexual desire. Although he claimed that his relationship with his wife of eight years had always been good, they were currently experiencing some problems because they could not conceive a child. After years of infertility treatment, they had given up trying. Jerry stated that he was content not to have children, but had problems dealing with his wife's disappointment. He reported that she frequently complained that he was unavailable to her emotionally, and that she felt like she was dealing with this loss alone.

(Continued)

(Continued)

Jerry was the youngest of three children. His older brother Tom, aged 44, was an alcoholic who worked sporadically at the machine shop. His older sister Jean, aged 40, was the office manager at the shop. Jerry stated that she was the one who kept things going. Jean was married with two children. Jerry stated that his father was an alcoholic who nonetheless managed to show up at the shop every day for 35 years. His mother stayed at home and was always 'pretty unhappy'.

When asked about significant childhood events, Jerry reluctantly revealed that at the age of 11 he had been molested in the park on his way home from school by two older boys whom he knew. They asked him to play a 'game' with them that resulted in each of them penetrating Jerry anally. Jerry was upset by the experience and told Tom about it. His brother responded by saying it 'sounded like fun' and then molested Jerry himself. This abuse by Tom, involving anal intercourse, occurred several more times. Tom said that if Jerry told their parents of their activities, he would deny it and would beat Jerry for telling; Tom had been physically violent when the brothers were younger.

The initial focus of counselling was on the abuse experience itself. Jerry dealt with issues of self-blame for not standing up to his brother and the other boys, anger toward Tom, and questions regarding his own sexuality. Much of Jerry's counselling also involved addressing the context of the sexual abuse. Jerry was encouraged by the counsellor to describe his family members, their relationships with each other, and major family events. In the following interaction, the counsellor introduces the idea that the experiences that accompanied the abuse could have had an important impact on Jerry's development.

Counsellor:	Jerry, you've worked hard dealing with your abuse experiences and the impact they've had on your life. I also wonder about other things that were occurring in your family at that time.
Jerry:	I'm not sure what you mean.
Counsellor:	Many things that children experience, not just abuse, can affect them in adulthood. What was your relationship with your parents like at that time?
Jerry:	Well, it was not good with my dad. I guess you could say he was a drunk.

The family did have many attributes of a dysfunctional family. Jerry's dad was an alcoholic and his mother was apparently chronically depressed. Jerry stated that his father drank 8–10 beers nightly until he passed out, although he never missed work. His mother would often complain about his father's drinking. When his dad's business associates called him in the evening, she would tell them that he was bowling or shopping; in fact, he had usually passed out. Because he would get quite irritable when drinking, she would keep the children quiet so as not to disturb him. Jerry claimed that no one outside of the family ever realized his dad had a drinking problem. His mother was always extremely tired and often tearful.

As a child, Jean did well in school and was actively involved in the family business at a young age. The family was 'shocked' when she got pregnant and married at the age of 16 because she had always been 'so good'. As a child, Tom was always in trouble at school and had several minor scrapes with the law for various violations (e.g. petty theft, disturbing the peace). Jerry described Tom as a bully who never obeyed their parents. On the other hand, Jerry described himself as a loner in school

(Continued)

(Continued)

who never caused the family any trouble. He stated that his family 'kind of ignored me'. He worked in the machine shop as a boy, but he never enjoyed the work.

In counselling, Jerry did some reading on chemically dependent families and became animated when discussing how classically his family members played the roles he read about. His mother's enabling behaviours were clear. He remarked that Tom was the scapegoat, Jean was the hero, and he was the lost child. Having this understanding of his family helped Jerry accept that he wasn't 'just a loser'. He recognized that his family's poor communication styles and isolation from the community, except through the business, were also characteristics of a dysfunctional family.

Dealing with his feelings toward his parents regarding the sexual abuse was more difficult for Jerry. He stated that he had never thought they knew of the abuse, but had begun to question why this was so. It was only after being in counselling for almost a year that he did begin to express disappointment and anger at his parents' failure to protect him from the abuse. He realized that he never told them of the abuse because he believed they could not have helped him. The following interaction represents Jerry's struggle with this issue.

Jerry:	I guess I always knew they [his parents] had problems of their own, but I never thought their problems affected me – or had anything to do with what my brother did to me. But maybe, I don't know, if they had not been messed up. I never told them, though.
Counsellor:	Remember yourself as a young boy. What kept you from telling them?
Jerry:	Well, I probably knew they couldn't – or wouldn't – do anything to stop Tom. He ran wild. They couldn't control him.
Counsellor:	It would have been futile to tell them?
Jerry:	Yes. When I talk about them they sound like losers. Now I guess I do wish they did something. Ya, I guess some parents might have done something, or noticed something happening, or found out. I wish mine had. I sure wish they had stopped it. They knew he beat me up and couldn't have cared less. [*Speaks softly, begins to fidget*] It's Tom's doing though, not theirs.
Counsellor:	Yes, only Tom is responsible for abusing you, and I know you've expressed the rage and hurt you feel toward him. It seems hard, however, for you to discuss your disappointment that your parents did not take action to stop him somehow.
Jerry:	Ya, I'm not sure why.

Jerry was able to connect his current concerns with the abuse situation in several ways. He recognized that he was dealing with the pain of infertility by withdrawing from his wife, much as he had withdrawn from his family as a child to try to avoid pain. Although the couple had been given a diagnosis of idiopathic, or unexplained, infertility, Jerry had attributed the infertility problems to himself. As an adolescent, he had extreme concerns about his sexual identity. He realized that currently, on some level, he thought the infertility reflected his lack of 'manliness'. Just as he blamed himself for not protecting himself from his brother's abuse by concluding that he was not a 'man', he blamed himself for the infertility by deciding that, regardless of what the doctors said, he was sterile. This served to reinforce his already poor self-concept.

(Continued)

(Continued)

Jerry's healing involved dealing with the abuse experience and the context within which it occurred. As a result of being the 'lost child' in his dysfunctional family, he felt insignificant and was left without the emotional resources to deal with his current crisis. Although much of Jerry's distress was related to the sexual abuse, general family issues clearly contributed to many of his concerns. Once he addressed these issues, he was free to begin to make changes in his life. These changes will be discussed in the following chapter.

8 Making Desired Life Changes

Once clients have addressed issues related to the sexual abuse experience and its context and have connected their childhood coping patterns with their current concerns, they often begin to make desired life changes and restructure their lives in ways they find more satisfying. This chapter will address some of the behavioural and lifestyle changes frequently made by survivors. Several experts have referred to this work as 'late phase treatment' because clients, having accomplished the goals of exploratory work, are free to focus on self-development and relationship concerns. Courtois stated:

> The gains achieved over the course of treatment, development of a self less encumbered by traumatic intrusions and effects, and continued development of interpersonal connections are consolidated and built upon in this third phase. (1999: 215)

Three areas of adult adjustment that are often addressed at this point in counselling are self-esteem, interpersonal functioning, and sexual functioning.

Self-esteem

Survivors often struggle with self-esteem concerns throughout the healing process. Although the reframing of the abuse experience (as previously discussed) can be effective in addressing the guilt and shame that underlie the survivors' negative self-image, dealing with self-esteem often remains a salient issue even late in counselling.

Although addressing self-esteem is frequently identified as a counselling goal, it is sometimes approached in an oversimplified manner (e.g. giving a client 'positive feedback'). Peplau proposed a model that can guide the counsellor in addressing self-esteem issues in depth (cited in O'Toole and Welt, 1989). This model suggests that there are three dimensions, or self-views, that comprise one's concept of the self.

The first dimension, the *self-views in awareness*, consists of conscious, familiar, and often articulated self-perceptions. These views reflect the messages about oneself that were heard frequently from significant others in childhood. The *self-views in awareness* of the client with a poor self-image are often that he or she is bad, worthless, or dirty.

The second dimension, the *maybe me self-views*, consists of self-perceptions that are not immediately in one's awareness. One may, however, apply these views to oneself if one's attention is directed toward them. These views reflect messages received only occasionally in childhood. For survivors of abuse, the *maybe me self-views* are often positive qualities that perhaps teachers or some other supportive adults in their lives acknowledged. A *maybe me self-view* of an abuse survivor might be that he or she was a good student and a child of some worth to someone.

The third dimension, the *not me self-views*, consists of self-perceptions that are out of awareness. Because these views are associated with severe anxiety, they are dissociated from the individual's experience. An abuse survivor's *not me self-view* might be that he or she is a worthy, valuable individual who possesses basic personal rights. Although these are positive perceptions, such self-views are at odds with the ways in which individuals with negative self-images are accustomed to perceiving themselves.

Counselling interventions

Survivors often make negative comments about themselves that reflect their low self-esteem and require intervention by counsellors. Peplau cautioned counsellors against challenging these negative self-views in awareness with laudatory comments regarding the client's value or worth in an effort to improve his or her self-esteem (see O'Toole and Welt, 1989). Although self-views in awareness are often negative, they are comfortable and expected. Simple compliments regarding positive qualities often reflect clients' *not me self-views*, which are associated with anxiety; these compliments, therefore, evoke defensiveness. Instead of praising clients, counsellors should first facilitate discussion of ways in which a self-view in awareness was noticed by the client or stated by others. Peplau called this method an investigative approach. Table 8.1 outlines a client statement exemplifying a negative self-view in awareness and non-facilitative and facilitative counsellor responses.

Peplau believed that this type of discussion will enable *maybe me* statements to emerge (see O'Toole and Welt, 1989). A *maybe me* statement is often a tentative or conditional positive self-statement. The counsellor can reinforce this statement with specific observations and have clients describe situations in which they have experienced the maybe me self-view. Table 8.2 outlines a client statement exemplifying a *maybe me self-view* and non-facilitative and facilitative counsellor responses.

Peplau emphasized the need for counsellors to address the anxiety that is likely to be associated with the expression of positive *not me self-views* (see O'Toole and Welt, 1989). Clients can be encouraged to describe feelings related to a self-view that is at variance with the self-view to which they are accustomed; they can then

Table 8.1   Interventions for statements reflecting the self-view in awareness

Client statement:	I am a slut. I'm not worth you helping me.
Non-facilitative counsellor response:	I think you are a worthwhile person and I look forward to helping you.
Facilitative counsellor responses:	1 Tell me who first told you that you were a slut. (Exploring when self-view was said.) 2 When did you first feel worthless? (Exploring when self-view was noticed.) 3 Tell me about a specific time that you felt like a slut. (Exploring when self-view was applied.)

Table 8.2   Interventions for statements reflecting the maybe me self-view

Client statement:	Well, I guess not everyone thinks of me as a slut just because that's what my stepfather told me I was. The other group members don't seem to see me like that.
Non-facilitative counsellor response:	Yes, they see you for the worthwhile human being you are.
Facilitative counsellor responses:	1 Yes, I've noticed they have commented that you have useful things to say. (Feedback-specific observation.) 2 Yes, I've noticed others in the group do treat you with respect. (Feedback-specific observation.) 3 Tell me about other people who do not consider you a slut. (Exploring when self-view is experienced.)

Table 8.3   Interventions for statements reflecting the not me self-view

Client statement:	I realize now that I am not a slut. I am a worthwhile human being.
Non-facilitative counsellor response:	I'm glad you've realized this. It will make a big difference in your life. I'm very happy for you.
Facilitative counsellor responses:	1 What is it like for you to think of yourself in this new way? (Exploring feelings.) 2 Tell me about a situation in which you have applied (or will apply) this new way of looking at yourself. (Exploring ways to apply this self-view.)

begin to consider how this new self-view can be applied. Table 8.3 outlines a client statement exemplifying a *not me self-view* and non-facilitative and facilitative counsellor responses.

Peplau's model, therefore, suggests that constructive, positive self-views emerge only after the more familiar self-views are processed, and only if the anxiety generated by the positive self-view is acknowledged and addressed. Positive self-views often do not emerge until late in counselling.

Interpersonal functioning

As the self-esteem of clients improves, they often begin to make changes in their current relationships. Interpersonal problems of survivors range from social isolation to involvement in relationships that are destructive or abusive. Because sexual abuse involves a disregard for the physical and emotional boundaries of children, typically by a supposedly trustworthy other, establishing boundaries between themselves and others, developing trust, and learning social skills are key relationship issues for survivors.

Counsellors may assist survivors in evaluating their current relationships by exploring how these relationships meet the survivors' needs for intimacy and socialization, and how the relationships enhance or detract from their growth and healing. Making connections between past abuse and current relationship difficulties can be important. Clients often discover, for example, that they are unable to express anger in their current relationships because they learned in childhood that the expression of anger resulted in negative consequences (e.g. a beating, further sexual abuse, rejection).

Establishing boundaries

The healing process for survivors often involves learning to establish personal boundaries. In the abuse situation, survivors were frequently part of an enmeshed family system in which they did not experience a sense of separateness from others. The family or the offender may have given the message that this enmeshment was a 'special closeness'. One survivor in the incest healing study (Draucker, 1992b) stated:

> I began to realize that my relationship with my father specifically wasn't what I wanted it to be or had always pictured it to be. There was a nurturing part of what we shared together and a real closeness. And I started hearing things about Daddy's little girl – red flag. Emotional enmeshment – red flag. You know, things that started sending up all these little signals in me, like, hmm, some of what I always felt was real special about our relationship may have actually been rather sick.

Establishing a way to separate the self from others becomes an important issue. The same participant described this process for herself in adulthood.

> You see, boundary issues in general are something that any incest survivor needs to deal with. Since my boundaries in almost every way were totally violated most of my childhood, you know, even emotionally. How far do I let people go with me …?

In order to address such issues, counsellors may ask for a description of situations in which the survivor experiences boundary dilemmas, assist the survivor in relating these current situations to the abuse experience, and support the survivor's attempts at establishing his or her personal boundaries. Counsellor responses to the above statement, for example, might include:

> Tell me about a situation you experienced recently in which your boundaries were threatened. How was that situation similar to (different from) your abuse experience? What did you do in the situation? In what ways would you have liked to have set limits on the other person's behaviour? What would it be like for you to set those limits?

Another participant in the incest healing study (Draucker, 1992b) related the following scenario:

> I went to him [a physician] last year and he was new, he was somebody new that I was just going to. And he pulled his stool very close to me and I felt myself extremely uncomfortable. I mean, I was sweating, I could feel my heart racing and I thought, 'Tell him to get away.' I kept establishing in my mind what I had a right to establish with people – that physical boundary. Something kept – I couldn't say it.

In response to a description of a situation such as this, the counsellor should support the client's desire to protect her physical boundaries. A possible counsellor response might be:

> Your physical space is very important, and the doctor invaded that space. I support your idea that you have a right to establish your boundaries. What would you like to have said to the doctor?

Establishing boundaries may include: rejecting unwanted sexual or physical contact; setting limits on intrusive or exploitative behaviours; establishing independent interests and becoming involved in activities separate from one's significant other; expressing one's opinions or beliefs; expressing negative feelings; and learning to meet one's own needs in a relationship. In some cases, survivors may choose to end relationships that are dysfunctional, destructive, or abusive. Counselling approaches that facilitate the above processes can include assertiveness training (or other interpersonal skills training), group counselling focusing on interpersonal dynamics, parenting skills training, and family or couples counselling.

Developing trust

For survivors, improving interpersonal relationships involves learning to trust others. The goal for survivors is not to indiscriminately trust all, but to be able to make judgements regarding who in their lives are trustworthy.

This process often begins with the counsellor. Clients may be told that the counsellor does not expect instant trust but will strive to act in a trustworthy manner (Sgroi and Bunk, 1988). For survivors, learning to trust others is often a question of accepting that trust is not an all-or-nothing aspect of a relationship; it is something that is built and maintained over time (Hall and Lloyd, 1989). One cannot evaluate another's trustworthiness by generalizing from one transgression or from one trustworthy act. Counselling can assist survivors in judging the trustworthiness of others by teaching them to evaluate objectively the other's behaviour in different situations and at different times. One participant in the incest healing study (Draucker, 1992b) described this process for herself:

> My parents have tried to teach me that you don't need anybody, you shouldn't have friends, and they don't have good friends. And, consequently, they're miserable, so they kind of brainwashed me that way. 'You shouldn't need anybody. You can't trust anybody.' Well, I'm not doing that. I like a lot of people and I've made a lot of new friends this semester ... I always thought people wouldn't like me so I always stayed away from people. I wouldn't go to parties, wouldn't go out to one of the bars. People liked me, but I've always been so afraid no one would like me. And it's not true. I have people tell me, 'I really like you. I'm glad I met you. You're nice. You're fun to be with', or 'You're really intelligent.' People get really verbally supportive of me and I really need that.

Learning social skills

For many survivors, reaching out to others involves developing and practising new communication and interpersonal skills. Because sexual abuse often disrupts the child's psychosocial development, he or she may not learn skills necessary to form and maintain satisfying interpersonal relationships in adulthood. These skills may include: appropriate self-disclosure (i.e. letting others know of one's personal self); the ability to express affection and caring to others; and the ability to receive affection and caring from others (Sgroi, 1989).

Social skills training may be helpful at this stage of treatment (Bolton et al., 1989). This training may involve: an assessment of the individual's strengths and weaknesses, attitudes and beliefs, and patterns of social behaviours; response acquisition activities (e.g. behavioural rehearsal through role playing, modelling); and guided practice in natural settings.

Some programmes focus on specific problem areas. Cloitre (1998), for example, proposed a two-phase treatment model for women who have had multiple experiences of victimization. The first phase focuses on affect and interpersonal regulation; the second phase focuses on the emotional processing of trauma memories. The aim of interpersonal regulation training is to help clients negotiate difficult interpersonal situations that require assertiveness and self-control. The ultimate goal of the training is to decrease interpersonal victimization. Role plays are recommended to help the client identify goals and feelings and express them in words and actions. Interventions for addressing negative self-perceptions and guilt and blame reactions that interfere with healthy interpersonal relationships are included. Gradual transitions to healthier social functioning are planned. Cloitre suggests that 'It is important for the client to experiment with new situations and new people, but this should be done in a way that maximizes success in these ventures: task demands should match the client's abilities and readiness' (1998: 297).

Sexual functioning

Once clients have addressed issues of self-esteem and interpersonal relationships, many choose to address concerns related to their own sexuality. The sexuality of survivors is often adversely affected by the childhood sexual abuse experience, during which they could not assert their interests, effect an end to the abuse, or understand what was occurring.

Female survivors and sexuality

Maltz and Holman (1987) suggested that due to sexual socialization, women often develop numerous misconceptions about sexuality and sex roles; these misconceptions are exacerbated by an abuse experience. Misconceptions may include the following: sexual relations should primarily meet the male's needs and desires; the role of the female in sexual activity is to be submissive and dependent; women are the property of men; women must satisfy the male's sexual desires, which are powerful and uncontrollable; and sexual activity is a prerequisite for receiving emotional nurturance.

Three aspects of sexuality are particularly influenced by the experience of childhood sexual abuse (Maltz and Holman, 1987). The first is the pattern of sexual emergence in adolescents or young adults. For abuse survivors, this often involves either sexual withdrawal (e.g. avoidance of dates) due to sexual fears and low self-esteem, or promiscuous or self-destructive sexual activity due to survivors' needs for attention or attempts to control their sexuality.

The second aspect of sexuality that is influenced by the sexual abuse experience is the choice of a same-sex or opposite-sex partner. Although the relationship between early childhood sexual abuse and sexual preference is unclear, a sexually victimizing experience can undoubtedly influence one's choice of sex partners. For example, heterosexual female survivors may choose women as sexual partners because they can be more supportive of the healing process (e.g. offer more nurturance, security, and empathy). Homosexual female survivors may choose a male partner if their victimization experience interfered with an awareness of their sexual preference (Maltz and Holman, 1987).

The third significant aspect of sexuality that is disrupted by childhood sexual abuse is sexual functioning. Survivors often experience disorders of sexual arousal, response, and satisfaction. Many report that sexual arousal is associated with feelings experienced during the abuse (e.g. disgust, panic) or with trauma symptomatology (e.g. flashbacks). In a qualitative study conducted in England, lesbian survivors of CSA reported similar experiences of sexual difficulties in adulthood including flashbacks and inability to express sexual needs (Hall, 1999).

Male survivors and sexuality

Although the sexual responses of males to victimization resemble the responses of female survivors in many ways, they are differentially influenced by male sex-role socialization and the frequency with which males are abused by males. Hypersexuality, compulsive sexual behaviours, and aggressive sexual behaviours may be exhibited by male survivors. Sexual identity concerns are frequently reported.

Counselling approaches to sexuality issues

Counselling related to sexuality can have an insight-oriented, cognitive, or behavioural focus. Initially, survivors need to make the connection between current sexual difficulties and their abuse experience, in much the same way as they do with other current difficulties. It is important to explore how their abuse experiences influenced their sexual development, their choice of sex partners, their sexual self-esteem, and their current sexual functioning.

Cognitive challenging or restructuring can be used to address the misconceptions of survivors regarding sex roles and sexuality (Becker et al., 1986; McCarthy, 1990; Westerlund, 1992). Maltz and Holman (1987) advised presenting the 'Bill of Sexual Rights' to survivors to challenge their sexual misconceptions. This 'Bill' 'includes basic premises, such as "I have a right to my own body", "I have a right to set my own sexual limits", and "I have a right to experience sexual pleasure" (1987: 83). Westerlund (1992) recommended that counsellors encourage survivors to use self-affirming statements related to their body image and sexuality.

Maltz and Holman (1987) outlined several behavioural strategies that can help survivors deal with sexual problems. These include: avoidance of triggers of the abuse experience (e.g. the smell of alcohol, cigarette smoke) during sex, having sex in a place that is not similar to the place where the sexual abuse occurred, or learning to say no or to stop sexual activities with one's partner in a non-rejecting manner. Jehu (1990) recommended a coping skills training programme to address phobic responses to sexual stimuli. The programme includes relaxation training, guided self-dialogue, imagery rehearsal (systematic desensitization), and cognitive restructuring. Westerlund (1992) describes image stopping or alteration techniques to deal with intrusive material evoked during sexual activities.

Behaviourally oriented sex therapy to treat specific sexual dysfunctions is often indicated. Counsellors should generally acquire specific training to employ some of these procedures. Sex therapy techniques may include Masters and Johnson's (1970) squeeze technique for premature ejaculation (i.e. the head of the penis is squeezed by the partner to inhibit ejaculation), sensate focusing (i.e. the pairing of pleasurable sensations with relaxation), and graded sexual contact (i.e. engaging in sexual activities from the least to the most threatening) for orgasmic dysfunction and impotence, and desensitization (e.g. relaxation, hypnosis, self-vaginal dilation) for vaginismus.

Hunter (1995) discussed counselling issues with survivors who exhibit compulsive sexual behaviours, including voyeurism, exhibitionism, compulsive masturbation, bestiality, sadism, masochism, bondage/discipline, affairs, anonymous sex, telephone sex, frotteurism (indecent or invasive touch), the compulsive use of pornography, and cross-dressing. He argued that:

> Overall, the therapeutic task when treating those with sexual compulsiveness is to help clients determine what is the reasonable, acceptable goal of the behaviour and then to find new, less emotionally expensive methods to obtain the goal. For example, if one is lonely, it is certainly acceptable to seek the company of others. However, if the only relationship that has been available is that with a character in a pornographic film, the loneliness will continue and even increase once the film has ended. The client would benefit from having access to a therapy group or mutual-help group so that intimate, mutually rewarding relationships could be formed that will lead to a decrease in the client's loneliness. (1995: 78)

Bolton et al. (1989) outlined behavioural techniques used in the treatment of deviant sexual responses. Covert sensitization, for example, involves relaxation, hierarchy construction, and using imagery to pair deviant responses with aversive consequences.

If the survivor has a committed sexual partner, counselling related to issues of sexuality may include the partner at some point. Partners may experience feelings of rejection, powerlessness, intense anger toward the survivor's family, or inadequacy for not being able to make the survivor 'better'. The goals of couples treatment, therefore, may include: helping partners understand and appreciate the impact of the incest on the survivor's life; encouraging the couple to consider that the sexual dysfunction relates to the abuse, not to either partner's inadequacy; and assisting survivors in responding to their partners' needs and concerns (Maltz and Holman, 1987). Couples often need to learn to communicate openly with each other regarding their sexual issues. Sex therapy, using some of the techniques discussed above, often requires that both partners participate actively in treatment.

Case example

The following case vignette illustrates how counselling techniques may be combined to address a sexual dysfunction experienced by a female incest survivor. Grace was a 30-year-old woman who sought counselling for vaginismus. When she was a young child, Grace had been sexually abused by her father for several years. Because Grace originally did not connect her sexual dysfunction with her sexual abuse experience, this issue was addressed at the start of counselling.

Grace: That [the abuse] happened so long ago. My problem now couldn't be related, could it?

Counsellor: Often, one's sexual life can continue to be affected by an abuse experience. As a child who was sexually abused, you could not control or understand what was happening to you. Your body was violated and you were engaged in sexual activity you did not choose and were not ready for.

Grace: Yes, maybe the tightening results from my not wanting to be violated again. But my boyfriend is kind, gentle.

Counsellor: Yes, although as an adult you've chosen a caring partner, the act of sex can trigger old memories and feelings.

Grace: Yes, sometimes after we try to have sex I do have nightmares. I have never truly enjoyed sex. Now that I have a nice boyfriend, I think I feel guilty. My father told me no one would love me for me. He called me a whore. Jack loves me, I know. But maybe I still feel dirty, after all these years.

Once Grace understood her sexual dysfunction in the larger context of her abuse experiences, more specific counselling interventions were used. Cognitive challenges were used to address Grace's belief that she was a 'whore' who did not deserve to have a good relationship or enjoyable sex. The belief that she had a right to sexual pleasure was extremely difficult for her to accept. She joined a women's sexuality group where this belief was reinforced by other group members. The use of relaxation techniques (e.g. warm baths, imagery) and self-vaginal dilation were used to treat the vaginismus. This symptom subsided after three months.

Survivors as offenders

For some survivors, the issue of sexual offending must be addressed. This issue may differ for female and male clients.

Lepine (1990) discussed her counselling experiences with female survivors who have also engaged in sexual offending behaviours. These women continued to experience overwhelming guilt even after working through survivor issues, and often would not disclose their offence to the counsellor for some time. Although the percentage of adult female survivors who subsequently sexually abuse others is believed to be very small, the author warned that counsellor denial of this possibility can interfere with the recovery of these survivors. Counsellors should neither minimize a survivor's guilt related to the offending behaviour nor 'join with, support, or exacerbate a disproportionate and disabling sense of guilt' (Lepine, 1990: 274). If the survivor was a child or adolescent at the time of the offence, the counsellor should help her consider the offence in the context of her develop-mental stage and her own abuse history.

Disclosure of offending behaviour is facilitated if clients have established a trusting relationship with the counsellor and if the counsellor introduces the issue. Lepine recommended an intervention such as: 'You know, when women have been sexually abused as children, they sometimes act out sexually against others, too' (1990: 275). The counsellor should respond calmly to a survivor's disclosure of offending behaviour. He or she should non-judgementally convey the message that, while the behaviour is unacceptable, the counsellor will not reject the client and will assist her in dealing with this issue. In certain instances (e.g. the ongoing abuse of a child), this might mean reporting the offence.

Counselling must address the survivor's feelings of guilt about abusing another person. Lepine (1990) recommended the use of the empty-chair technique, in which survivors speak vicariously with their victims. Survivors may acknowledge the offence and its consequences, apologize and ask for forgiveness, and share their own abuse experience. They may also communicate these messages to their victims through the use of the unsent letter. Actual contact with a victim, however, should be thoughtfully considered before being carried out. Issues to be explored include: the survivor's motives (e.g. survivors should not expect the victim to resolve their guilt); the consequences (e.g. legal actions, the survivor's reputation); the victim's potential reactions (e.g. trauma symptomatology if the experience had been repressed); and the survivor's potential reactions.

The counselling of male survivors who have engaged in sexually offending behaviour has also been addressed. In many cases, the typical disclosure process differs from that of female survivors. Female survivors often begin counselling to deal with their abuse, and later in the process reveal the offending behaviour. Male survivors, on the other hand, often enter counselling because of a sexual offence, and reveal their own victimization experience later in the process. These differences may reflect social role expectations. Because women are socialized to care for and protect others, offending behaviours may be less frequent, less traumatic, and more likely to cease when they are adults (Lepine, 1990). Males, who are socialized to act out their feelings and deny their experience of victim-ization, may be more likely to offend into adulthood in ways that will result in some contact with the criminal justice system.

The percentage of male victims who become offenders is unclear. However, the assumption that most male survivors engage in sexually offending behaviours is a destructive myth that can interfere with the healing of survivors. Gerber suggested that, 'It seems more reasonable to acknowledge that according to research, it [tran-sition from victim to offender] occurs with some frequency and causation is attrib-utable to a variety of variables' (1990: 154). Childhood sexual abuse factors associated with later offending behaviours include: bizarre sexual acts; sexual acts accompanied by the threat of violence; the use of a 'seductive, covert, pre-sexual conditioning process' (1990: 155) by the offender; and a long duration of abuse. Certain personality characteristics (e.g. passive dependency) and chemical depen-dency are also thought to contribute to the transition from victim to offender.

The counselling of male survivors who are also perpetrators requires that both the offending behaviour and the childhood sexual abuse be addressed.

Counselling typically begins with perpetrator issues and progresses to issues related to childhood victimization. Counselling offenders may occur in four stages, which are described by Carlson (1990).

The first stage is the focus on perpetrator characteristics, attitudes, and self-concept. Counselling interventions include: setting limits; providing structure; and confronting the perpetrator's denial, his view of himself as a victim of the system or of his family, and his tendency to project negative characteristics on to others (e.g. calling his abused daughter a 'slut').

The second stage in counselling is the reinforcement of the client's positive characteristics and the development of his strengths. Counselling interventions include assisting the survivor to develop extra-familial support systems, strengthen his own boundaries (e.g. develop assertiveness skills), and learn to delay gratification. Counsellors should reinforce other positive behaviours, such as the survivor's accepting responsibility for his actions, expressing his feelings, and communicating his needs in a direct manner.

The third stage, treating the 'victim within', occurs when issues related to the client's victimization begin to emerge. During this stage, the counsellor provides support, education, and validation related to the client's victimization experiences. The client is encouraged to describe these experiences fully. He can then appreciate that his own victimization was a source of his victimizing behaviour, although this does not relieve him of the responsibility for his offences. When the survivor gets in touch with his own feelings of victimization, he can begin to develop empathy for his victims.

The fourth stage of counselling is called 'returning the parental role', as the client again assumes responsibility for his own behaviour. He begins to set his own boundaries (e.g. respecting others' privacy, determining appropriate limits with his children) and to determine for himself what constitute appropriate sexual behaviours. He also identifies available sources of support following treatment, methods by which he will care for himself, and a plan of action if he feels he is in danger of reoffending.

Case example

The case of Jerry, who was discussed in the preceding chapter, exemplifies the process of making desired life changes once the connections between childhood experiences and adult functioning have been made. Jerry made changes in his self-concept, his relationships with his wife and family of origin, and his job.

Much of counselling focused on Jerry's self-esteem. Jerry originally described himself as an 'insignificant failure'. He also believed himself to be 'unmanly', a self-perception that was probably related to his abuse experiences involving same-sex offenders. The following client–counsellor interaction, based on Peplau's model (see O'Toole and Welt, 1989), shows how self-esteem issues were addressed with Jerry:

Jerry:　I guess I'm not much of anything. I'm certainly not much of a man. [*Self-view in awareness*]

Counsellor:　Where did you get the message that you are not much of anything?

(Continued)

(Continued)

Jerry:	I guess from my family. My dad never bothered with me much, except to yell when he was drunk, or to tell me what to do at work. My mom, well, she thought it best we kids be 'seen and not heard'. She was pretty weak. I wanted more to do with her but she was always sick.
Counsellor:	So both of your parents gave you the message, in one way or another, that you were not very important. Tell me about an experience you had when you felt particularly unimportant.
Jerry:	Once, I brought home a table I made in shop, you know, woodworking class. I thought it was good. I put it in the living room. I thought my mom would be happy but instead she had me put it out in the garage so my dad 'wouldn't be upset with such clutter'. I was disappointed because the instructor had said the table was really good.
Counsellor:	I can see why a young boy would not feel very important in this situation. Something you made yourself, which had received praise, was discarded in the interest of keeping your dad calm.
Jerry:	Yes, and shop was the only thing I was really good in. [*Maybe me self-view*]
Counsellor:	You had a talent that was not recognized by your parents, but was recognized by your teacher. Were there other situations like this – instances when your parents did not attend to you, but others did?
Jerry:	Jean, of course. She was good to me, until she left home. No one else until Jane …
Counsellor:	Although your parents gave you the message you weren't very important, Jean, and later Jane, showed that you were important to them.

Jerry described receiving messages from his parents indicating that he was not considered a significant member of the family, and that it was best if he just stayed out of the way. Once Jerry recognized that his self-perceptions stemmed from these messages rather than from his own inherent worthlessness, he considered other ways of viewing himself. He concluded that he was special to Jean, who clearly cared for him a great deal. He was thus worthwhile in someone's eyes. Jerry also gradually began to consider his strengths – that he had survived his childhood, had maintained a basically sound marriage, and had developed many skills related to his trade. Some of these views were associated with anxiety as they were incongruent with Jerry's accustomed self-perceptions. For example, Jerry was initially very resistant to considering himself a skillful tradesperson as this meant he might be valued outside the family shop and, therefore, vocational opportunities might exist for him away from his family.

Eventually, Jerry was seen in counselling with his wife Jane. He had never told her of the abuse, and chose to do so during a counselling session. She was extremely supportive, although some tension did develop between Jane and Jerry when she expressed anger toward his family, whom she 'never liked anyway'. She had trouble understanding why Jerry should have any loyalty remaining toward them. Nonetheless, she was able to assure Jerry that she did not blame him for the

(Continued)

(Continued)

infertility, nor did she see him as 'unmanly'. She did, however, need him to understand her feelings of loss. Once Jerry stopped blaming himself for the infertility, he was able to be more emotionally available to her. Jerry felt unable, however, to 'talk about his feelings', as this was discouraged in his family of origin. Thus, the development of new communication skills became the focus of couple counselling. Both Jerry and Jane became more successful in expressing their needs and feelings in ways the other could hear. Because their sexual relationship improved as their communication skills developed, the couple did not require behaviourally-oriented sex therapy.

   Jerry chose not to confront his parents or his brother Tom about the abuse, but did identify the need to separate from his family. He made the difficult decision to leave the machine shop, and began work at a different plant. He interacted with his family only occasionally, when he chose to do so. He did well in his new position and was ultimately appointed as shift supervisor.

9 Addressing Resolution Issues

Once survivors have begun successfully to employ new coping mechanisms and make desired life changes, they often deal with issues related to the resolution of the childhood sexual abuse experience. Resolution does not indicate that the experience of abuse is forgotten, or that the healing process is finished. Indeed, many survivors believe that healing can be a lifelong process (Draucker, 1992b). Resolution refers to the process by which the childhood sexual abuse experience is integrated into the individual's identity, but is no longer the primary force that guides his or her adult life. Sgroi (1989) refers to this as relinquishing the survivor identity. The individual views himself or herself from a variety of perspectives. The issues discussed below are frequently related to the process of resolution.

Forgiveness

After clients have experienced some healing from the sexual abuse experience, many struggle with the issue of whether or not to forgive the offender. Some survivors believe that forgiveness is a prerequisite to true recovery; others believe they must forgive the offender because of their religious or social beliefs. It can be important for counsellors to help clients determine what forgiveness means to them. Maltz and Holman (1987) discussed two styles of forgiveness. In the first style, survivors release the offender from responsibility for the abuse because they have determined that the offender's actions were justifiable in some way. Such forgiveness may represent a survivor's attempts to deny repressed anger, hurt, or betrayal toward the offender, and may be a form of self-blame or minimization. The second style of forgiveness involves coming to appreciate the offender's 'humanness, limitations, and history' (1987: 31). This may include achieving an understanding of the offender's own childhood abuse experiences or his or her adult weaknesses or pathology. The authors suggest that this style of forgiveness can be beneficial for survivors, as it can help them develop compassion and forgiveness for themselves.

Hall and Lloyd (1989) suggested that forgiveness occurs when survivors accept their feelings related to the abuse, especially their anger, but no longer seek revenge. This type of forgiveness can free survivors from their ties to the offender. If they no longer need to avenge the offence, the offender becomes less relevant in their healing process; survivors can then begin to accept responsibility for their adult happiness.

The survivors' religious or philosophical beliefs related to forgiveness must be discussed, acknowledged, and respected. Forgiveness, however, that stems from true acceptance of one's feelings, insight into the offender's childhood experiences and adult limitations, and personal healing that has moved one beyond the need for revenge is usually more therapeutic than forgiveness that is dictated by religious or social prescriptions.

Counsellors can help clients determine the personal meaning they attach to forgiveness and the role forgiveness might play in their healing. They may choose, for example, to forgive a non-offending parent, but not the offender. Counsellors should stress that forgiveness is not a prerequisite to their healing, but a personal choice some survivors may make as they begin to move toward a resolution of their abuse experience.

The following client–counsellor interaction illustrates a survivor's struggle with the issue of forgiveness. Pamela is a 23-year-old woman who was sexually abused as a child by her older brother.

Pamela:	My visit [to her family] did not go well this weekend. I was talking to my mother and she said she believes to be truly healed I must forgive my brother. She's brought this up before.
Counsellor:	What is it like for you when your mom says this?
Pamela:	I get really angry. I think she wants this whole thing to be over and done with so he can come back into our lives, and we can pretend it [the abuse] never happened. I don't know, though, maybe at some point I will be able to forgive him. Not now, but at some point maybe. I don't know.
Counsellor:	You were angry at your mom because you sense her push for you to forgive your brother comes more from her needs to reunite the family than from her concern about your healing?
Pamela:	Yes, all along she has been more concerned about getting things back to normal. I'm not saying I'll never forgive him. I'm just not ready yet. And I don't want to be pushed. But some day I hope I will reach a point of forgiveness.
Counsellor:	People mean different things when they talk about forgiveness. When you say at some point you may be able to forgive your brother, what do you mean?
Pamela:	Well, not that I'll say that the abuse was OK. I'll never say that. It wasn't. It hurt me deeply and that will never change. Maybe at some point, though, I won't feel as much hatred. At one point, I wanted him dead. I know he did to me what was done to him. Yet, that doesn't make it OK. I don't know. I'm confused.
Counsellor:	Yes, one meaning of forgiveness is that one forgives and forgets the abuse, coming to believe it was unimportant and should be forgotten. Perhaps you believe this is what your mom wants you to do. Another meaning of forgiveness is that one reaches some understanding of why the abuse occurred, and then moves beyond needing retribution. One can still feel angry, but no longer be driven by bitterness.
Pamela:	Yes, it was somehow helpful to know Grandpa abused Tim [her brother]. Although that didn't make what he did to me OK, it somehow helped make things make sense, if you know what I mean. I would like to be able to be in the same room with him without freaking. Maybe then I'll feel more like he can't pull my strings any longer.

Reintegrating into the family of origin

Many survivors discontinue or limit contact with their family of origin when they begin the healing process. In some cases, survivors need distance from the dysfunctional nature of their family in order to appreciate how the family dynamics influenced their development. Some survivors break off contact because family members continue to engage in behaviours that are deleterious to their recovery (e.g. blaming the survivor for the abuse, disapproving of the survivor's therapy). For example, one survivor in the incest healing study (Draucker, 1992b) reported that, 'I didn't talk to my family for two years. I withdrew from them after a really severe confrontation about counselling, which they really objected to.'

After they have experienced some healing, many survivors decide to re-establish contact with their family of origin. The same survivor stated:

> And as soon as my counselling sessions had ended, I found out my mom had cancer, so it was like, you were able to spend two years away in healing and getting over it, then it was like time to go back and slay the dragons and see my brothers and sisters and talk to my mom and try and work through some of the problems and feelings that I had with them, which I thought I did pretty well.

Survivors need to approach their family from the perspective of the changes they have made in the healing process, rather than interacting with their family based on old roles and patterns. Participants in the incest healing study stressed that the re-establishment of contact with their family had to be, in some way, on the survivors' terms, which were often specific and definite. One woman maintained a relationship with her brother, the offender, as long as he remained in therapy. Another participant, who had been abused by her stepfather, discussed re-establishing a relationship with her mother, which she planned to discontinue if her mother engaged in any of the hurtful or destructive behaviours from which she had agreed to refrain (e.g. blaming the survivor for the abuse).

Reintegrating into the family of origin, based on changes the client has made, can be an important resolution issue. It is helpful to explore whether a client has any unrealistic expectations related to his or her family, such as that the family will have changed to meet the client's needs. Typically, families will attempt to repeat old, familiar patterns to maintain the status quo. Survivors should guard against allowing the actions of their families once again to control their sense of well-being. Counselling may be helpful in assisting survivors to maintain realistic expectations regarding their family's responses, while focusing on what survivors can control when re-entering the family or re-establishing a relationship with a family member.

Davis (1990) proposed an activity that assists survivors in establishing new ground rules or setting limits when interacting with their families. She asks survivors to determine what things they would no longer do with their family (e.g. care for an inebriated parent), as well as what things they will no longer discuss with their family (e.g. the survivor's sexual life). Davis also encourages survivors to specify the conditions under which they will have contact with their family (e.g. only at the survivor's residence; at the family's home, only if the offender is not present). Counsellors can also discuss how clients can best communicate these ground rules to their family, what the experience of setting limits might be like for them, what their contingency plan will be if the ground rules are not respected, and how they anticipate their family will respond. Family members will usually test the limits; survivors should be prepared for this.

It is most important that survivors do not engage in old family dynamics in which they are exploited, manipulated, ignored, or belittled. In some instances, contact continues to be destructive and survivors may again choose to break off their relationship with the family. This decision is often accompanied by sadness and grief, feelings that must be validated by the counsellor. Letting go of the family of origin or coming to terms with its limitations can be a significant part of the resolution process.

Finding meaning in the experience

Taylor theorized that one way to cope with a traumatic or a victimizing event is to search for meaning in the experience. She defined the search for meaning as 'an effort to understand the event: why it happened and what impact it has had' (1983: 1161). Research has suggested that this is important for sexual abuse survivors and may facilitate the resolution of the abuse experience (Draucker, 1989, 1995, 1997; Silver et al., 1983).

Understanding the cause of the event is referred to as causal attribution. This process has been discussed primarily in relation to survivors' reattributing the cause of the abuse from themselves to the offender. Although holding the offender responsible for the abuse is important in addressing issues of self-blame, it does not seem to be sufficient explanation for many survivors. Many question why the offender did what he or she did, why the abuse occurred in their family, and, ultimately, why society permits the widespread occurrence of childhood sexual abuse.

In the study of incest survivors (Draucker, 1992b), many participants indicated that they had answered these questions for themselves. Several reported that they had learned that their offenders were impaired in some way (e.g. alcoholic, psychotic). One participant said, 'My father was an alcoholic who was raised in a time when women were inferior. He was also sick.' Other clients attributed the actions of the offenders to the offenders' own history of abuse. One stated: '[It was my] older brother taking out aggressions on me, most likely caused by his own molestation from our paternal grandmother.' Several survivors attributed the cause of the abuse to family dynamics. For example, a participant stated, 'I realize that the incest experience was because of my dysfunctional family, not because of me.' One survivor placed the blame for the incest on society, saying that she had come to believe that the incest was part of 'an extreme exploitation of females commonly practiced in the USA'.

Whether or not certain types of attribution are more helpful in facilitating healing is uncertain. What is important in regard to resolution of trauma is that individuals come up with a causal explanation that is satisfactory to them. Janoff-Bulman (1992: 127) argued that attributions fit into the larger, richer efforts of survivors to rebuild their inner world following traumatic life events. This is only one piece of the greater picture, yet it is a reflection of the larger task – to integrate their victimization by somehow getting it to fit better with prior self- and world-views.

In the late phase of counselling, survivors often seek closure on the question of *why* they were abused. In some cases, it is helpful for the counsellor to provide factual or theoretical material to aid in this quest. For example, discussing incestuous family dynamics, as outlined by Gelinas (1983), may help survivors understand the functioning of their family. Discussing incest from a feminist perspective (e.g. according to Herman, 1981) may help survivors put their childhood sexual abuse in a larger societal context. Reading literature can also facilitate this. Daugherty (1984), for example, wrote a book for survivors of childhood sexual abuse entitled *Why Me?* In one chapter, the author addresses the issue of understanding individuals who sexually abuse children. This helps survivors with their need to know why the abuser did what he or she did.

Taylor (1983) also indicated that in order to find meaning, one must understand the significance the traumatic event has had in one's life. She suggested that this could involve construing positive meaning from the experience by reappraising one's life, developing a new attitude toward life, or gaining increased self-knowledge. Survivors of childhood sexual abuse who participated in a survey study on coping (Draucker, 1992a) described these processes as part of healing. They indicated that, because of the abuse, they are stronger, more self-reliant, or independent; have a greater self-awareness of their emotional or spiritual life; have acquired a sense of purpose in life; or have developed a better understanding of human nature in general. Wiehe, who conducted a survey of 150 victims of sibling abuse, reported that some of the respondents saw a 'silver lining in the dark cloud of their abuse' (1990: 132) and used their abuse experience for personal growth.

Resolving the abuse issue may involve the 'rethinking of one's attitude or priorities to restructure one's life along more satisfying lines' (Taylor, 1983: 1163). This does not mean that survivors conclude that they were glad the abuse occurred, or that the offender actually 'did them a favour' and is, therefore, exonerated. Rather, they conclude that the abuse was a negative experience, but from that experience, or from the healing after that experience, they were able to grow personally in some way. One survivor (Draucker, 1992b) stated, 'It [the abuse] has forced my growth in areas that would have been neglected otherwise. I have to examine how much of our behaviour is choice versus reactions – where's the balance?'

In the following client–counsellor interaction, a survivor struggles with the issue of finding meaning in her incest experience. Rosalie is a 55-year-old woman who was sadistically sexually abused as a child by her uncle.

Rosalie: You know, I realized that as much suffering as I have experienced – it's been almost 50 years of suffering – I don't think I would be as strong as I am today if it hadn't been for what he did.

Counsellor: In what ways are you stronger than you would have been?

Rosalie: After being in therapy, I now know that I can handle just about anything. If I lived through what I did as a youngster, I can live through anything. I never realized that before. My friend Eleanor falls apart at every family crisis. In fact, the other day someone called me a 'tough cookie'. I think that's true. I am a tough cookie. I wouldn't wish what happened to me on a dog, but it did make me strong.

Counsellor: So having survived a horrible experience as a child …

Rosalie: Yes, I survived because I was strong. I feel good about myself now. I like who I am. Someone asked me if I'm glad the abuse happened. That's nonsense. Of course I'm not glad. I work to stop abuse. But it was one of the many things that made me who I am today. And I like me.

The process of helping others

The need to help others who have been abused, or the need to make the world a safer place more generally, seems to be a key part of the resolution process for many survivors. In the incest healing study (Draucker, 1992b), for example, the majority of participants identified that having a positive impact on their world – by helping other victims personally, being an advocate for victims, or choosing a helping vocation (e.g. teaching) – was an important aspect of their own recovery. In a study that investigated the process of construing benefit from a negative experience of incest, Draucker (1992a) found that the majority of survivors who derived any benefit from the experience listed the ability to help others as a positive outcome. As a result of their incest experience, these women indicated that they were able to help others in ways that non-abused individuals could not. They had acquired a special ability to empathize with those who were suffering, the courage to speak out against injustice, a unique skill to detect abuse in their work settings (e.g. a paediatric emergency room), and a particular vigilance, which they used to protect their own children from abuse.

Helping activities seem to be beneficial for survivors only when they have worked through a number of issues in their own healing process (e.g. caretaking issues, setting boundaries with others, dealing with issues of blame). For example, it can be a devastating experience for survivors to speak publicly about their abuse when they have not worked through their feelings of shame. If survivors choose to help other survivors before they have learned to define their own boundaries or to set interpersonal limits, they tend to feel burdened or overwhelmed. The counsellor may help survivors explore the role that helping others can play in the healing process, and support these activities when they contribute to the resolution of the abuse experience.

Addressing identity issues

The key resolution issue for incest survivors is establishing a clear sense of their own identities. Much of the healing process has focused on giving up the role of victim by taking control of one's own thoughts, feelings, and actions. When survivors perceive that they have given up this role, they often mourn the loss; the victim role probably defined their identities for some time. Along with the role of the victim, survivors also often abandon caretaking roles they find oppressive. These roles may have shaped their interpersonal relationships and perhaps even their vocational choices. Counselling may provide survivors with an opportunity to deal with feelings of loss and anxiety associated with these changes.

Sgroi (1989) maintained that, ultimately, clients can also give up the survivor identity. They recognize their strengths and weaknesses, and integrate the sexual abuse experience into their total identities. They have found success in adopting new coping mechanisms and have assumed responsibility for their own happiness; therefore, they no longer need to define themselves by their childhood sexual abuse experience. Sgroi (1989) suggested that this stage can be elusive for survivors. In the later stages of treatment, counsellors might discuss the process of giving up the survivor identity. One participant in the incest healing study (Draucker, 1992b) discussed this:

> Another thing I think I dealt with was to try to get rid of the role of incest survivor. I used to play with it by saying, no, I was a survivor. Because of it, a lot of good things were given to me. I understand, I could empathize, I could do a lot of things that way and I was a survivor. I was getting on with my life and all that ... . Dr Susan Forward was in this area and a lot of women were calling [to a radio programme] and she would talk to them and she had been an incest victim herself and had written a book which I had read and her idea was to get out of the role of being an incest survivor and do your life without having to be in that role. I liked that idea. I worked very hard on trying to just not constantly come from, dwell on, be, an incest survivor.

Termination of counselling

Along with resolution comes the process of terminating counselling. This, of course, can represent a significant loss for the survivor, but also a transition consistent with relinquishing the survivor identity. The termination process may include: a review of the healing process; reminiscence about the highlights of counselling; sharing of feelings between counsellor and client regarding the relationship and termination; and an exploration of the client's future plans. Many counsellors choose to extend an invitation to survivors to keep in touch with them because survivors often profit from sharing ongoing life changes with the counsellor.

Case example

The following case exemplifies how reintegrating into the family of origin can be related to resolution for survivors.

Candy was a 22-year-old college student who had attended counselling for approximately one year to deal with having been sexually abused by her brother, Ken. The abuse occurred intermittently for approximately a year, when she was 7 and he was 15. The sexual activities primarily included genital fondling, although Candy believed vaginal penetration was attempted on some occasions. Ken had been adopted at the age of two, at a time when Candy's parents believed they could not have any biological children. Ken exhibited significant behavioural problems (e.g. being expelled from school, minor scrapes with the law, unruliness at home) throughout most of his childhood. He was ultimately diagnosed as having foetal alcohol syndrome. As an adult, he continued to live with his parents, worked at a local service station, and spent most of his time with his local 'buddies'.

After being in counselling for over six months, Candy decided to tell her parents about the abuse during one of her visits home. She reported to her counsellor that her father responded only by saying, 'I should kill him next time I see him.' Candy's mother initially became 'hysterical' and was unable to discuss Candy's experience with her. However, on their next contact, Candy's mother began to defend Ken and

(Continued)

(Continued)

minimize the abuse. She suggested to Candy that the abuse was normal child's play, that Ken probably did not mean any harm, and that perhaps the counsellor was making too big a deal of the issue. Candy's father would not discuss the abuse further.

Although Candy had spent time in counselling preparing for this disclosure, she stated that she was nonetheless devastated by her parents' response and decided to limit her weekly visits with them. Initially, she would see them occasionally, on major holidays; when holiday visits became stressful, she ceased these visits as well. Candy's mother wrote to her frequently, begging her to come home. Her mother's letters often contained references to her ill-health and despondency over Candy's break from the family.

Her parents' reactions to her disclosure prompted Candy to examine their roles as non-offending parents. Although she had initially assumed that they had no knowledge of the abuse, she eventually began to wonder if her mother 'knew on some level'. Candy believed that she did not tell her mother about the abuse at the time it occurred because her mother pampered Ken. As a child, Candy believed her mother would fall apart if she knew 'what her children were doing'. Candy stated that she would never have considered telling her father, who was seldom at home and who would not 'talk about personal things anyway'.

Candy struggled for some time in counselling to understand her parents' role in the abuse situation, as well as their reactions to her disclosure of the abuse. This led to a discussion of her parents' family backgrounds. Candy reported that her mother grew up in poverty and was raised by several aunts, at least two of whom worked as prostitutes. She had spent her later years in a foster home and met her husband, Candy's father, during her last year of high school. Candy knew less of her father's history, other than that he came from a strict, but 'respectable', military family. Candy's parents tried to have a child for many years and finally adopted Ken through a Catholic adoption agency. Candy herself was a 'late miracle' baby.

Candy indicated that her mother always seemed overwhelmed by childcare responsibilities with Ken: 'She was always going to school or to court or to counselling to deal with his problems'. Candy suspected that her mother had become overly involved with her son, whereas her father withdrew, having little to do with Ken or with the family. Candy, as a child, was quiet and caused no problems. As an adolescent, she became her mother's confidante. Her mother frequently complained to Candy about the lack of support she received from Candy's dad, a 'workaholic', and the troubles she continued to have with Ken.

Candy surmised that her mother had probably married her father to gain the respectability and stability she lacked as a child. Although her mother's marriage provided those things, her father showed little nurturance and caring. When Ken began to have problems, her mother took total responsibility for him. Candy guessed that her mother probably felt like a failure because she had invested so much in having the 'all-American' family and was unable to 'make Ken better'. As Ken's problems increased, her father withdrew further, adding to her mother's feelings of burden and abandonment. Her pregnancy with Candy, which at one time would have been welcomed, was unplanned and probably added to her mother's stress.

After achieving some understanding of these dynamics, Candy decided to resume contact with her mother. In the following interaction, she and the counsellor discuss this issue:

(Continued)

(Continued)

Candy:	I have decided to see my mom again. I feel better myself and I miss her. I don't need to see Dad, but I do want to see Mom. I've been away long enough. When I see her though, I'm afraid I'll slip back. That's what kept me from calling her. I've come so far myself. But I also want to talk with her about some of what we've been talking about, you know, her background and stuff.
Counsellor:	I know you've been wanting to be involved with your mom again; it's important to you. In what ways are you afraid you'll slip back if you see her again?
Candy:	Well, it hurt me so much last time when my mom defended Ken and made light of the abuse. Then she got sick. Remember … I got real depressed. That could happen again. That's why I hope she's changed.
Counsellor:	We discussed your mom's response when you told her about the sexual abuse and I know you've determined that her defence of Ken and denial of the abuse probably results from her longstanding need to have a normal, perfect family and that it is her pattern to withdraw from her problems by becoming ill.
Candy:	I know, but maybe she's changed and can face it now. Maybe my staying away shook her up enough … Maybe she'll stand up to my brother to show me she really believes he did something wrong. That would help me and she says she wants to help me.
Counsellor:	Facing the abuse and dealing with your brother in a way that would be helpful for you would be a major change in your mom's way of dealing with things.
Candy:	Yes, it's highly unlikely, I know.
Counsellor:	You are hoping for a significant change. Although your mom loves you and may sincerely want to help you, there is a strong pull for family members to stay the same. To change is threatening.
Candy:	I so wish she would be different. She probably won't be. I guess I know that on some level.
Counsellor:	When you resume contact with your family, you cannot make them change in ways you would like them to. No one has that control over others. You may hope for certain changes while also considering what's realistic.
Candy:	I'm afraid if I go back, and she hasn't changed, she'll just make light of the whole thing again.
Counsellor:	Although you cannot control how your mom responds to you, you can control how you respond to her.
Candy:	I know what's coming. [*Smiles*] Because she makes light of the whole thing, I don't have to.
Counsellor:	Yes, you've made many changes. One change is that you no longer blame yourself for what happened. You seem to hold that belief very strongly now. You accept that the abuse was a traumatic event in your life. Your mom cannot take that away.
Candy:	No, she cannot. I do believe that. I guess I also know that without some kind of help, like counselling, she won't change. That makes me sad. I wish she would get help, to understand what did

(Continued)

(Continued)

	happen to me, and to help herself as well. Otherwise, although I'll never blame myself again, if she defends Ken, I will get frustrated with her and probably stay away again. If only she would get help, I think that's the only way we can be really close again.
Counsellor:	Although you cannot make her go to counselling, you can ask her to do that and decide how you will proceed with your relationship based on her response.
Candy:	Yes, she needs counselling before we really get back together.

This interaction reaffirmed Candy's belief that the abuse was a significant, traumatic experience, and that contact with her mother could no longer jeopardize this belief. She concluded, however, that her mother would need to confront what had happened to Candy before they could have a meaningful relationship. Candy agreed to have contact with her mother at this point only if her mother agreed to attend counselling. Although her mother consented to this and found a counsellor she liked, she was extremely reluctant and missed several early sessions due to illness. She eventually became very involved with counselling, however. With the support of her counsellor, she confirmed much of what Candy had inferred about her mother's background. Her mother shared with Candy that she had suspected the abuse but could not face it. She confessed that she had feared that if her husband had found out what Ken was doing, he would have forced Ken to leave the home, something he often threatened to do as Ken's problems increased. At this point, Candy expressed anger toward her mother because she had chosen to protect Ken rather than Candy. Her mother was not only able to tolerate Candy's expression of anger, but admitted that she had, in fact, sacrificed Candy due to her own limitations and fears (e.g. of her husband, of Ken, of what others would think). This event was significant for Candy as it cemented many of the issues she had addressed earlier in counselling related to her own self-blame. Her mother also acknowledged that she believed that the abuse was a traumatic experience for Candy and she deeply regretted not intervening to stop it.

Candy eventually agreed to visit the family home again, something she had not done since her initial disclosure of the abuse to her parents. In the following client–counsellor interaction, Candy discusses her concerns about visiting her family in their home, and decides what ground rules she wishes to establish.

Candy:	My parents want me to come home and I want to go there, I think, I'm not sure. My brother will be there and I'm not ready to see him yet. He's loud and butts into all our conversations, whether they involve him or not. He invades my space. Everyone just puts up with it. Also, I'm ready to see my dad, I think, but I feel really uncomfortable because my mother fusses over him so. She waits on him hand and foot. I'll be expected to do that too. You know, bring him coffee, soda, when he can get it himself. My mother does this for my brother sometimes as well. It makes me sick.
Counsellor:	You are concerned, then, that if you go home things will be the way they were before. And that you will fall into old habits, such as putting up with your brother's behaviour or waiting on your father.
Candy:	Yes, but now I couldn't stand doing those things.
Counsellor:	Yes, because you've made changes. Putting up with your brother's behaviour is a passive thing to do, and you've been

(Continued)

(Continued)

	working on actively setting limits on the intrusive behaviours of others. Waiting on your dad is a deferent behaviour, also something you've been working on avoiding.
Candy:	I'm so afraid in that house I'll fall back into doing those things.
Counsellor:	Again, you cannot control what others do, but you can decide what you will or will not do and what you will or will not tolerate there.
Candy:	OK, then, I decide here and now that I will not wait on my dad or my brother. And I will tell them this up-front.
Counsellor:	Yes, you cannot decide if your mother will wait on them, but you can decide whether you will or not. What will it be like for you to set this limit?
Candy:	It was scary when I heard myself saying it. But it feels good. I know I can do it. I can say no. 'Dad, I will not get your coffee when I'm visiting.' Wow. That felt good. If they don't accept that, I'll leave. My brother is a different story, though. I think his very presence will bother me a lot. Especially since I'm not ready to confront him about the abuse.
Counsellor:	What would you like to do about your brother?
Candy:	Really, I don't want to see him at all.
Counsellor:	How can you have that happen?
Candy:	Well, I can visit when he's not there. I can agree to go only when he's out. A ground rule will be that if Ken's there, I won't be. I won't have him there until I'm ready. If Mom wants me home, she'll have to ensure that Ken will not be there.

Candy identified unhealthy family patterns in which she no longer wanted to participate and determined how to avoid such participation by specifying what she would not do (i.e. wait on the men in the family) and by establishing an important ground rule (i.e. she would not visit when her brother was present). On several occasions, Candy recognized attempts by family members to test her limits. For example, during one visit her mother was carrying a coffee cup to her dad in the living room and stopped to answer the phone. Without saying a word, she handed the cup to Candy. At that point, Candy realized she could put the cup down or bring it to her father. She chose to put the cup on the counter, reinforcing her choice not to wait on him. On one occasion, the family 'forgot' to make arrangements for Ken to be away from the home for Candy's visit. Consistent with her contingency plan, Candy left immediately and visited a high school friend instead of spending the afternoon with her family.

Eventually, Candy chose to confront Ken about the abuse. He responded by becoming sullen and withdrawn, but did not deny the abuse had occurred. Candy grew very aware of his limitations and, although she did not address the issue of forgiveness, she claimed that she had got in touch with how 'pathetic' her brother had become.

After this confrontation, Candy began to visit her family less frequently, having decided that she needed to work on developing friendships at school. She was now withdrawing from her family because it was the 'normal thing to do at [my] age'. However, she believed that reintegrating into her family in a healthy way (e.g. by no longer keeping the incest secret, by setting limits based on her own needs) gave her the freedom to move on and establish her own adult relationships.

10 Dynamics and Disruptions in the Therapeutic Alliance

Researchers have consistently demonstrated that the quality of the relationship between the counsellor and the client, referred to as 'the therapeutic alliance', is a key factor in treatment success, regardless of population or treatment modality (Safran and Muran, 2000). Gaston (1990) identified four components of the therapeutic alliance: (a) the client's affective relationship with the therapist; (b) the client's capacity to work purposely in therapy; (c) the therapist's empathic understanding; and (d) client–therapist agreement on the goals and tasks of therapy. The counselling relationship is especially important in work with survivors of childhood sexual abuse, a trauma that occurs in an interpersonal context, as it serves as the secure base from which clients explore their trauma and provides a corrective emotional experience for clients who have experienced a significant betrayal of trust.

A therapeutic relationship involves a series of personal negotiations between two individuals seeking affiliation (Frankel, 2000). Because tensions are inherent in the negotiation of any relationship, disruptions and strains in therapeutic relationships are inevitable. Counsellors must develop effective strategies to address relationship disruptions that lead to therapeutic impasses. Disruptions have been referred to as ruptures or disjunctions. Safran and Muran describe ruptures as 'disagreements about the tasks or goals of therapy or of problems in the bond dimension' (2000: 16). Frankel refers to disruptions in the therapeutic process as disjunctions, which are 'intervals in psychotherapy ... when therapists and patients miss and confuse each other, or are deflected from their goal because they collude in order to minimize their differences' (2000: 2).

With adult survivors of childhood sexual abuse, disruptions in the therapeutic alliance must be understood in the context of abuse dynamics. Childhood sexual abuse influences many dimensions of interpersonal functioning, such as the ability to develop trust and establish intimacy in relationships, including those with clinicians (DiLillo, 2001). Adult clients who were sexually abused may associate love with abuse, have distorted relational boundaries, and re-enact earlier traumatic dynamics in adult relationships (Harper and Steadman, 2003). Research indicates that traumatized clients often report that their therapists disappoint or betray them. Eighty-four clients who sought therapy for perceived trauma-related symptoms were interviewed about their perceptions of therapy. Forty-eight of the participants indicated that they had experienced a serious betrayal by one or more therapists (Dalenberg, 2000).

Counselling adult abuse survivors involves interpersonal challenges for the counsellor as well. Dalenberg (2000) recommends that counsellors be especially attuned to reactions such as disapproval, disgust, dominance, and rejection that might be triggered by the clients' histories and symptoms. In a study examining how clinicians experience trauma work, several types of reactions were identified, including intrusive preoccupation with the nature of trauma work, avoidance and detachment, and over-involvement and identification with the client's situation (Wilson and Thomas, 2004). Wilson and Thomas caution:

> As the therapist gets pulled into the patient's inner world of traumatization and the magnetic force of his or her trauma story and personal state of injury, the stark reality and devastating extent of the patient's trauma experience may become so real that it seems like the therapist's own experience. Realities and boundaries may blur, creating states of confusion. This phenomenon has been variously labeled vicarious traumatization, secondary traumatization, empathic distress, compassion fatigue, trauma-related countertransference, and affective overloading. (2004: 34)

Attachment theory

Because childhood sexual abuse most often occurs within the context of early family experiences, attachment difficulties are thought to underlie problematic dynamics in therapeutic relationships with survivors of childhood abuse. Attachment theory, as developed by Bowlby (1980), explains the nature of fundamental affectional bonding between human beings (Goodwin, 2003). While the original focus of attachment theory was on mother–infant bonding, this work has been extended to address adult attachment. According to Bowlby, attachment behaviour is 'any form of behaviour that results in a person attaining or retaining proximity to a differentiated and preferred individual' (Goodwin, 2003: 36). Attachment behaviours are activated by stressful, unfamiliar, or frightening situations. They lead to the development of affectional bonds and provide a secure base from which children explore or experience the world. Internal working models of attachment, developed during early family life experiences and resulting in childhood attachment patterns, are carried into adult life and influence the quality of interpersonal relationships (Goodwin, 2003).

Using an experimental paradigm referred to as the Strange Situation, Ainsworth and colleagues (1978) studied attachment. During a 20-minute laboratory procedure, 12-month-old infants stay with their mother, their mother and a stranger, a stranger, and then alone. The children are observed as they are separated from and then reunited with their mothers. Observers note how the infants seek proximity to their mothers when the two are reunited, how easily the infants are soothed if they are distressed, and how rapidly they return to exploratory play after the reunion. This work led to the identification of four types of attachment (Ainsworth et al., 1978; Goodwin, 2003; Main and Goldwyn, 1998; Siegel, 1999). Children with secure attachments are distressed by separation from their mothers, greet their mothers when reunited, allow themselves to be comforted if they are upset, and resume play easily. Three types of insecure attachment have been identified. Children with avoidant attachments show little distress on separation, ignore the mothers when reunited, and focus on toys throughout the procedure. Children with resistant or ambivalent attachments show wariness prior to the procedure, experience high distress and preoccupation with their mothers on separation, fail to be comforted by their mothers when reunited, and fail to return to exploratory play after the reunion. Children with disorganized attachments exhibit confused or disoriented behaviours both in their mothers' presence and when reunited. Secure attachment is associated with later indices of successful adolescent and adult functioning, including emotional maturity, peer relationships, and academic performance (Main, 1996; Siegel, 1999).

Research has also been conducted on adult attachment. The Adult Attachment Interview (AAI) (Main et al., 1985) is a tool that assesses adults' states of mind or internal working models with respect to attachment. Patterns are observed in the way in which individuals narrate the stories of their early family life and relationships with parents or caregivers. This research has resulted in a classification system of four types of adult attachment patterns (Ainsworth et al., 1978; Hesse, 1999; Main and Solomon, 1990).

Secure/autonomous attachment is reflected in discourse that is coherent and consistent with respect to both favourable and unfavourable attachment-related experiences. Attachment relationships or events are valued and described objectively. Individuals with this pattern seem to live in the present, balance positive and negative aspects of relationships, and enjoy rewarding connections with others (Goodwin, 2003; Hesse, 1999; Siegel, 1999).

Dismissing attachment is reflected in discourse that is not consistently coherent and gives little consideration to attachment-related experiences and events. Narratives are typically brief and include generalized representations of experiences (e.g. my childhood was 'very normal') that are inconsistent with episodes recounted. Individuals with this pattern are prone to being emotionally distant, rejecting relationships and have restricted emotional lives (Goodwin, 2003; Hesse, 1999; Siegel, 1999).

Preoccupied attachment is reflected by long, often incoherent, narratives that include convoluted sentences and vague use of words. Preoccupied adults wish for closeness with others, but have an intense fear of abandonment. They believe others will not be able to meet their needs and experience ongoing emotional turmoil (Goodwin, 2003; Hesse, 1999; Siegel, 1999).

Unresolved or disorganized attachment is reflected by discourse that includes long discussions of loss or abuse. The narratives indicate disorganized reasoning and include long silences and eulogistic speech. These individuals often experience unresolved trauma or grief that continues to cause pain and suffering. They exhibit disorganized behaviour and chaotic shifts in states of mind (Goodwin, 2003; Hesse, 1999; Siegel, 1999).

Research indicates that the attachment classifications of infants in the Strange Situation experiments are strongly correlated with the mothers' AAI scores and predict their own AAI scores later in life (Hesse, 1999; Siegel, 1999). A basic tenet of attachment theory is that children's early experiences with caregivers influence future relationships by the development of internal working models of attachment that become generalized interactional styles (Goodwin, 2003). If, for example, children do not receive warm and predictable care from a caregiver, as is often the case with childhood maltreatment, they may develop a dismissive style of attachment which results in isolation and social incompetence in adulthood. If parents are preoccupied by their own emotional states and are not consistently attuned to the emotional states of their child, the child may develop an ambivalent style of attachment, longing for connection with others but experiencing new relationships as unreliable.

Attachment and therapeutic relationships

The theoretical formulation of attachment provides a foundation for understanding dynamics and difficulties in the counselling relationship with survivors of childhood sexual abuse. Clients' attachment styles will influence their ability to engage in the therapeutic alliance, and specific counsellor strategies may be required to enhance engagement. Eames and Roth (2000) found that clients' attachment styles are related to the formation of the alliance early in treatment. Secure attachment is related to high levels of therapist-rated alliance, and fearful avoidance is related to low levels of alliance. Preoccupied attachment is related to low levels of alliance at the beginning of treatment and higher levels toward the end. Korfmacher et al. (1997) found that women who had secure attachment styles were more involved in therapy than those with dismissing styles. Women with unresolved attachment styles were likely to have a crisis orientation to treatment. Women with dismissive attachment styles were likely to be unengaged with treatment.

The attachment style of the counsellor is likely to influence the counselling relationship as well. Researchers found that clinicians with insecure attachment styles attended more to the dependency needs of preoccupied clients than they did with dismissing clients. Clinicians with preoccupied styles intervened with clients in greater depth than did clinicians with dismissing styles (Dozier et al., 1994). Tyrell and Dozier (1998) measured behaviours of deactivation (associated with dismissive states of mind) and hyperactivation (associated with preoccupied states of mind). They found that clients who were more deactivating had stronger alliances with clinicians who were less deactivating; clients who were less deactivating had better alliances with clinicians were who more deactivating. The authors suggest that this is due to a noncomplementary process whereby clinicians can more successfully challenge clients with behaviours that are not concordant with the clinicians' attachment styles. The findings also indicate that clinicians with insecure attachment styles have difficulty providing effective treatment, regardless of the client's attachment style.

Repairing therapeutic ruptures

Difficulties in attachment are experienced by both the client and the counsellor, and can result in problems in the counselling relationship. Safran and Muran (2000) identified two types of ruptures in therapeutic relationships. Ruptures may occur due to: disagreements that occur between therapist and client over tasks and goals of therapy; or problems associated with relational bonds or the affective relationship between the client and the therapist. These authors identified several types of interventions that therapists can use to address these types of ruptures.

As discussed previously, the therapist and the client negotiate a contract early in counselling about the goals and tasks of treatment. As counselling proceeds, however, it is not uncommon for disagreement on treatment goals and tasks to emerge. When this happens, Safran and Muran (2000) recommend that therapists reiterate or clarify the treatment rationale and explore the client's reaction. If clients respond to this discussion with either skepticism or confusion, therapists must distinguish between a surface lack of understanding and confusion that reflects a basic mistrust. In the case of the latter, clients need to explore their underlying concerns and acknowledge their feelings about the counselling process (Safran and Muran, 2000).

Therapists can also respond to disagreements about tasks and goals by reframing their meaning so that they are more acceptable to the client. A goal for a particular behaviour change, for example, increasing assertiveness with others, may have been agreed upon at the start of counselling, but might later be rejected by the client. The goal of assertiveness can be reframed as an experiment – something the client can try and then assess how it went, what it felt like, and whether it would be worth trying again. A client may perceieve an experiment as less threatening than a behaviour change (Safran and Muran, 2000).

Therapists can agree on new tasks and goals that are more in line with the client's wishes. For example, a therapist and client may have agreed to work on the client's interpersonal relationships at work; the client, however, decides whether he or she would rather work on a particular symptom, such as anxiety during presentations. Accommodating the client and focusing on symptom reduction may establish trust, thereby enabling the relationship issues to be explored at a later time (Safran and Muran, 2000).

Similar approaches can be used when the rupture is related to an interpersonal conflict between the counsellor and the client, referred to as a 'bond rupture'. Clients often experience anger, disappointment, and frustration with the therapist or the process of therapy. One intervention for a bond rupture is to clarify misunderstandings on a surface level. Clients are encouraged to identify the therapist behaviours or interactions they perceive as problematic. It is critical that therapists acknowledge their role in the conflict and work with the client to improve interactions. Negotiating a change in an interaction pattern on a surface level will allow a temporary strain to be repaired so other therapeutic tasks can be addressed (Safran and Muran, 2000). For example, a client may complain about the therapist's inattentiveness. The therapist would ask the client to describe the inattentive behaviours and how he or she felt during these interactions. The counsellor would examine his or her own responses that might contribute to the interaction (e.g. boredom, anxiety) and find ways of showing more active interest in the client's situation. The client's role in such interactions might be examined at a later time.

Therapists can also intervene by framing the client's responses to the relationship as adaptive. The therapist can indicate that defensive behaviours are adaptive ways of avoiding pain, and that mistrust is an appropriate response until the relationship has been established. Therapists may also work toward repairing bond ruptures by acting in ways that contradict the client's negative expectations (e.g. being consistent and available), thereby providing a new relational experience (Safran and Muran, 2000).

Exploring core relational themes

At a deeper level, disruptions can provoke explorations of the client's characteristic behaviour patterns and attachment styles. Alliance ruptures occur at the
'intersection between the patient's and the therapist's core organizing principles'
(Safran and Muran, 2000: 85). Ruptures can, therefore, be considered glimpses into
the clients' relational schemas rather than obstacles to successful treatment. In
counselling, abuse survivors may act in ways that test their negative views of
themselves and others, with the underlying hope that these views may be proven
incorrect. Thus, the therapeutic relationship may become a re-enactment of the
traumatic developmental experiences of the client, with the therapist playing
the role of the perpetrator. Conversely, individuals who have been mistreated by
others may treat the counsellor as they have been treated, putting the counsellor
in the role of victim.

Exploring disruptions in the therapeutic relationship in the context of abuse
dynamics can reveal these core relational themes. If the dynamics of the current
relationship are explored, the characteristic relational patterns of the client can be
highlighted and addressed.

Metacommunication

Metacommunication is the intervention used to address core relational processes
in the context of alliance ruptures and therapeutic impasses. Metacommunication
is defined as:

> An attempt to step outside of the relational cycle that is currently being enacted by treat-
> ing it as the focus of collaborative exploration: that is, communication about the transac-
> tion or implicit communication that is taking place. (Safran and Muran, 2000: 108)

Metacommunication is grounded in the therapist's immediate experience of some
aspect of the here-and-now relationship, rather than an interpretation of the interaction based on the client's past history. Safran and Muran (2000) outline a number
of principles of metacommunication related to a therapist–client interaction or
dynamic. To facilitate exploration of the therapist–client interaction in the moment,
they recommend that the therapist: (a) communicate observations about the interaction in a tentative manner; (b) invite the patient to join collaboratively in an exploration of an interaction; (c) emphasize the subjectivity of the therapist's perception
or response to the interaction; (d) accept responsibility for his or her contribution to
the interaction; and (e) keep the focus on the here-and-now, referring to both the
therapist's and client's concrete and specific behaviours. The therapist needs to evaluate the client's response to and experience of the intervention.

Safran and Muran (2000) have presented two stage-process models to guide
clinicians in resolving ruptures in the therapeutic alliance. They identify two types
of ruptures: withdrawal ruptures occur when clients disengage from the therapist,
their own emotions, or the therapeutic process; confrontation ruptures occur
when clients express anger, resentment, or dissatisfaction with the therapist or
the therapeutic process. A rupture marker is a statement or behaviour that signals
the rupture.

Withdrawal ruptures

Safran and Muran (2000) identify five stages for resolution of withdrawal ruptures. They indicate that the stages are presented as discrete steps for heuristic purposes only; in actuality, therapists and clients cycle back and forth throughout the stages. Safran and Muran's stages are described below, followed by a client example provided by Draucker and Martsolf.

Stage 1: Withdrawal marker

Clients signal withdrawal from the therapy process by any number of actions. They may deny feelings, respond to an open-ended question with a short answer, shift the topic, describe an experience in an overly intellectual manner, story-tell, or talk about other people rather than themselves (Safran and Muran, 2000).

> Sally, a woman whose father ignored her childhood sexual abuse by an uncle, is working with a counselor who is planning an extended vacation and wants to cover some important material before he leaves. After he tells her about the vacation, Sally begins to provide only short, one-word responses to any questions he poses.

Stage 2: Disembedding and attending to the rupture marker

The therapist points out the marker, invites exploration of feelings that underlie the marker, and maintains a curious and empathic stance to the client's negative feelings. The therapist directs the client to the here-and-now by asking for comments about what is happening between the two of them in the present situation. The therapist remains aware of his or her own feelings and actions and acknowledges his or her own participation in the process. The goal of this stage is to facilitate a collaborative exploration about how the therapeutic relationship is being enacted (Safran and Muran, 2000).

> Sally's counselor states, 'I am feeling anxious to talk more about your abuse before I go on my vacation. I'm thinking I might be pushing too hard. I have a vague sense that your short answers to any questions might be a way to slow me down or let me know you have concerns about my vacation. How are you feeling about our interactions during this session?'

Stage 3: Qualified assertion

The client begins to express previously avoided feelings and thoughts related to underlying unmet needs in the therapeutic relationship. The client continues to retain some aspects of the rupture marker, however, by tempering his or her expressions. For example, the client may convey anger at a comment made by the therapist but then indicate that it is 'no big deal'. The therapist supports the client's assertion by expressing interest and curiosity in the negative emotion expressed by the client or by providing feedback about how the client softens his or her negative statements. If the client expresses conflict related to a negative emotion, the therapist acknowledges both sides of the conflict and then focuses on the emotion that the client is having difficulty owning (Safran and Muran, 2000).

> Sally acknowledges that she is irritated about the length of the counselor's vacation, but states 'everyone deserves time to get away.' She then mutters, 'but why now?' The

counselor responds, 'It sounds like you have two reactions to my leave. One part of you thinks I am entitled to a vacation, but the other part of you is irritated that I am leaving for such a long time at such an important juncture in our work. I would like to hear more about the part of you that is irritated.'

Stage 4: Avoidance

The exploration of the rupture experience becomes blocked. The client fears that expression of negative emotions will evoke either retaliation or withdrawal by the therapist and responds by changing the topic and avoiding focus on the current situation. The therapist expresses empathy and continues to encourage the client to explore his or her experiences in the moment. The client may also block exploration by engaging in self-criticism. The therapist points out the shift from assertion to self-criticism (Safran and Muran, 2000).

Sally indicates that she regrets bringing up her irritation because 'it is just my own neediness.' The counselor responds, 'I notice you pull back from talking about your irritation by chalking it up to your being needy. Tell me what was happening before you pulled back.'

Stage 5: Self-assertion

The client expresses underlying wishes and needs and conveys an acceptance of responsibility for those needs. This is in contrast to Stage 3, during which the client may demand that the therapist meet his or her needs. The therapist empathizes with the client's expression and facilitates ongoing self-assertion (Safran and Muran, 2000).

Sally, who is able to talk about her irritation, then becomes free to discuss her underlying fears of abandonment.

Confrontation ruptures

The authors also identify stages for resolution of confrontation ruptures (Safran and Muran, 2000), which are summarized below and followed by a client example.

Stage 1: Confrontation marker

A confrontation rupture begins with a client's comments or actions that reflect dissatisfaction with the therapist's skills or competencies, the activities of therapy, the parameters of the sessions (e.g. inconvenience, time, cost), or the lack of progress in therapy. Because clients have often had experiences of being let down, exploited, or disappointed by others, they expect the same from the therapist. It is critical that the therapist responds to the confrontation marker without criticism or defensiveness (Safran and Muran, 2000).

Jeffrey, who was molested by his parish priest, often complains that his counselor, who recently graduated from a counseling program, is incompetent, stating, 'I need some one who has been around the block to handle this. I don't know if I made a mistake coming to you.'

Stage 2: Disembedding

The therapist disembeds the confrontation marker by remarking on the current struggle. The therapist may feel compelled to defend against the attack or convince the client of the value of therapy; instead, the therapist must acknowledge his or her contribution to the rupture. Interventions include: remarking on the marker; articulating the therapist's experiences related to the rupture; inviting the client to reflect on the current interaction; providing feedback for the client regarding the impact of the client's aggression on the therapist; and helping the client confront the therapist directly (Safran and Muran, 2000).

> Jeffrey's counselor states, 'I'm feeling pressured to assure you that I can help you, but I have a sense I may not be able to convince you that I can do so. Does that fit with your experience?'

Stage 3: Exploration of construal

The therapist explores how the client construes the interaction and the rupture. Descriptions of the client's conscious experiences of the interaction and those 'on the edge of awareness' (Safran and Muran, 2000: 160) are solicited. The client's overt feelings of anger, hurt, or disappointment are accepted and validated by the therapist. The client is encouraged to share his or her perceptions of how the therapist contributed to the rupture. This exploration may free the client to explore feelings related to underlying needs or desires (Safran and Muran, 2000).

> Jeffrey continues to maintain that the counselor is not fit to help him. The counselor requests, 'Tell me some things that I have done or said in this session that fueled your concerns that I might not have the experience I need to help you.' Jeffrey mentions that on two occasions the counselor had referred to his abuser as a minister, when in fact he was a priest.

Stage 4: Avoidance of aggression

The client may shift between feelings of aggression and feelings of guilt over anger expressed toward the therapist. The client may attempt to defuse the situation by justifying his or her actions or by attempting to depersonalize the situation. The therapist assists the client in becoming aware of these states and the internal processes that cause the shifts (Safran and Muran, 2000).

> Following an interaction in which Jeffrey tries unsuccessfully to reveal some details of the abuse, including some sadistic violence, he angrily calls his counselor 'clueless' and 'wet behind the ears.' He later qualifies his remarks by saying that any counselor would have a hard time 'with my case.' The counselor says to Jeffrey, 'You soften the blow of calling me "clueless" by letting me off the hook, saying other counselors might also not "get it." Tell me what happens when you switch from expressing frustration that I am clueless to cutting me some slack by suggesting it is not just me ...'

Stage 5: Avoidance of vulnerability

The client becomes more aware of vulnerable feelings, such as sadness or fear of abandonment. At times, the client may experience these feelings as intolerable and shift back to an aggressive stance in interactions with the therapist. The therapist should be aware of these shifts and call the client's attention to the internal triggers that produce them (Safran and Muran, 2000).

> During one session, Jeffrey reveals that he experienced terror as the abuse became more violent. When the counselor tries to ask more about the terror, Jeffrey responds, 'You just don't get it, do you?' The counsellor states, 'I had the sense you began to share just how terrifying your abuse was, and then suddenly you shifted to being angry at me. Any sense of what caused the shift?'

Stage 6: Vulnerability

The client explores needs and wishes that underlie aggressive feelings, including despair, terror, and longing for nurturance. The therapist empathizes when the client shares pain and distress (Safran and Muran, 2000). This process typically occurs after a period of time in which the therapist takes the client's aggression seriously and trust develops.

> Jeffrey begins to share feelings of rage over being exploited and, at the same time, reveals how much he craves closeness and support from someone who knows about the abuse but does not reject him.

Case example

The following case example by Draucker and Martsolf reveals how dynamics and difficulties arise in the therapeutic alliance. Safran and Muran's (2000) stage model for repairing ruptures is used to exemplify how counsellors might address withdrawal ruptures with survivors of childhood sexual abuse.

Jenny was a 35-year-old woman who taught third grade at the local elementary school. She sought counselling following a divorce from her husband of five years. Although she sought help for her grief and depression over the divorce, soon after beginning counselling she shared a history of multiple types of childhood maltreatment.

Her mother, Abigail, gave birth to Jenny when Abigail was 16. Abigail was the oldest of seven children. Abigail's father, Jonathon, was a strict minister whose wife had died several years before Jenny was born. When he heard of Abigail's pregnancy, he flew into a rage and beat Abigail severely. She fled her father's home to avoid more violence, as well as to protect the identity of the father, Jim, Abigail's long-time friend.

For three years, Abigail travelled about with Jenny, finding part-time jobs and temporary housing situations. At times Abigail would resort to prostitution to support herself and Jenny. Abigail began to abuse alcohol and barbiturates. Abigail loved Jenny and tried to provide the care she needed. When Abigail was drinking or working, however, she would often fail to feed or bathe Jenny. Occasionally she left Jenny alone or with acquaintances, and lived in fear that Jenny would be taken away from her.

Tired of living on the streets, Abigail reluctantly returned home at age 19 and begged Jonathon to support her and Jenny while she 'got on her feet'. He agreed to do so but continued to rail against Abigail's 'sins' because of her 'bastard child'. Initially he ignored Jenny but by the time Jenny was six, however, he began to fondle

(Continued)

(Continued)

her when he had been drinking. He would tell her that this was her 'contribution' to the family, and if she wanted to have a roof over her head she had best not tell Abigail. Abigail continued to abuse alcohol and barbiturates. On several occasions, she sought substance abuse treatment, leaving Jenny with her grandfather and Abigail's siblings. Several times Abigail would disappear for long periods of time. When she was sober, she was a loving and devoted mother. For a reason that was not clear to Jenny, Jonathon stopped molesting her when she was eight.

Jenny did well in school, but was very shy. She had few friends but played in the band, which she experienced as a refuge from her chaotic family situation. She would often talk with school counsellors but never revealed the molestation by her grandfather or her mother's troubles. She remembers spending long periods of time alone in her room.

Abigail died from an alcohol overdose when Jenny was 18. Jenny believes Abigail never knew of the abuse by Jonathon. Jenny won a college scholarship to a local state-funded university, where she got her degree in education. She lived in the dorm and never returned to her grandfather's home.

After graduation, Jenny got a job teaching in an elementary school in a nearby community. She had a few close friends, but complained that as soon as she got close to women, they would find boyfriends and desert her. When she was 29, she met her husband Harry at an education conference. He was the superintendent of a school system in a neighbouring community. They married after a short courtship and moved into a home Harry had shared with his first wife Pamela, who had died of cancer. Jenny worried constantly that Harry would never love her as much as he loved Pamela. Harry was an avid golfer and had a wide circle of friends. Jenny told the counsellor that he divorced her after five years because she was too clingy. She told Harry little of her early family experiences for fear that he would reject her because of her troubled past.

Jenny always attended counselling sessions promptly. She was often tearful and frequently bemoaned the fact that she would never get over Harry and would never find someone else who loved her. She revealed experiencing depression 'off and on' for most of her life. After being in counselling for a short time, she revealed the trauma of the molestation. She held Jonathon responsible for her mother's death. She believed that if he had not driven Abigail away as a young, unwed mother, both Abigail's and Jenny's lives would have been much less troubled. Although Jenny indicated she had been intensely in love with Harry, the marriage had been a turbulent one. She stated she would have 'done anything' for him, but he did not appreciate her attention and would seem to look for ways to get out of the house. She revealed that she could never bring herself to be intimate with Harry, as she believed sex to be 'dirty'. She believed this was one of the reasons he left her.

Jenny exhibited a style of preoccupied attachment. The only person to whom she had ever felt emotionally close was her mother. Her mother provided some love and nurturance, but her care was inconsistent and at times neglectful. Jenny's sexual abuse by her grandfather left her feeling worthless and dirty. As an adult, she desired closeness with others, both friends and lovers, but felt no one could meet her needs for love and protection. She had been unable to maintain any long-term relationships, other than her five-year marriage to Harry. Despite being a well-respected teacher with a long tenure in the school system, she experienced a good deal of turmoil throughout her adult life.

(Continued)

(Continued)

During the early sessions, Jenny praised the counsellor, often stating that he was the only one who ever really listened to her and understood her pain. She was early for sessions and sometimes asked to schedule additional sessions because she was so distraught about losing Harry. After several months of counselling, Jennifer and her counsellor experienced what Safran and Muran (2000) would consider a withdrawal rupture. The marker was Jenny's changing the topic when the counsellor brought up her mother.

Counsellor:	You were telling me about your relationship with your mother around the time you started school and your grandfather began to molest you...
Jenny:	Yes, school was good though. I did well and the teachers liked me.
Counsellor:	And your mother...
Jenny:	Those were rough times for both of us. That was the time I had tonsillitis and had to go the hospital. My first grade teacher and all the kids in the class made a card for me. I gave it to my aunt to bring home and of course she lost it. I couldn't have anything nice. She probably threw it away thinking it was just a silly card. She never took care of anything that was mine...

The counsellor was aware that he was becoming frustrated because Jenny would not talk about her mother, a topic that the counsellor felt was essential to Jenny's healing. Being attuned to his own feelings, he decided to disembed and attend to the rupture marker. His goals were to communicate his observations about their interactions in a tentative manner and invite Jenny to explore their relationship in the here-and-now.

Counsellor:	I note that when I brought up your mom a few moments ago, you talked about your aunt instead. I wonder what you were feeling while we were having that interaction.
Jenny:	I was thinking about my aunt. I never did like her. Is it not ok to talk about her?
Counsellor:	I would like to hear more about her, but I was curious about what was occurring between you and me. I have a vague sense that by changing the topic from your mom to your aunt you might be telling me I was treading on ground you didn't want me to tread on.
Jenny:	If you want me to talk about my mother, I will. You know I will do whatever it takes to get better.
Counsellor:	We probably will need to talk about your mom at some point. Right now I am curious about how you felt a few minutes ago when I brought her up.
Jenny:	I thought you were going to blame her for everything. Just like my grandfather.
Counsellor:	And that felt...
Jenny:	Awful.
Counsellor:	Perhaps we can figure out what to do when I am treading where you don't want me to tread. My treading caused you to feel awful and I would like to understand more about what awful feels like for you...

(Continued)

(Continued)

Jenny: Awful feels like…I need to protect her. I get the feeling you want me to bad-mouth her. She wasn't perfect but I dread it when you keep pushing me about her. I thought you understood me and would be there just to listen. It feels threatening when you bring up my mother and I can't go there…

In this intervention, the counsellor pointed out the marker (switching topics), encouraged Jenny to describe her feelings underlying the marker, invited her to explore the here-and-now interaction, and acknowledged his part in the rupture ('treading where you don't want me to tread'). Jenny revealed that the therapist was pushing the topic of her mother too much and that this made her feel threatened. As the interaction went on, however, Jenny began to qualify her feelings.

Jenny: You do keep bringing up my mother, who was a good woman, but I know you have to – that – it is your job. I feel threatened by you sometimes, but I shouldn't. I want to get well. You care about me.

Counsellor: You were able to tell me that when I encourage you to talk about your mom, or maybe push you to talk about your mom is a better way to put it, you feel threatened. That is a tough way to feel when you are trying to get help. You softened your feedback for me, however, by saying that my pushing you is understandable because I am doing my job. I would like to hear more about what it is like for you to feel threatened in our work together.

In this interaction, the counsellor empathized with Jenny's feelings of being threatened and provided feedback about how she softens her negative statements. His goal was to acknowledge both sides of her conflict, while expressing interest and curiosity in the feelings she was having difficulty addressing. Although Jenny articulated that she felt threatened when the counsellor pushed her to talk about her mother, the exploration of the interaction became blocked. In the next session, she resumed her praise of the counsellor and emphasized how much help he had been.

Jenny: I was really looking forward to the session today. Last week was really helpful.

Counsellor: Last week we talked about interactions we have had in which I pushed too much about your mom, and how you feel threatened.

Jenny: Last week was just a bad week. I had gotten the divorce papers and well, it was just a bad week. Harry tells me I avoid talking about anything of substance, and that's what I was doing last week. Anything that is a little threatening, I turn wimpy.

Counsellor: Last week you were able to let me know that you felt threatened by some things I did and I recognized that I was pushing and prodding. Today I get the sense you are pulling back a little from the feedback you gave me last week. Could you tell me what you are experiencing now?

The counsellor recognized that Jenny's self-criticism ('I turn wimpy') blocked the exploration of the here-and-now. He again invited her to explore their interactions in an attempt to understand her shift from self-assertion to self-criticism. Later, Jenny began to reveal her fear of abandonment by the counsellor and this became the focus of their work.

(Continued)

(Continued)

Jenny: I am afraid that if I turn you away by whining, I will have no one. I cannot be alone again. I want this. I want therapy. I do not want to be alone.

Counsellor: The fear of being left alone can be very powerful. You fear that if you say what you really think and feel in our sessions I will call it quits. Actually, if you share with me what you think and feel about my approach, I can better gauge my work with you.

11 Case Study: The Counselling Process with an Adult Survivor of Childhood Sexual Abuse

This chapter illustrates counselling principles by describing the counselling experience of Sue, an adult survivor of childhood sexual abuse who sought counselling at a community agency. Sue was in individual counselling for approximately a year and a half. This was her first counselling experience.

Background

Sue was a 44-year-old woman who sought counselling for complaints of general life dissatisfaction and concern about her drinking habits. Because she broke several scheduled appointments, she did not come for an intake session for several months after her initial call to the agency. She claimed that she had cancelled the appointments to take her mother to various doctor's appointments.

When Sue finally did attend a scheduled appointment, she told the counsellor that she was very anxious. She stated, 'I never thought I would be the type of person to do this [seek counselling].' She began by describing herself as a 'plain Jane old maid'. Sue revealed that she got up one morning and realized that she was unhappy with her life and did not want to 'live the next 20 years like I lived that last 20'. However, she was unable to articulate what changes she wanted to make in her life other than to 'get out more with people'. She did report that she had completely stopped drinking over two months before, when she made the initial call for a counselling appointment.

An assessment revealed that Sue was living with her 76-year-old mother, who was in poor health due to long-standing heart problems. Sue reported that she had been taking care of her mother for many years by doing her shopping and housekeeping and making her doctor's appointments. She described their relationship as strained and conflict-ridden. She claimed her mother was very 'cranky' and would usually complain that Sue was not doing things right. At times, Sue resented the fact that her mother depended on her so much. Sue's father and mother had been separated for approximately 33 years. Her father lived in a distant part of the country. Sue would call him periodically, but he would usually be drunk when she called.

Sue had two older sisters and one younger brother. Her sisters were both married and living in another area. They visited infrequently, usually during the holidays. Sue stated that her younger brother, John, had emotional problems and was currently living in a nearby rooming house. When he ran out of money, he would sometimes return to live with Sue and her mother. Sue said this arrangement was problematic as John was 'difficult to control' and at times would become violent when angry. Although he did not attack Sue or her mother, he would destroy their belongings (e.g. smash dishes, break furniture). Sue stated that he would also get drunk, steal from the family, and stay away for days at a time. Sue's mother would insist that Sue 'keep an eye' on John when he stayed with them.

Sue was employed as the receptionist and secretary for a small local industry. She had been at her job for over 26 years, since graduating from high school. Although she was reluctant to compliment herself, Sue indicated that her work was highly regarded by her employer. She had not missed a day of work since she was hired. Although her work could be monotonous at times, she basically enjoyed her job and her relationship with co-workers.

After work, Sue would usually stop at a local restaurant for dinner and a few drinks. She would then come home to watch television and have a few more drinks. She stated that she had no friends outside of work other than Jim, a young man who lived in the apartment above hers. She described him as a 'shy loner – much like me'. Jim would suggest from time to time that they get married, but Sue denied any interest in Jim that was 'more than friends'. Sue reported that she had always been isolated from anyone outside her family.

Sue was somewhat vague when answering questions about her childhood. She denied any abuse, although she did claim that her father was 'very strict' with the other children, 'whipping them when they needed it'. She 'got off the hook' because she never got into any trouble. Her dad 'drank too much sometimes' and 'had quite the temper'. Sue described her family as very conservative and religious. She stated that they had few friends outside of the church. Sue's mother was often sick. Sue laughed, 'I guess things haven't changed much – I was calling the doctor for her even back then.'

Sue remained somewhat hesitant about counselling, but stated, 'I'm depressed, lonely, and bored and need to do something.' Sue and the counsellor agreed to work on Sue's social relationships and her conflicted relationship with her mother.

Disclosing an experience of childhood sexual abuse

During the second session, Sue appeared very anxious and avoided eye contact with the counsellor. She began the session by stating, 'I think I had better tell you about some weird dreams I've been having.' Sue revealed that she had had several dreams in which she is a little girl and a 'shadowy figure' climbs into bed with her. Sometimes this figure would have a knife or a spear. She experienced these dreams as very frightening. She feared that having these 'dirty' dreams meant that she was 'some kind of pervert'. In the following interaction, Sue discusses the dreams and reveals that she was sexually abused by her father as a child.

Sue: I think it's strange I would have such a weird dream. It is so bizarre. I must be some kind of weirdo. I wasn't just in bed with him. It was like, well, sexual. It's like the figure touches me, in my private parts. The dreams are fuzzy, I cannot remember everything.

Counsellor:	What do the dreams mean to you?
Sue:	It's just bizarre. I know people have weird dreams, but this is too strange. You must think I'm perverted.
Counsellor:	No, I don't. People can have dreams like this for any number of reasons. I can see it was hard for you to tell me about these dreams, however, and I respect your courage for bringing them up.
Sue:	Maybe I should tell you. I wasn't completely honest with you last time. [*Long pause*] I think it happened in real life. My father did stuff to me. I do not remember all the details, but I do know he would come to my bed and would, you know, fondle me. That I do remember. This is probably hard for you to believe. For a long time I pretended it did not happen. I'm embarrassed to tell you. This is not why I am here. It's not important. It is my mother who drives me crazy, not my father.
Counsellor:	I can appreciate that it was hard for you to tell me about this. I am glad you chose to share this. We may decide to explore these childhood experiences and see how they may be related to the concerns you have now.

Upon further questioning, Sue revealed that her father had fondled her in her bed about once a week for a period of two years, starting when she was about eight. It usually occurred when he was drunk and her mother was asleep. He convinced her never to tell her mother, by telling Sue that she was his 'special girl'. The nightmares began when she stopped drinking.

Discussion

Sue's initial presentation was consistent with a possible undisclosed history of sexual abuse. She presented with issues common to sexual abuse survivors: social isolation, substance abuse, and being in a caretaking role that she clearly resented. In addition, she also described a history of parentification in which she had cared for a sickly mother from a young age. The family was isolated and her father was impulsive, violent, and chemically dependent. Sue indicated that her other siblings had been beaten by their father, but she was vague when asked about her own treatment by him. While the counsellor did not suggest that trauma was a factor related to Sue's current concerns, she did formulate an index of suspicion.

During the second session, Sue disclosed a possible trauma-related symptom, an ongoing intrusive nightmare. When the counsellor assured Sue that she did not consider her 'perverted' because of her dreams, Sue disclosed long-term sexual abuse by her father. The counsellor responded to this disclosure with calm concern, and suggested that they explore the significance of this abuse in Sue's life.

Focusing on the abuse experience

The counselling agreement

Sue at first denied that the sexual abuse by her father was a significant childhood event related to her current concerns. After a few sessions, however, the nightmare of the 'shadowy figure' became more frequent and more violent in content. Sue described waking up just as the figure was about to stab her. She decided to focus on the abuse experience after the following interaction with her counsellor:

Sue:	I'm 44. I'm lonely. I've stopped drinking and yet I'm still miserable. Now, on top of this, I've been thinking about my dad as a dirty old man who messed with me. Bringing this up has not helped me. In fact, it's made me more depressed. I still have the problem I came here with. I'm alone and I don't know what to do about it. The abuse happened, but so what?
Counsellor:	An abuse experience like the one you suffered as a child may be related in some way to the struggles you have now.
Sue:	How can this be? As nearly as I can figure out, it happened almost 36 years ago.
Counsellor:	Being sexually abused as a young child by a parent can affect how the child relates to others when he or she grows up. Or – the way the child learns to cope with the abuse continues to be the way he or she copes with things as an adult.
Sue:	Like – I always hid out in my room as a kid. Now I know I was probably trying to get away from what was happening. I played alone for hours and had no friends. I still hide out in my room now in a way. Instead of Barbie dolls, I leaned on my bourbon [Whiskey]. I still have no friends. Maybe my messed-up childhood does have something to do with all this. How will talking about it help, though?

Discussion

In this interaction, the counsellor explored a possible connection between the abuse and Sue's current difficulties. For Sue, making the connection between hiding out in her room as a child and 'hiding out' as an adult was a powerful experience. If she had not made a connection between the abuse and her current concerns, she probably would not have chosen to continue to deal with the abuse issue in counselling. At this point, the counsellor described the purpose of the exploratory work (e.g. translation of memories into a narrative, making sense of her life story, experiencing emotions at a pace that is safe and manageable) and answered questions Sue had about the abuse-focused approach to counselling. Because Sue had made a connection between her past and present, and thereby ceased to minimize the abuse, she contracted with the counsellor to focus on the abuse experience as a way of better understanding her current difficulties.

Preparing for exploratory work

Both Sue and the counsellor were concerned about Sue's drinking history. Sue readily agreed that her drinking was one way she had coped with the pain in her life and her feelings of loneliness and boredom. Although she was proud that she had stopped drinking on her own, she realized that she might be tempted to drink once she began to explore the abuse. She agreed to attend AA, both to address her abuse of alcohol and to decrease her social isolation. In time, she became an avid AA member.

Sue and the counsellor also discussed the relationship between Sue's nightmares and the abuse. The counsellor informed Sue that the nightmares might become more troubling as they began to explore the abuse in greater depth. Together they planned how Sue could manage the nightmares if this occurred. Sue placed an award that she had received at work as 'Employee of the Year' on her nightstand. When awakened by a nightmare, she would reach out for this plaque and it would ground her to present reality. This associational cue worked particularly well as it clearly reflected Sue's competency as an adult.

For Sue, the preparatory period was brief. She had been sober for several months and was functioning relatively well. Some experts may argue for a longer period of sobriety before exploring the abuse in depth. The counsellor felt that Sue was ready to begin the exploratory work after about four sessions. Although Sue had been reluctant to discuss the abuse when she first came to counselling, once she decided that exploring this issue would help she was determined to get started.

Exploratory work

Several approaches were used to help Sue explore her abuse. She remembered many abuse incidents but was 'fuzzy' about the details. Discussing general childhood events provoked more detailed memories of the abuse. For example, when Sue talked about her mother's preoccupation with health issues, the counsellor inquired as to what impact this had on Sue as a child. Sue revealed that her mother had taken her to the doctor for even the most minor ailments. During one visit, the doctor told her mother that Sue must have fallen off her bike as she had injuries 'down there'. At the time, Sue felt confused about this because she had not had any such accident. She remembered being concerned that her mother might have thought that she had sex at school, but her mother never mentioned the doctor's comments again. Looking back, Sue concluded that the vaginal injuries were probably the result of the sexual abuse, and that her mother did not respond to the doctor's revelation because she did not want to deal with what Sue's father had done. As Sue discussed this incident, memories of some abuse incidents became clearer and she recalled incidents of penetration as well as fondling.

Sue began to discuss the abuse incidents in some detail, but complained of feeling numb and 'distant from' the memories. The counsellor recommended that Sue bring in an old family photograph taken at a time when she was eight years old. Sue found only one old photo of her family. In the photo, she was eight years old. Sue asked her mother if there were other photos and her mother told her that the family had never owned a camera and that the photograph Sue had found was taken by her grandmother. The photograph provoked several fruitful discussions about Sue's family. While viewing the photo, Sue discussed her father's alcoholism and his severe physical abuse of her brother, much of which Sue had witnessed. She also revealed that her mother did not seem to notice her brother's beatings. When discussing these family dynamics, Sue began to have an emotional response to her memories:

> *Sue:* You know you can tell something is wrong with this family even by looking at this photo. No one is smiling. You know how families always smile in pictures. We all look miserable. No wonder we never had our own camera. Look at my brother. He looks mad! No wonder. My father beats him and my mother couldn't care less.

Counsellor: What do you think when you look at yourself in the picture?
Sue: I look dumb, I think. We all look weird. Other families stand close to each other or touch each other. We look wooden. My father even looks mean; my mother looks frail; I look spaced out.
Counsellor: Spaced out?
Sue: Ya, like not there. I have such a blank look.
Counsellor: What do you make of that?
Sue: It's like I checked out. I don't look happy. I don't look sad. I just look there. That's how I felt. I was just there. I don't remember being happy, but I don't remember being sad either. When my father beat my brother, I think I would kind of pretend that it wasn't happening. Like I made myself numb.
Counsellor: What do you think of when you look at your family as a whole?
Sue: Looking at this picture I realize this family is not normal. My father did what he wanted, my mother didn't notice, and I was spaced out. Like I was in a coma. [*She begins to cry softly.*] What a waste of a childhood.

Through discussions about her family's functioning, Sue concluded that her sisters, who both left home immediately after high school, might have been sexually abused. Her father had been extremely strict with her oldest sister, flying into a rage whenever she brought dates home. Sue, who by this time had read a good deal of material on incestuous families, concluded that her father's response to her sister's dates reflected a 'possessive jealousy', which is often characteristic of a sexually abusive father.

Sue decided to call her sisters and ask if they had been sexually abused by their father. The counsellor requested that they first spend time discussing Sue's plans (e.g. her motives, possible risks and benefits for both herself and her sisters). After these discussions, Sue remained determined to contact her sisters. She first called Jill, the younger of the two sisters, who denied abuse by her father and was quite critical that Sue should even suggest such a 'dirty-minded' thing. Despite having previously considered that this might be Jill's response, Sue nonetheless felt devastated at her sister's reaction to her disclosure and request for help. (It was later revealed by Sue's mother that all the girls had been sexually abused by their father.)

Sue's older sister Paula responded quite differently. When Sue told her the purpose of the call, Paula became very quiet and started to cry. Paula revealed that she had been abused by their father from the ages of 10 to 16, when she left home. She stated that she had hoped that Sue had been spared his abuse, but she had always wondered. Paula decided to visit Sue, and Sue invited her to one of the counselling sessions. Both sisters were very supportive of one another. They cried together and commiserated that although they had both suffered, until now they had not been able to share each other's pain.

Discussion

While Sue had some initial amnesia about the details of the abuse incidents (e.g. the vaginal penetration), these memories returned spontaneously through free narrative recall as she described other childhood experiences. Even when she began to discuss abuse incidents, she maintained good control over her intrusive nightmares and remained sober. However, she complained of being 'stuck', i.e. having little emotional response to the discussions of the abuse. This is an example of defensive dissociation, in which memories are disconnected from overwhelming affect. The counsellor felt that they were 'undershooting' the therapeutic window as Sue continued to employ avoidant defences and was therefore describing, but not processing, the traumatic material. The counsellor decided to increase the use of exploratory interventions.

Several techniques were used, including viewing old photographs and processing Sue's interactions with her sisters. Although the counsellor did not recommend that Sue contact her sisters, she did acknowledge Sue's desire to do so and stressed the importance of first discussing the risks and benefits for all concerned. With the support of the counsellor and her older sister, Sue did begin to experience first sadness, then rage, toward her father. Although it was difficult to have these feelings, she claimed that she began to feel 'alive'. As she continued to discuss the abuse and her feelings regarding it, her nightmares began to subside. She remained sober throughout the process.

Reinterpreting the sexual abuse experience from an adult perspective

Because her father abused all his children, either sexually or physically, Sue blamed her father, not herself, for the abuse relatively early in her healing process. She did not struggle as intensely with responsibility issues as do some survivors. Following her interactions with her sisters, Sue quite clearly stated her belief that her father was a 'very sick man' and that she and her siblings were not to blame for the abuse.

She did deal, however, with the issue of sexual responsiveness. In her dream, she responded sexually to the shadowy figure. Sue asked, 'I know I was too young to ask for it [the abuse], but did I enjoy it?' When her sexual response was reframed by the counsellor as a natural physiological reaction, rather than an indication that she had enjoyed the activity, Sue was able to resolve this issue.

Addressing the context of the sexual abuse

Addressing the context of the sexual abuse experience was an important issue for Sue. In addition to the sexual abuse, her father's alcoholism and explosive temper and her mother's illnesses, obsession with the physical health of the family, and denial of the family violence had a significant impact on Sue's childhood development. Sue avidly read anything she could get her hands on regarding sexual abuse and alcoholic families. She identified herself as the 'family hero' (Wegscheider-Cruse, 1985), because she was always the child who did well at school and who had assumed the responsibility of caring for her mother. Sue was able to see how she continued to play these roles as an adult by being extremely responsible at work (e.g. never missing a day, 'doing the work of two people') and providing for her mother's, and now her brother's, needs. She recognized that she was unable to meet her own needs and, thus, had ultimately become very dissatisfied with her life.

Sue was especially interested in the concept of the closed family system (Satir, 1988). Her family's isolation had been profound. Her parents never socialized with others and discouraged the children from having friends. Sue recognized that Paula's attempts at dating, in addition to making her father jealous, had broken an unspoken family rule against interacting with outsiders. For this offence, Paula had been punished with her father's rage. Other attempts by the parents to discourage the children from having friends were more subtle. Often her parents would simply 'badmouth' other children with whom Sue or her siblings became friendly. Sue recognized that her isolation as an adult resulted in part from this deep distrust of those outside the family. Exploring her mother's role in the abuse was also important to Sue. While she acknowledged the rage she felt toward her father, she stated that she did not know how to feel toward her mother. After discussing her mother's behaviour during Sue's childhood (e.g. pretending not to notice John's beatings; ignoring the doctor's revelation of Sue's 'accident'), Sue concluded that her mother knew something of the abuse, but did not intervene. In the following counsellor–client interaction, Sue reaches this conclusion and decides to discuss her suspicions with her mother. The counsellor again recommends that Sue plan for this confrontation before carrying it out.

Sue: I can't believe she let this happen. But she must have. She never left the house. How could she not know? When the doctor told her about my 'accident', she never asked about it again. She must have known what really caused it or she would have asked me about it. Yes, she knew. She just ignored it.

Counsellor: What has it been like for you to reach this conclusion about your mom?

Sue: I don't know. I need to know for sure. Now, I can't feel anything. I mean if I really knew I would be angry. I need to ask her. After everything I've done for her. I was the only one to stick by her. I'm going to ask her when I get home.

Counsellor: I can see it's important for you to find out whether your mother knew what your father was doing, and asking your mom directly would, of course, be a way to find out. It would be helpful to plan this ahead – what you will say to your mom, what you hope will happen, what it might feel like for you to do this, what effect it would have on her. That way it feels more in your control.

Sue: OK, I won't run home and do it tonight.

Counsellor: Let's start by discussing what it might be like for you to confront your mom.

Sue recognized that the confrontation in itself would be very difficult for her. She was accustomed to protecting her mother from anything unpleasant and, in this instance, she would be bringing up a painful issue. She hoped that her mother would confirm what Sue really believed to be true, i.e. that her mother knew of the abuse, but felt powerless to stop it. Sue knew this would be very hard to hear but would be a 'step in the right direction' toward sorting out her feelings regarding her mother's involvement in the abuse dynamics. Sue also explored her possible reactions if her mother denied knowledge of the abuse. She guessed that if her mother did not 'take responsibility and admit the truth', she would feel very resentful.

Before confronting her mother, Sue practised exactly what she wanted to say. She decided to begin the conversation with this statement, 'Mom, I now know Dad abused me by having sex with me when I was little. I do not question that it happened. Would you tell me if you were aware he was doing this to me? It is important to me that I know.'

When Sue confronted her mother, her mother did admit that she had known what the father was doing to all the kids (i.e. sexually abusing the girls and physically abusing John). Sue's mother confirmed Sue's belief that she felt powerless to stop the abuse because of her husband's violent temper, the family's dependency on his paycheck, and her own ill-health. Sue's mother became very tearful and yet 'somehow calm' as she said that she had hoped that Sue had been too young to realize what was happening to her. Her mother told Sue that one of the reasons her father had left the house when he did was because he was afraid Paula would tell the authorities of her abuse.

Sue initially felt enraged with her mother. She became very resentful that she had been her mother's caretaker all these years, whereas her mother had not protected her when she was a young child. Eventually, Sue came to appreciate her mother's limitations, which Sue called her 'extreme weakness of character'. Sue stated that she did not forgive her mother for not protecting her from the abuse. She did, however, resolve her own feelings toward her mother by coming to understand why she had not taken action. She was, therefore, no longer consumed with needing to know what her mother knew about the abuse and felt less bitterness as time went on.

Sue began to identify the unhealthy aspects of their relationship and decided to make changes in the way she interacted with her mother. She realized, for example, that many of the things she did for her mother (e.g. arranging doctor's appointments) were things her mother could do for herself. Ultimately, despite protests from her mother, Sue decided to move to her own apartment and gradually gave up much of the caretaking role. She also set limits on John's behaviours, although she continued to bail him out of trouble from time to time.

Discussion

Counselling interventions that were aimed at helping Sue explore the context of the abuse included facilitating a discussion related to dysfunctional families. When Sue recognized that she had assumed the role of the responsible, but joyless, child in her family and that the family system in which she grew up was extremely closed, she came to appreciate that her social isolation, her main presenting concern, was in many ways an extension of her family's history. Having this insight freed her to make other choices regarding social relationships as an adult.

Sue needed to explore her mother's role in the abuse dynamics. As with Sue's sisters, the counsellor did not advise a confrontation. Once Sue had chosen this course of action, however, the counsellor did help her plan and process the experience. Sue confirmed what she had suspected about the extent of her mother's knowledge of the abuse and dealt with her feelings related to this. She was then able to decide what kind of relationship she would like to maintain with her mother.

Making desired life changes

Even prior to beginning counselling, Sue had made a major life change: achieving and maintaining sobriety. However, she continued to feel lonely and isolated, often seeing only her mother, her brother John, and a few co-workers during the course of a day. As previously mentioned, she realized that she was continuing a family pattern of social isolation. Sue also recognized that the abuse and the family dynamics that surrounded it had made her feel poorly about herself, believing she would have very little to offer if she did make any friends. She continued to complain, 'I'm a plain Jane old maid.' In the following client–counsellor interaction, this self-perception was challenged.

Sue:	I look at other people, you know, married people. Or people having fun, going on dates. I'm so plain, so boring. The original old maid.
Counsellor:	I've noticed that you often refer to yourself as a 'plain old maid'. Tell me who first told you in some way that you were plain.
Sue:	Who first told me? Well, it must have been my parents, of course. I've always been ugly, even as a child. My father called me an 'ugly duckling'. I didn't mind. I was a tomboy, unlike Paula who was really pretty.
Counsellor:	So, your mom and dad first gave you the message that you were plain?
Sue:	Yes. I guess being plain looking actually saved me some of the pain Paula went through. I told you what happened because she had dates. You know, I remember my mother going through the ceiling when she came home one day with make-up. My father also went wild. I remember him scrubbing it off her face.
Counsellor:	What do you make of that now, looking back?
Sue:	Well, it fits in with what we've been talking about. Being attractive or wearing make-up gets you noticed. Our parents didn't want us noticed.
Counsellor:	Being a 'plain Jane' was what your family wanted you to be. It was what they expected.
Sue:	Yes, but I am plain. Plain and dumpy. I did let myself get dumpy. My mother used to say heavy girls are virtuous, and 'shapely' girls are sluts. Jim tells me that I have nice eyes. That's what they tell fat people, nice eyes.
Counsellor:	In your family you were expected to be plain and that's how you learned to see yourself. You tried to live up to those expectations, maybe by gaining weight. Yet those outside your family, like Jim, have seen something different, like your attractive eyes.
Sue:	I can see where this is leading. I can make choices about how I look as an adult. I don't need to meet my parents' expectations. I'm not sure I believe that, but maybe I could spruce up a bit. I've lost weight since I stopped drinking and it does feel good. You also think I have nice eyes? [*Laughs*]

A similar interaction addressed Sue's perception of herself as boring. In fact, she revealed that some of her co-workers liked to talk with her at lunch because she was so well read and kept up an interesting conversation. Also, Sue had a real sense of determination, which was probably what allowed her to stop drinking and deal with the sexual abuse issue so doggedly. Through discussions in counselling she became aware of this trait, an aspect of her personality to which she had never given credence. Exploring these strengths was a fruitful endeavour for Sue.

Having made progress in dealing with self-esteem issues, Sue then focused on her interpersonal relationships, the main issue that brought her to counselling. She decided that risking hurt was worth being less lonely. She joined an active, reputable singles' club – a major step for her. Attending the first few planned activities was very difficult for Sue, but she soon began to get to know several of the members, both male and female. Within a month of joining the club, she was asked out on a date. She began to see one of the members, Jake, on a regular basis. She eventually decided to end the relationship, realizing Jake had a 'drinking problem' and had begun to push for a sexual relationship that Sue did not want. Although she was disappointed that the relationship ended, she was well entrenched in the club and felt confident that she would meet someone else.

Discussion

Making life changes was an important aspect of Sue's healing. Stopping drinking, feeling better about herself, and becoming more active socially were all significant changes for her. Counselling interventions that challenged Sue's negative self-views and facilitated her increased awareness of her positive self-views were used to address self-esteem issues. Supportive interventions, such as encouraging Sue to discuss her new activities, were helpful as she risked new social interactions. In this phase of counselling, Sue expressed her belief that 'things were really happening'.

Addressing resolution issues

In the final stages of counselling Sue dealt with several resolution issues, the search for meaning being the most predominant. At this point, she claimed that she no longer hated her father – although she did hate what he had done to her, her mother, and her siblings. Sue also reported that she no longer wished her father harm, as she once had. However, she expressed a strong need to know 'why he did what he did'. Her attempt to understand the cause of the abuse became the focus of several counselling sessions. In the following interaction, Sue begins to seek an answer to this question and the counsellor encourages her search:

Sue: I just cannot understand why anyone would do that to his little girls. Was he sick or was he evil? He'll have to pay in hell, one way or the other. Maybe it was the alcohol. I guess it really doesn't matter, it happened.

Counsellor: I know I've heard you wonder before why your father did what he did, so perhaps it is an important question for you. There may not be a definite answer – and whatever the answer, the abuse was wrong. However, many individuals who have had a traumatic experience wonder why it happened.

Sue: I do wonder a lot. I think about him a lot now. I know he was an alcoholic, but there are many alcoholics who don't abuse their children. I've read that sometimes those who abuse their children were abused themselves. I suspect that might be true of my father. I do know my grandfather was in jail for a long stretch; I think it was for assaulting someone in a bar. Maybe even for killing someone. So he could not have been a model parent. My grandmother, she was weird. She was a cold fish.

Counsellor: So you would guess that your father had some pretty poor parenting himself.

Sue:	I'm sure he did. I suspect he was beaten, probably a lot.
Counsellor:	That might be a possibility. Sometimes, those who abuse others were abused themselves.
Sue:	You know I wouldn't be surprised if my mother was also abused. Both her parents died of alcoholism – you know, liver problems – so at the very least she probably had a miserable childhood. Us kids probably didn't stand a chance of getting good parents.

Sue also found meaning in her experience by coming to believe that some benefit had come from her healing process. In the following interaction, she comes to this conclusion:

Sue:	Now that I'm doing so well, someone in AA asked me the other day if I'm glad the abuse happened because it made me tough.
Counsellor:	What did you say?
Sue:	No, I'm not glad. That's silly. This has been too painful and I lost too many good years of my life because of it. But, as bad as it was to be abused and to be a hermit for all those years, something good has come from this. Paula and I are close in a way we have never been before. Did you know I'm going to see her over my vacation? Also, now I know I'm strong. Everyone told me this, but now I believe it.

Relinquishing the survivor identity was also a significant step for Sue, as reflected in the following interaction with the counsellor:

Sue:	It's funny, for most of my life I never thought of myself as an incest victim. Then, for a year, it was all I could think about. I was obsessed with it. Now, things are good. I have other things to think about. I'll never forget it [the abuse] of course, but it doesn't rule my life.
Counsellor:	Yes, your abuse is an important part of your history. Due to your strength and all the work you've put into dealing with it, however, it no longer guides your life. You've moved beyond thinking of yourself primarily as an incest survivor.

Shortly after this interaction, Sue decided to end counselling. She spent several more sessions reviewing her progress, stating future goals, and saying goodbye to the counsellor. She said she believed that she would continue to expand her circle of friends and was contemplating beginning college. She visited her mother periodically, but was no longer her caretaker. Although she was sad and a bit scared to be ending counselling, Sue believed she had made significant progress and stated that she now felt healthy.

Discussion

The counselling interventions used at this stage validated Sue's need to search for meaning. Because Sue's search involved deciding why her father had abused her, exploring possible causes of his abusive behaviour (e.g. his own childhood abuse) enhanced the resolution process. The counsellor also facilitated discussion of two other resolution issues for Sue: finding benefit from her healing experience (e.g. her strength, her close relationship with Paula) and giving up the survivor role.

12 Future Directions and Trends

The six healing processes thought to be necessary for recovery from childhood sexual abuse have been described to provide a model for counselling adult survivors. In addition to considering basic healing processes, counsellors must remain abreast of emerging and relevant areas of scholarship related to the phenomenon of childhood sexual abuse. Three such areas of scholarship will be addressed in this chapter. First, much is being learned about the neurobiology of trauma and childhood maltreatment. This information is essential to an appreciation of the experiences of adult survivors, and also has implications for treatment planning. A brief overview is provided, with an emphasis on how interpersonal relationships influence brain development. While the processes are described in an orderly, step-wise manner, the counselling process will be fluid and guided by each client's unique needs and the unfolding of the therapeutic relationship. The cultural backgrounds of clients contribute to their uniqueness. Although a comprehensive discussion of multicultural counselling is beyond the scope of this book, a brief discussion of multicultural counselling theory and practice techniques is included. Finally, there is an overview of trauma-based treatment approaches that may be incorporated to address specific symptoms, concerns, and co-morbid disorders encountered during phase-oriented counselling.

Neurobiology of trauma

Childhood sexual abuse is an adverse developmental experience that has profound effects on the immature brain, causing alterations that may create vulnerability for a host of adult neuropsychiatric symptoms (Kendall-Tackett, 2003; Perry, 2001). Counsellors should be aware of the ways in which childhood trauma influences brain development and the normal stress response. They must also consider how interpersonal experiences, including the counselling relationship, can affect the neurobiology of adults (Siegel, 1999).

During a traumatic event, neural systems that provide for emotional, behavioural, cognitive, and physiological survival responses are activated (Perry, 2001). These systems include the hypothalamic-pituitary-adrenal (HPA) axis and the noradrenergic (NA) and dopaminergic (DA) systems. The thalamus, located in the diencephalon region of the brain, directs information to the cerebral cortex to be evaluated. In the prefrontal cortex, meaning is attached to events. In the limbic system, the hippocampus controls memory and learning and the amygdala controls emotional response. The anterior cingulated cortex activates additional brain circuits that control emotions (Kendall-Tackett, 2003). If an event is perceived as non-threatening, the amygdala activates the adrenal medulla system; if the event is perceived as threatening, the hippocampus activates the hypothalamic-pituitary-adrenal axis (HPA) (Kendall-Tackett, 2003). The hypothalamus releases corticotrophin-releasing factor (CRF) in response to the stressful event. CRF coordinates the neuroendocrine stress response by activating the pituitary-adrenal axis and the sympathetic nervous system. CRF stimulates the pituitary to release adrenocorticotrophic hormone (ACTH), which signals the adrenal glands to release cortisol, a glucocorticoid that stimulates cortical arousal, improves concentration, and increases energy on initial activation (van Voorhees and Scarpa, 2004). The adrenal medulla secretes epinephrine and norepinephrine, catecholamines that are responsible for the fight–flight response, into the bloodstream (Kendall-Tackett, 2003).

When the stressor is severe or of long duration, as is often the case in childhood maltreatment, the stress response becomes overactivated and can no longer restore homeostasis. Chronic stress creates long-term alterations in the connections between the frontal lobes and the limbic system and between the brainstem and the central nervous system. The neural systems of children who sustain long-term maltreatment adapt to the chaotic environment, and the children develop a generalized physiological hyperarousal (Kendall-Tackett, 2003). As a result, subsequent stressors create an overreaction and the children's neural systems are activated by less environmental stimulation and minor or non-dangerous triggers (Perry, 2001). Changes in the HPA axis are evidenced by abnormal levels of norepinephrine and cortisol, specific changes in receptors of these hormones, and structural changes in the hippocampus. High levels of cortisol may cause hippocampal atrophy, resulting in elevated CRF. Hypersecretion of CRF and ACTH results in adrenal and pituitary hypertrophy (Kendall-Tackett, 2003).

Abnormal functioning of the HPA axis has been associated with emotional disturbances, including anxiety, depression, and PTSD, as well as learning and memory deficits (van Voorhees and Scarpa, 2004). Researchers have found that the degree of HPA dysregulation in children who have experienced childhood trauma is influenced by a number of factors, including the nature, duration, and pattern of the stressor; the age of the child at the time of the trauma; the child's characteristics (e.g. genetic predisposition, history of previous stress); and the caregivers' responsiveness (Perry, 2001; van Voorhees and Scarpa, 2004). Experts suggest that secure attachment to a parent may mitigate the effects of trauma on the HPA axis. Behaviourally-inhibited children, for example, have higher cortisol reactivity to novel events, but only if they have insecure attachment relationships with their caregivers (van Voorhees and Scarpa, 2004).

Knowledge of the neurobiology of trauma, therefore, supports the need for programmes that provide prevention and early intervention for children who have experienced trauma and maltreatment.

Neurobiology and interpersonal relationships

Experts suggest that interpersonal relationships, such as those that occur between client and counsellor, can influence the brain functioning of trauma survivors. Siegel (1999) has proposed the neurobiology of interpersonal relationship, based on three fundamental principles:

1 The human mind emerges from patterns in the flow of energy and information within the brain and between brains.
2 The mind is created within the interaction of internal neurophysiological processes and interpersonal experiences.
3 The structure and function of the developing brain are determined by how experiences, especially within interpersonal relationships, shape the genetically programmed maturation of the nervous system. (1999: 2)

Siegel argues that life experiences, particularly interpersonal relationships, alter the activity and structure of neuronal connections and shape circuits responsible for processes of the mind, including memory, emotion, and self-regulation. Interpersonal relationships have a significant influence on brain development throughout life because the neuronal circuits that are responsible for social perception are closely linked to those which integrate the creation of meaning, bodily states, memory, and the capacity for communication.

Early relationships with caregivers activate pathways that strengthen existing neuronal connections and create new ones (Siegel, 1999). Different patterns of child–parent attachment result in different physiological responses and affect the capacity of the child's developing mind to integrate experiences and adapt to stressors. Emotional attunement between an infant and caregiver, based on the caregiver's sensitivity and responsiveness to the infant's signals, allows the child to integrate mental processes; this enables a functional flow of states of mind across time. This central integrative process is best reflected in a coherent autobiographical narrative.

Trauma experiences early in life alter brain structures that are responsible for regulatory and integrative capacities. Unresolved trauma leaves the individual with a sense of incoherence in autonoetic consciousness, which includes a recollection of the self in the past, an awareness of the self in the present, and projection of the self to the future. Siegel believes that interpersonal processes, including psychotherapy, can alter physiological responses resulting from trauma:

> It may be the case that certain individuals – whether because of genetic factors, early traumatic experiences, or some combination of inherited vulnerability and stressful environmental conditions – have developed such maladaptive brain structures and self-organization capacities that intensive psychotherapy and/or medication are essential. It is important to keep in mind, however, that the limbic regions of the brain (especially the orbitofrontal cortex) may continue to be open to further development throughout the lifespan, and thus remain open to experience-dependent maturational processes. Psychotherapy can utilize this potential in helping facilitate the further development of the mind. (1999: 295)

The brains of individuals who did not have optimal attachment experiences as children may be open to further growth and development. Experiences of emotional attunement throughout the lifespan can allow individuals to acquire new integrative capacities (Siegel, 1999). Psychotherapy that creates secure attachment allows traumatized clients to experience and tolerate dysregulated states and eventually regulate them to improve adaptation. The counsellor's attunement allows the trauma survivor to make 'left-hemisphere verbally mediated sense out of right-hemisphere autobiographical representations' (1999: 297). Siegel argues that this integrative process affects the capacity of the right hemisphere to regulate emotional states. Self-integration occurs, therefore, through the interaction of neurophysiological processes and the therapeutic relationship.

Multicultural counselling

Although this book presents a general approach to counselling survivors of child-hood sexual abuse, clients' unique characteristics, including their national origin and cultural background, should be considered by counsellors. Violence against women has been identified by international health groups, including the World Health Organization, the American Medical Association, and the Royal College of Nursing, as a significant international public health problem (Watts and Zimmerman, 2002). Child sexual abuse is one of the most common ways in which violence is manifested worldwide. Finkelhor (1994) reviewed prevalence studies from 20 countries that indicated that 7–36 per cent of girls and 3–29 per cent of boys reported histories of childhood sexual abuse. In a study conducted in Haiti, Martsolf (2004) indicated that 53.4 per cent of males and 20.6 per cent of females seeking primary health care in an internal medicine clinic reported having expe-rienced childhood sexual abuse at a moderate to severe level. Worldwide immi-gration rates are high, with the number of international migrants estimated to be 175 million in the year 2000. This represents approximately 2.9 per cent of the world's population (United Nations, 2003). Thus, it is very likely that survivors of childhood sexual abuse might present for mental health services in a setting in which no counsellors of similar cultural or ethnic background are available to provide services.

Although some groups argue that therapist–client ethnic/cultural match is extremely important, others have suggested that ethnic/cultural matching does not ensure desired therapeutic outcomes. In fact, ethnic/cultural differences between therapists and clients can be advantageous, especially when the client requests a therapist from a different cultural group (Tseng, 2001). In these cases and in cases in which a therapist–client ethnic/cultural match is not possible, understanding and use of multicultural counselling techniques are imperative. Multicultural counselling is defined as 'preparation and practices that integrate multicultural and culture-specific awareness, knowledge and skills into coun-selling' (Richardson and Jacob, 2002: 33).

Multicultural counselling theory and practice techniques have been developed to address several concerns. Mental health services are known to be under-utilized by members of minority groups (Gray et al., 1997), and ethnic minority group members tend to terminate services early (Tseng, 2001). It is important to train counsellors to meet the needs of individuals who are diverse in terms of culture, ethnicity, race, gender, age, disability, sexual orientation, and religious and spiritual backgrounds in order to ensure that minority groups utilize appro-priate services and continue in treatment. Furthermore, therapeutic outcomes are affected by the communication and alliance that is established between ther-apist and client. This alliance is enhanced when therapists consider the cultural viewpoints and life ways of individuals whose backgrounds are different from their own.

Sue et al. (1992) have developed a model of competencies for multicultural counsellors. In this model, the culturally-competent counsellor: develops self-awareness of personal biases, assumptions, and values; strives to understand the worldview of the culturally different client; and develops therapeutic strategies and techniques that are culturally appropriate. According to Sue and colleagues, each of these three counsellor characteristics has three dimensions: beliefs and attitudes; knowledge; and skills. Thus, the model includes nine competency areas for multicultural counselling. Further expansion of the model has yielded 31 multicultural counsellor competencies (Roysircar, 2003). The competent counsellor:

- has cultural awareness and sensitivity;
- understands influence of culture on experiences;
- recognizes limitations;
- is comfortable with differences;
- is aware of negative emotional reactions to client;
- is aware of stereotypes and preconceptions;
- respects diverse religious or spiritual beliefs and values;
- respects indigenous helping practices and networks;
- values bilingualism;
- is aware that cultural heritage affects the definition of normality;
- acknowledges racist attitudes, beliefs, and feelings;
- knows about variations in communication styles;
- has specific knowledge of the particular group with which he or she is working;
- understands the impact of culture on personality, preferences (e.g. vocation, counselling style);
- understands sociopolitical influences;
- is sensitive to conflicts between counselling vs. cultural values;
- understands institutional barriers;
- is aware of bias in assessment;
- understands family structure, hierarchies, values, and beliefs;
- knows discriminatory practices in society/community;
- seeks out educational, consultative, and training experience and recognizes limits of competencies;
- actively propagates nonracist identity;
- is familiar with relevant research and findings;
- pursues non-professional social involvement with minority individuals;
- conveys accurate and appropriate nonverbal messages;
- intervenes institutionally;
- consults with traditional healers and spiritual leaders;
- interacts in the client's language;
- appropriately uses traditional assessment with diverse clients;
- works to eliminate bias, prejudice, and discrimination; and
- educates and informs clients. (Roysircar, 2003: 19)

Multicultural counselling theorists espouse at least two different views of multicultural counselling (Sue and Sue, 2003). In the first view, the therapist–client relationship and development of a therapeutic alliance is thought to be paramount. Thus, each relationship is thought to be a specific cross-cultural experience, and cross-cultural communication techniques are of greatest importance (Tseng, 2001). Clients who feel safe, understood, and comfortable with a therapist whom they perceive to be trustworthy, warm, genuine, and empathic can experience positive therapeutic outcomes. The therapist does not need to share the client's worldviews or cultural life experiences, but should respect and understand the client's beliefs (Wilson and Sandhu, 2002).

In the second view, general cross-cultural awareness is thought to provide a foundation for cross-cultural counselling. However, members of each ethnic group are seen as developing self-identity and developing psychologically in a manner common to that group, and based on the history and social struggles of that group. Ibrahim and Ohnishi (2001) suggest that ethnic minorities may experience trauma based on race and class discriminations. Thus, psychological health or lack of health is culture-bound and defined by each cultural group (Wilson and Sandhu, 2002). From this viewpoint, the counsellor must acquire knowledge about the particular group with which an individual client identifies, thereby enabling the counsellor to understand the psychological processes of that individual in the context of cultural background (Herring and Salazar, 2002).

Laungani (2003) describes a case of an adolescent girl of Sikh background whose family had emigrated to London. The client had suffered almost 10 years of sexual abuse perpetrated by her uncle. Laungani methodically describes the cultural context of Sikh families, including the reluctance of the girl's father to press charges against the perpetrator because of the probable ramifications of family division and economic disaster in the tightly-knit Sikh business community in London. Laungani outlines the course of counselling with this young girl, and describes how use of hymns and poems from Sikh holy literature were the mechanism by which he was finally able to form a therapeutic alliance with the client.

A second example details the relationship between religious background and reactions to childhood sexual abuse. Within the Christian community, Kennedy (2000) suggests that some beliefs increase distress related to sexual abuse. The command to 'honor father and mother' causes tremendous conflict for children, especially when the abuser is a parent, and children can perceive themselves as 'bad' or sinful as a result of the abuse. Furthermore, when the father is the perpetrator, survivors of abuse often equate God the Father as an abusing figure. Even the idea of forgiveness (as suggested in Chapter 9) can be misused in order to obtain premature closure to the resolution process. Counsellors should understand the spiritual background of the survivor in order to confront distortions and support faith that is healing.

Multicultural counselling techniques are often taught in graduate counselling programmes, either as a separate course or integrated into courses throughout the curriculum (Richardson and Jacob, 2002). Numerous books and journals are dedicated to this topic. The reader is encouraged to consult recent textbooks for deeper insights into this trend in counselling (see Baruth and Manning, 2003; Ponterotto et al., 2001; Pope-Davis and Coleman, 2001; Sue and Sue, 2003; and Trusty et al., 2002).

Complementary treatment approaches

Although a phase-oriented treatment approach, as presented in this book, is considered the treatment of choice in counselling adult survivors of childhood sexual abuse, counsellors may wish to incorporate aspects of other therapeutic approaches in their work with survivors. These approaches might be used to address specific symptoms, co-morbid disorders, or particular psychosocial concerns. Several emerging and complementary techniques that are likely to be useful with survivors of childhood sexual abuse are discussed here.

Effective treatments for PTSD

Because survivors of CSA so frequently experience symptoms of post-traumatic stress disorder (PTSD), several effective therapies for PTSD are discussed. Practice guidelines for effective treatment of PTSD were developed by the PTSD Treatment Guidelines Task Force, which was established by the Board of Directors of the International Society for Traumatic Stress Studies (Foa et al., 2000). The Task Force acknowledged that treatments for PTSD are not well developed for survivors of childhood sexual abuse, who exhibit a wide range of relational and interpersonal problems in addition to trauma symptoms and typically require multimodal treatment, often over an extended period of time. The approaches discussed below, therefore, might be incorporated into counselling survivors of childhood abuse who experience PTSD symptoms, but might not provide the comprehensive treatment they often require.

Cognitive-behavioural therapy (CBT)

A variety of cognitive, behavioural, and combined techniques have been used to treat PTSD. We will discuss only those approaches that have been supported by empirical research, including exposure therapy (EX), stress inoculation training (SIT), cognitive processing therapy (CPT), and cognitive therapy (CT) (Rothbaum et al., 2000).

Exposure therapy (EX)

This approach involves prolonged exposure to trauma-related, anxiety-producing stimuli and is not accompanied by other anxiety-reduction techniques, such as those used in systematic desensitization. In imaginal exposure therapy, clients discuss the trauma in detail for an extended period of time; in *in vivo* exposure therapy, clients are exposed to real-life stimuli. The rationale for exposure therapy is that continuing exposure to threatening stimuli will diminish anxiety, leading to a decrease in escape and avoidance behaviours that were previously maintained by negative reinforcement. Following an extensive review of the therapy outcome literature on exposure therapy, Rothbaum and colleagues conclude, 'Compelling evidence from many well-controlled trials with a mixed variety of trauma survivors indicates that EX is quite effective. In fact, no other treatment modality has evidence this strong indicating its efficacy' (2000: 75). Exposure techniques for PTSD have been outlined by Foa and Rothbaum (1998).

Stress inoculation training (SIT)

This approach is based on the rationale that anxiety conditioned during the traumatic event is typically generalized to a variety of other situations. A number of techniques are used to help clients manage anxiety in order to decrease avoidance behaviours (Rothbaum et al., 2000). SIT includes education, muscle relaxation training, breathing retraining, role playing, covert modelling, guided self-dialogue, and thought stopping. Rothbaum and colleagues reviewed four studies that had evaluated SIT with trauma clients. They concluded, 'Only two [studies] were well-controlled and all were with female assault survivors, leaving open the question of SIT's efficacy with other trauma populations' (2000: 76). Stress inoculation training techniques have been outlined by Meichenbaum (1985).

Cognitive processing therapy (CPT)

This approach incorporates elements of cognitive and exposure therapies and has been used primarily with rape survivors. Based on principles of cognitive therapy, clients are trained to challenge problematic cognitions related to issues of safety, trust, power, esteem, and intimacy. They are also asked to write a detailed account of the assault, to be read in therapy and at home. The narratives reveal 'stuck points', i.e. aspects of the assault that conflict with previously-held beliefs, and these points become the focus of the cognitive work (Rothbaum et al., 2000). This approach has been shown to be effective in reducing post-traumatic symptoms in one study of female sexual assault survivors (Rothbaum et al., 2000). CPT procedures are discussed by Resick and Schnicke (1993).

Cognitive therapy (CT)

CT is an approach in which clients are taught to identify thoughts that are dysfunctional or erroneously biased; to challenge those that are deemed to be inaccurate or unhelpful; and replace them with more beneficial thoughts (Rothbaum et al., 2000). Cognitive therapy was originally developed by Beck (1972) for the treatment of depression and was modified for the treatment of anxiety (Beck et al., 1985). Thoughts related to safety, trust, and self-views are often challenged in work with trauma survivors. Rothbaum et al. (2000) report that CT has been shown to be effective with trauma survivors in two controlled studies.

Eye movement desensitization and reprocessing (EMDR)

Chemtob et al. described EMDR as an 'emerging therapy for psychological trauma' (2000: 139). EMDR is an approach in which clients engage in saccadic (back and forth) eye movements while retrieving trauma-related imagery and aversive cognitions (Blake and Sonnenberg, 1998). In EMDR:

> The trauma survivor identifies a traumatic event on which he or she wants to work, provides a SUDs rating (a 0–10 or 0–100, from least to most, of subjective units of discomfort or distress) to indicate how much discomfort he or she feels while recalling the event, creates, articulates positive and negative self-statements related to the event, provides a 'validity of cognitions' (VoC) rating for how strong he or she believes each of the two self-statements, and describes a 'safe place' where he or she can return to mentally at the end of the session. (1998: 17)

A review of the outcome research reveals that EMDR is an effective treatment for trauma symptoms, but it is unclear whether it is another form of exposure treatment or a novel approach (Shalev et al., 2000).

An integrative behavioural approach

Follette et al. (2004) have proposed an integrative behavioural approach for individuals with a history of interpersonal victimization. Their approach is based on a combination of dialectical behaviour therapy (DBT) (Linehan, 1993), acceptance and commitment therapy (ACT) (Hayes et al., 1999), and functional analytic psychotherapy (FAP) (Kohlenberg and Tsai, 1991). Although an in-depth description of these approaches is beyond the scope of this chapter, central constructs of each approach will be discussed briefly.

Dialectical behaviour therapy (DBT)

DBT was developed initially to treat suicidality in patients with borderline personality disorder (Linehan, 1993). The DBT therapist focuses on acceptance and change simultaneously. The desire to change painful experiences is balanced with efforts to accept the unavoidable pain of living. Clients are encouraged to experience, rather than escape, distressing emotions. Mindfulness practice is a core element of DBT. Mindfulness practice is 'the intentional process of observing, describing, and participating in reality nonjudgmentally, in the moment and with effectiveness . . .' (Robins et al., 2004: 37). Mindfulness involves awareness and engagement in both private and public experiences, without distractions, distortions, and judgmentalness (Follette et al., 2004). Acceptance involves acknowledging distress as an understandable outcome of reality, rather than as a solvable problem. Clients are encouraged to focus on the current moment and accept reality. If one views reality without defensiveness or blindness, one can then act to change the environment by choosing 'the path of least resistance' (Robins et al., 2004: 40). DBT skills training addresses emotion regulation, distress tolerance, and interpersonal effectiveness (Follette et al., 2004).

Acceptance and commitment therapy (ACT)

ACT is an approach to therapy that was developed by Hayes and colleagues (1999), and is based on a view that language causes direct experience to fuse with cognition. Because humans respond to the literal content of the thought (e.g. 'I can't do this') as reality, they avoid situations or emotions that give rise to painful thoughts. Avoidance of unpleasant private experiences interferes with effective living (Follette et al., 2004). The ACT therapist encourages the defusion of self and language. The goal of ACT is to promote psychological flexibility, which is the ability to alter language processes and respond behaviourally in ways that achieve valued ends. Clients are encouraged to think and feel what they 'directly feel and think already, as it is, not as what it says it is, and to . . . move in a valued direction, with all of their history and automatic reactions' (Hayes, 2004: 17).

Functional analytic psychotherapy (FAP)

FAP is a treatment approach developed by Kohlenberg and Tsai (1991). This approach focuses on clinically relevant behaviours (CRBs) that occur during the therapy session. The rationale of FAP is that behaviour is shaped and maintained by reinforcement. Because reinforcement has a greater effect when it is closer in time to a behaviour, the natural reinforcement of behaviours that occur in the therapy session can yield desired treatment outcomes. Kohlenberg and colleagues argue, 'In this view, the client–therapist relationship is a social environment with the potential to evoke and change actual instances of the client's problem behaviour in the here and now' (2004: 97).

Follette et al. (2004) discuss how principles from these three treatment approaches can be used with individuals who have experienced trauma and who experience a complex array of problems. They recommend a contextual behavioural assessment that seeks to understand how clinically relevant behaviours develop, function, and are maintained, given the client's historical and environmental contexts. Treatment strives to eliminate ineffective avoidance behaviours and develop effective behavioural responses to intense emotions. Arguing that traditional exposure treatment targets individuals who have experienced a circumscribed traumatic event, as opposed to complex and extended interpersonal trauma, they propose an approach of acceptance-based exposure. This approach utilizes techniques from DBT, ACT, and FAP and emphasizes:

> (1) assessing the function of both private and public behavior, looking for behaviors that function as avoidance of private experience; (2) identifying classes of private experiences most routinely avoided, including thoughts, feelings, physical sensations, memories, and so on; (3) assessing whether the effort to change or control aversive private experience is a workable solution; (4) exposing clients to specified classes of aversive private experience, while coaching them on accepting the experience as it is in the moment rather than avoiding the experience; (5) emphasizing the importance of living in accordance with identified life values rather than making choices in life based on the content of aversive private events; and (6) helping clients to clarify their own set of life values and make behavior commitments toward those values. (Follette et al., 2004: 203)

Creative therapies

A variety of creative arts therapies, including art therapy, dance/movement therapy, drama therapy, music therapy, poetry and bibliotherapy, and psychodrama have been used to treat psychological trauma (Johnson, 2000). Clinicians have found these approaches to be useful in addressing trauma symptoms, co-morbid syndromes, and psychosocial concerns. Creative therapies are often used as adjuncts to other treatments. While there is clinical consensus that these approaches may complement other treatment approaches, especially when traditional treatment seems stalled, their efficacy has not been established by empirical research (Johnson, 2000).

Narrative therapy

Narrative, or constructive, therapies are emerging approaches in the treatment of trauma and have been used with adult survivors of childhood sexual abuse. Narrative therapy is a treatment approach in which clients are encouraged to create life narratives that are meaningful and fulfilling (Freedman and Combs, 1996). The theory of social constructionism provides the foundation for narrative approaches to psychotherapy. The basic premise of social constructionism is that:

the beliefs, values, institutions, customs, labels, laws, divisions of labor, and the like that make up our social realities are constructed by the members of a culture as they inter-act with one another from generation to generation and day to day. That is, societies construct 'lenses' through which their members interpret the world. (1996: 16)

Narrative therapists argue that society has cultural narratives, which are shared stories that promote social norms and influence the meaning individuals ascribe to events in their lives (Freedman and Combs, 1996). These narratives often function to maintain the distribution of power in our society and may, therefore, be oppressive to individuals. Prevailing sociocultural narratives may prevent individuals from living their preferred narratives (White and Epston, 1990). The key to narrative therapy is that life stories that are hurtful or limiting can be changed by discourse that introduces alternate meanings to storied events or highlights previously un-storied events. Freedman and Combs state, 'Narrative therapy is about the retelling and reliving of stories' (1996: 33).

Techniques of narrative therapy include: listening and understanding clients' problem-saturated stories without intensifying the painful or pathological aspects; and asking questions and making comments that encourage clients to objectify, rather than personalize, their problems and place them in their sociocultural context. This dialogue allows new constructions and meanings to emerge and opens space for new, less problematic narratives. Adams-Westcott and Isenbart (1996) have described how narrative techniques can be used to help survivors of childhood sexual abuse create stories about relationships based on connections.

References

Adams-Wescott, J. and Isenbart, D. (1996) 'Creating preferred relationships: The politics of recovery from child sexual abuse', *Journal of Systemic Therapies*, 15 (1): 13–30.

Agosta, C. and Loring, M. (1988) 'Understanding and treating the adult retrospective victim of child sexual abuse', in S. M. Sgroi (ed.), *Vulnerable Populations, Vol. 1: Evaluation and treatment of sexually abused children and adult survivors*. Lexington, MA: Lexington Books. pp. 115–36.

Ainsworth, M. D. S., Blehar, M. C., Waters, E. and Wall, S. (1978) *Patterns of Attachment: A psychological study of the strange situation*. Hillsdale, NJ: Erlbaum.

Alexander, P. C., Neimeyer, R. A., Follette, V. M., Moore, M. K. and Harter, S. (1989) 'A comparison of group treatments of women sexually abused as children', *Journal of Consulting and Clinical Psychology*, 57 (4): 479–83.

Allen, C. V. (1980) *Daddy's Girl*. New York: Berkeley Books.

American Psychiatric Association (1994) *Diagnostic and Statistical Manual of Mental Disorders* (4th edn). Washington, DC: Author.

Anderson, M. (1998) 'Active forgetting: Evidence for functional inhibition as a source of memory failure', in *Conference on Trauma and Cognitive Science*. Eugene, OR: University of Oregon.

Andrews, B., Brewin, C. R., Rose, S. and Kirk, M. (2000) 'Predicting PTSD symptoms in victims of violent crime: The role of shame, anger, and childhood abuse', *Journal of Abnormal Psychology*, 109: 69–73.

Angelou, M. (1971) *I Know Why the Caged Bird Sings*. New York: Bantam Books.

APA Working Group on Investigation of Memories of Childhood Abuse (1998) 'Final conclusions of the American Psychological Association working group on investigation of memories of childhood abuse', *Psychology, Public Policy, and Law*, 4: 933–40.

Apolinsky, S. R. and Wilcoxon, S. A. (1991) 'Symbolic confrontation with women survivors of childhood sexual victimization', *Journal of Specialists in Group Work*, 16: 85–9.

Armstrong, L. (1978) *Kiss Daddy Goodnight*. New York: Pocket Books.

Bagley, C. and Mallick, K. (2000) 'Prediction of sexual, emotional, and physical maltreatment and mental health outcomes in a longitudinal cohort of 290 adolescent women', *Child Maltreatment*, 5: 218–26.

Bagley, C. and Ramsey, R. (1986) 'Sexual abuse in childhood: Psychological outcomes and implications for social work practice', *Journal of Social Work and Human Sexuality*, 4: 33–7.

Bagley, C. and Young, L. (1998) 'Long-term evaluation of group counseling for women with a history of child sexual abuse: Focus on depression, self-esteem, suicidal behaviors and social support', *Social Work with Groups*, 21 (3): 63–73.

Baruth, L. G. and Manning, M. L. (2003) *Multicultural Counseling and Psychotherapy: A lifespan perspective* (3rd edn). Upper Saddle River, NJ: Merrill Prentice Hall.

Bass, E. and Davis, L. (1994) *The Courage to Heal: A guide for women survivors of child abuse* (3rd edn). New York: HarperPerennial.

Bass, E. and Thornton, L. (eds) (1983) *I Never Told Anyone: Writings by women survivors of child sexual abuse*. New York: Harper and Row.

Beck, A. T. (1972) *Depression: Causes and treatment*. Philadelphia, PA: University of Pennsylvannia Press.

Beck, A. (1994) 'Workshop on cognitive therapy of personality disorders'. Evolution of Psychotherapy Conference, Hamburg, Germany.

Beck, A. T., Emery, G. and Greenberg, R. L. (1985) *Anxiety Disorders and Phobias: A cognitive perspective*. New York: Basic Books.

Beck, A. T. and Steer, R. (1993) *Manual for the Beck Depression Inventory*. San Antonio, TX: The Psychological Corporation.

Becker, J. V., Skinner, L. J., Abel, G. G. and Cichon, J. (1986) 'Level of postassault sexual functioning in rape and incest victims', *Archives of Sexual Behavior*, 15 (1): 37–49.

Beitchman, J. H., Zucker, K. J., Hood, J. E., daCosta, G. A., Akman, D. and Cassavia, E. (1992) 'A review of the long-term effects of child sexual abuse', *Child Abuse and Neglect*, 16: 101–17.

Bernstein, D. P., Fink, L., Handelsman, L., Foote, J., Lovejoy, M., Wenzel, K., Sapareta, E. and Ruggiero, J. (1994) 'Initial reliability and validity of a new retrospective measure of child abuse and neglect', *American Journal of Psychiatry*, 151 (8): 1132–6.

Berstein, E. M. and Putnam, F. W. (1986) 'Development, reliability, and validity of a dissociation scale', *Journal of Nervous and Mental Disease*, 174 (12): 727–35.

Bifulco, A., Brown, G. W. and Adler, Z. (1991) 'Early sexual abuse and clinical depression in adult life', *British Journal of Psychiatry*, 159: 115–22.

Blake, D. and Sonnenberg, R. (1998) 'Outcome research on behavioral and cognitive-behavioral treatments for trauma survivors', in V. M. Follette, J. I. Ruzek and F. R. Abueg (eds), *Cognitive Behavioral Therapies for Trauma*. New York: Guilford Press. pp. 14–47.

Blake-White, J. and Kline, C. M. (1985) 'Treating the dissociative process in adult victims of childhood incest', *Social Casework: The Journal of Contemporary Social Work*, 66: 394–402.

Bolton, F. G., Morris, L. A. and MacEachron, A. E. (1989) *Males at Risk: The other side of child sexual abuse*. Newbury Park, CA: Sage.

Bowlby, J. (1980) *Attachment and Loss, Vol. 3: Loss: sadness and depression*. New York: Basic Books.

Brady, K. (1979) *Father's Days*. New York: Dell.

Braun, B. G. (1988) 'The BASK model of dissociation', *Dissociation: Progress in the Dissociative Disorders*, 1 (1): 4–23.

Briere, J. (1989) *Therapy for Adults Molested as Children*. New York: Springer.

Briere, J. (1992) *Child Abuse Trauma: Theory and treatment of lasting effects*. Newbury Park, CA: Sage.

Briere, J. (1995) *Trauma Symptom Inventory: Professional manual*. Odessa, FL: Psychological Assessment Resources.

Briere, J. (1996) 'A self-trauma model for treating adult survivors of severe child abuse', in J. Briere, L. Berliner, J. A. Bulkely, C. Jeeny and T. Reid (eds), *The APSAC Handbook on Child Maltreatment*. Thousand Oaks, CA: Sage. pp. 140–57.

Briere, J. (1997) 'Assessment of child abuse effects in adults', in J. P. Wilson and T. M. Keane (eds), *Assessing Psychological Trauma and PTSD*. New York: Guilford Press. pp. 43–68.

Briere, J. and Conte, J. (1993) 'Self-reported amnesia for abuse in adults molested as children', *Journal of Traumatic Stress*, 6 (1): 21–31.

Briere, J. and Elliott, D. M. (1993) 'Sexual abuse, family environment and psychological symptoms: On the validity of statistical control', *Journal of Consulting and Clinical Psychology*, 61: 284–8.

Briere, J. and Runtz, M. (1988) 'Post sexual abuse trauma', in G. E. Wyatt and G. J. Powell (eds), *Lasting Effects of Child Sexual Abuse*. Newbury Park, CA: Sage. pp. 85–99.

Briere, J. and Runtz, M. (1990) 'Differential adult symptomatology associated with three types of child abuse histories', *Child Abuse and Neglect*, 14: 357–64.

Brower, K. J., Blow, F. C. and Beresford, T. P. (1989) 'Treatment implications of chemical dependency models: An integrative approach', *Journal of Substance Abuse Treatment*, 6 (3): 147–57.

Brown, D., Scheflin, A. W. and Hammond, D. C. (1998) *Memory, Trauma Treatment, and the Law: An essential reference on memory for clinicians, researchers, attorneys, and judges.* New York: Norton.

Brown, D. P. and Fromm, E. (1986) *Hypnotherapy and Hypnoanalysis.* Hillsdale, NJ: Erlbaum.

Brown, L. S. (2004) 'Memories of childhood abuse: Recovered, discovered, and otherwise', in B. J. Cling (ed.), *Sexualized Violence Against Women and Children.* New York: Guilford Press. pp. 188–212.

Browne, A. and Finkelhor, D. (1986) 'Impact of child sexual abuse: A review of the research', *Psychological Bulletin,* 99: 66–77.

Bruckner, D. F. and Johnson, P. E. (1987) 'Treatment for adult male victims of childhood sexual abuse', *Social Casework: The Journal of Contemporary Social Work,* 68: 81–7.

Bushnell, J. A., Wells, J. E. and Oakley-Browne, M. A. (1992) 'Long-term effects of intra-familial sexual abuse in childhood', *Acta Psychiatrica Scandinavica,* 85 (2): 136–42.

Calam, R. and Slade, P. D. (1987) 'Eating problems and sexual experience: Some relationships', *British Review of Bulimia Anorexia,* 2 (1): 37–43.

Calam, R. M. and Slade, P. D. (1989) 'Sexual experience and eating problems in female undergraduates', *International Journal of Eating Disorders,* 8 (4): 391–7.

Cameron, C. (1994) 'Women survivors confronting their abusers: Issues, decisions and outcomes', *Journal of Child Sexual Abuse,* 3 (1): 7–35.

Campbell, J. A. and Carlson, K. (1995) 'Training and knowledge of professionals on specific topics in child sexual abuse', *Journal of Child and Sexual Abuse,* 4: 75–86.

Carlson, S. (1990) 'The victim/perpetrator: Turning points in therapy', in M. Hunter (ed.), *The Sexually Abused Male, Vol. 2: Application of treatment strategies.* Lexington, MA: Lexington Books. pp. 249–66.

Carson, D. K., Gertz, L. M., Donaldson, M. A. and Wonderlich, S. A. (1990) 'Family-of-origin characteristics and current family relationships of female adult incest victims', *Journal of Family Violence,* 5 (2): 153–71.

Carver, C. M., Stalker, C., Stewart, E. and Abraham, B. (1989) 'The impact of group therapy for adult survivors of childhood sexual abuse', *Canadian Journal of Psychiatry,* 34: 753–8.

Ceci, S. J. and Bruck, M. (1993) 'Suggestibility of the child witness: A historical review and synthesis', *Psychological Bulletin,* 113 (3): 403–39.

Ceci, S. J., Huffman, M. L. C., Smith, E. and Loftus, E. F. (1994) 'Repeatedly thinking about a non-event: Source misattributions among preschoolers', *Consciousness and Cognition,* 3: 388–407.

Chard, K. M., Weaver, T. L. and Resick, P. A. (1997) 'Adapting cognitive processing therapy for child sexual abuse survivors', *Cognitive and Behavioral Practice,* 4: 31–52.

Chemtob, C. M., Tolin, D. F., van Der Kolk, B. A. and Pitman, R. K. (2000) 'Eye movement desensitization and reprocessing', in E. B. Foa, T. M. Keane and M. J. Friedman (eds), *Effective Treatments for PTSD.* New York: Guilford. pp. 139–54.

Chu, J. A. (1998) *Rebuilding Shattered Lives.* New York: Wiley.

Chu, J. A. and Dill, D. L. (1990) 'Dissociative symptoms in relation to childhood physical and sexual abuse', *American Journal of Psychiatry,* 147 (7): 887–92.

Clarke, K. M. (1993) 'Creation of meaning in incest survivors', *Journal of Cognitive Psychotherapy: An International Quarterly,* 7 (3): 195–203.

Clarke, S. and Llewelyn, S. (1994) 'Personal constructs for survivors of childhood sexual abuse receiving cognitive analytic therapy', *British Journal of Medical Psychology,* 67: 273–89.

Cloitre, M. (1998) 'Sexual revictimization: Risk factors and prevention', in V. M. Follette, J. I. Ruzek and F. R. Abueg (eds), *Cognitive Behavioral Therapies for Trauma.* New York: Guilford Press. pp. 278–304.

Cloitre, M. and Koenen, K. C. (2001) 'The impact of borderline personality disorder on process group outcome among women with posttraumatic stress disorder related to childhood abuse', *International Journal of Group Psychotherapy*, 51 (3): 379–98.

Cole, C. H. and Barney, E. E. (1987) 'Safeguards and the therapeutic window: A group treatment strategy for adult incest survivors', *American Journal of Orthopsychiatry*, 57: 601–9.

Conte, J. (1999) 'Memory, research, and the law: Future directions', in L. M. Williams and V. L. Banyard (eds), *Trauma and Memory*. Thousand Oaks, CA: Sage. pp. 77–92.

Courtois, C. A. (1999) *Recollections of Sexual Abuse: Treatment principles and guidelines*. New York: Norton.

Coxell, A. W., King, M. B., Mezey, G. C. and Kell, P. (2000) 'Sexual molestation of men: Interviews with 224 men attending a genitourinary medicine service', *International Journal of STD and AIDS*, 11: 574–8.

Crowe, M. and Bunclark, J. (2000) 'Repeated self-injury and its management', *International Review of Psychiatry*, 12: 48–53.

Cunningham, R. M., Stiffman, A. R., Dore, P. and Earls, F. (1994) 'The association of physical and sexual abuse with HIV risk behaviors in adolescence and young adulthood: implications for public health', *Child Abuse and Neglect*, 18 (3): 233–45.

Dalenberg, C. J. (2000) *Countertransference and the Treatment of Trauma*. Washington, D.C.: American Psychological Association.

Daugherty, L. B. (1984) *Why Me?* Racine, WI: Mother Courage Press.

Davis, L. (1990) *The Courage to Heal Workbook*. New York: Harper and Row.

Demaré, D. (1993) 'The childhood maltreatment questionnaire'. Unpublished manuscript. University of Manitoba, Winnipeg, Canada.

Derogatis, L. R. (1992) *SCL-90-R Administration, Scoring and Procedures Manual for the Revised Version*. Towson, MD: Clinical Psychiatric Research.

DiLillo, D. (2001) 'Interpersonal functioning among women reporting a history of childhood sexual abuse: Empirical findings and methodological issues', *Clinical Psychology Review*, 21: 553–76.

Dozier, M., Cue, K. L. and Barnett, L. (1994) 'Clinicians as caregivers: Role of attachment organisation in treatment', *Journal of Consulting and Clinical Psychology*, 62: 793–800.

Draucker, C. B. (1989) 'Cognitive adaptation of female incest survivors', *Journal of Consulting and Clinical Psychology*, 57: 668–70.

Draucker, C. B. (1992a) 'Construing benefit from a negative experience of incest', *Western Journal of Nursing Research*, 14 (3): 343–57.

Draucker, C. B. (1992b) 'The healing process of female adult survivors: Constructing a personal residence', *Image: Journal of Nursing Scholarship*, 24 (1): 4–8.

Draucker, C. B. (1995) 'A coping model: adult survivors of childhood sexual abuse', *Journal of Interpersonal Violence*, 10 (2): 159–75.

Draucker, C. B. (1996) 'Family-of-origin variables and adult female survivors of childhood sexual abuse: A review of the research', *Journal of Child Sexual Abuse*, 5 (4): 35–63.

Draucker, C. B. (1997) 'Early family life and victimization in the lives of women', *Research in Nursing and Health*, 20: 399–412.

Draucker, C. B. and Petrovic, K. (1996) 'The healing of adult male survivors of childhood sexual abuse', *Image: Journal of Nursing Scholarship*, 28 (4): 325–30.

Draucker, C. B. and Petrovic, K. (1997) 'Therapy with male survivors of sexual abuse: The client perspective', *Issues in Mental Health Nursing*, 18: 139–55.

Drossman, D. A., Leserman, J., Nachman, G., Li, Z., Gluck, H., Toomey, T. C. and Mitchell, C. M. (1990) 'Sexual and physical abuse in women with functional or organic gastrointestinal disorders', *Annuals of Internal Medicine*, 113: 828–33.

Eames, V. and Roth, A. (2000) 'Patient attachment orientation and the early working alliance: A study of patient and therapist reports of alliance quality and ruptures', *Psychotherapy Research*, 10: 421–34.

Edmond, T., Rubin, A. and Wambach, K. G. (1999) 'The effectiveness of EMDR with adult female survivors of childhood sexual abuse', *Social Work Research*, 23 (2): 103–116.

Edwards, J. J. and Alexander, P. C. (1992) 'The contribution of family background to the long-term adjustment of women sexually abused as children', *Journal of Interpersonal Violence*, 7 (3): 306–20.

Elliott, D. M. (1992) 'Traumatic events survey'. Unpublished psychological test, Harbor-UCLA Medical Center, Los Angeles.

Elliott, D. M. and Briere, J. (1992) 'Sexual abuse trauma among professional women: Validating the Trauma Symptom Checklist-40 (TSC-40)', *Child Abuse and Neglect*, 16: 391–8.

Elliott, D. M. and Briere, J. (1993) 'Childhood maltreatment, later revictimization, and adult symptomatology: A causal analysis'. Paper presented at the 101st Annual Meeting of the American Psychological Association, Toronto, Canada, August.

Elliott, D. M. and Briere, J. (1995) 'Post-traumatic stress associated with delayed recall of sexual abuse: A general population study', *Journal of Traumatic Stress*, 8: 629–47.

Erikson, E. (1968) *Identity: Youth and crisis.* New York: Norton.

Etherington, K. (1997) 'Maternal sexual abuse of males', *Child Abuse Review*, 6: 107–117.

Etherington, K. (2000) 'Supervising counsellors who work with survivors of childhood sexual abuse', *Counselling Psychology Quarterly*, 13: 377–89.

Evans, M. C. (1990) 'Brother to brother: Integrating concepts of healing regarding male sexual assault survivors and Vietnam veterans', in M. Hunter (ed.), *The Sexually Abused Male, Vol. 2: Application of treatment strategies.* Lexington, MA: Lexington Books. pp. 57–78.

Faria, G. and Belohlavek, N. (1984) 'Treating female adult survivors of incest', *Social Casework*, 65: 465–71.

Farmer, S. (1989) *Adult Children of Abusive Parents.* Chicago, IL: Contemporary Books.

Farrell, D. and Taylor, M. (2000) 'Silenced by God: An examination of unique characteristics within sexual abuse by clergy', *Counseling Psychology Review*, 15: 22–31.

Felitti, V. J. (1991) 'Long-term medical consequences of incest, rape, and molestation', *Southern Medical Journal*, 84 (3): 328–31.

Finkelhor, D. (1990) 'Early and long-term effects of child sexual abuse: An update', *Professional Psychology: Research and Practice*, 21 (5): 325–30.

Finkelhor, D. (1994) 'The international epidemiology of child sexual abuse', *Child Abuse and Neglect*, 18 (5): 409–17.

Finkelhor, D. (1997) 'Child sexual abuse', in O. W. Barnett, C. L. Miller-Perrin and R. D. Perrin (eds), *Family Violence across the Lifespan.* Thousand Oaks, CA: Sage. pp. 69–104.

Finkelhor, D., Hotaling, G. T., Lewis, I. A. and Smith, C. (1990) 'Sexual abuse in a national survey of adult men and women: Prevalence, characteristics, and risk factors', *Child Abuse and Neglect*, 14: 19–28.

Finkelhor, D. and Russell, D. (1984) 'Women as perpetrators: review of the evidence', in D. Finkelhor (ed.), *Child Sexual Abuse: New theory and research.* New York: Free Press. pp. 171–87.

Foa, E. B., Keane, T. M. and Friedman, M. J. (2000) 'Introduction', in E. B. Foa, T. M. Keane and M. J. Friedman (eds), *Effective Treatments for PTSD.* New York: Guilford Press. pp. 1–17.

Foa, E. and Rothbaum, B. O. (1998) *Treating the Trauma of Rape: Cognitive-behavioral therapy for PTSD.* New York: Guilford Press.

Follette, V. M., Palm, K. M. and Rasmussen Hall, M. L. (2004) 'Acceptance, mindfulness, and trauma', in *Mindfulness and Acceptance: Expanding the cognitive-behavioral tradition.* New York: Guilford Press. pp. 192–208.

Foy, D. W., Sipprelle, R. C., Rueger, D. B. and Carroll, E. M. (1984) 'Etiology of post-traumatic stress syndrome in Vietnam veterans: Analysis of premilitary, military, and combat exposure influences', *Journal of Consulting and Clinical Psychology*, 52 (1): 79–87.

Frankel, S. A. (2000) *Hidden Faults: Recognizing and resolving therapeutic dysjunctions.* Madison, CT: Psychosocial Press.

Frankland, A. and Cohen, L. (1999) 'Working with recovered memories', *The Psychologist*, 12: 82–3.

Freedman, J. and Combs, G. (1996) *Narrative Therapy: The social construction of preferred realities.* New York: Norton.

Freyd, J. J., DePrince, A. P. and Zurbriggen, E. L. (2001) 'Self-reported memory for abuse depends upon victim-perpetrator relationship', *Journal of Trauma and Dissociation*, 2: 5–17.

Friedman, M. A. and Brownell, K. D. (1996) *A Comprehensive Treatment Manual for the Management of Obesity.* New York: Plenum Press.

Friedman, M. J. and Schnurr, P. P. (1995) 'The relationship between trauma, posttraumatic stress disorder, and physical health', in M. J. Friedman, D. S. Charney and A. Y. Deutch (eds), *Neurobiological and Clinical Consequences of Stress: From normal adaptation to PTSD.* Philadelphia, PA: Lippincott-Raven. pp. 507–24.

Fromuth, M. E. and Burkhart, B. R. (1989) 'Long-term psychological correlates of childhood sexual abuse in two samples of college men', *Child Abuse and Neglect*, 13 (4): 533–42.

Fry, R. (1993) 'Adult physical illness and childhood sexual abuse', *Journal of Psychosomatic Research*, 37 (2): 89–103.

Garbarino, J., Guttman, E. and Seeley, J. W. (1986) *The Psychologically Battered Child: Strategies for identification, assessment and intervention.* San Francisco, CA: Jossey-Bass.

Garner, D. M. and Garfinkel, P. E. (1997) *Handbook of Psychotherapy for Anorexia and Bulimia* (2nd edn). New York: Guilford Press.

Gaston, L. (1990) 'The concept of the alliance and its role in psychotherapy: Theoretical and empirical considerations', *Psychotherapy*, 27: 143–53.

Gelinas, D. J. (1983) 'The persisting negative effects of incest', *Psychiatry*, 46: 312–32.

Gerber, P. N. (1990) 'Victims becoming offenders: A study of ambiguities', in M. Hunter (ed.), *The Sexually Abused Male, Vol. I: Prevalence, impact, and treatment.* Lexington, MA: Lexington Books. pp. 153–76.

Gold, E. R. (1986) 'Long-term effects of sexual victimization in childhood: An attributional approach', *Journal of Consulting and Clinical Psychology*, 54: 471–5.

Gold, S. N. and Brown, L. S. (1997) 'Therapeutic responses to delayed recall: Beyond recovered memory', *Psychotherapy*, 34 (2): 182–91.

Gold, S. N., Hughes, D. and Hohnecker, L. (1994) 'Degrees of repression of sexual abuse memories', *American Psychologist*, 49 (5): 441–2.

Golding, J. M. (1994) 'Sexual assault history and physical health in randomly selected Los Angeles women', *Health Psychology*, 13 (2): 130–8.

Gonsiorek, J. C., Bera, W. H. and LeTourneau, D. (1994) *Male Sexual Abuse: A trilogy of intervention strategies.* Thousand Oaks, CA: Sage.

Goodwin, I. (2003) 'The relevance of attachment theory to the philosophy, organization, and practice of adult mental health care', *Clinical Psychology Review*, 23: 35–56.

Gordon, M. and Alexander, P. C. (1993) 'Introduction of special issue: Research on treatment of adults sexually abused in childhood', *Journal of Interpersonal Violence*, 8 (3): 307–11.

Gordy, P. L. (1983) 'Group work that supports adult victims of childhood incest', *Social Casework: The Journal of Contemporary Social Work*, 64: 300–307.

Gorski, T. (1992) *Understanding the Twelve Steps.* New York: Simon and Schuster.

Gray, S., Higgs, M. and Pringle, K. (1997) 'User-centered responses to child sexual abuse: The way forward?', *Child and Family Social Work*, 2: 49–57.

Greenwald, E., Leitenberg, H., Cado, S. and Tarran, M. J. (1990) 'Childhood sexual abuse: Long-term effects on psychological and sexual functioning in a nonclinical and nonstudent sample of adult women', *Child Abuse and Neglect*, 14: 503–13.

Gudjonsson, G. H. (1984) 'A new scale of interrogative suggestibility', *Personality and Individual Differences*, 5 (3): 303–14.

Hall, J. (1999) 'An exploration of the sexual and relationship experiences of lesbian survivors of childhood sexual abuse', *Sexual and Marital Therapy*, 14 (1): 61–70.

Hall, L. and Lloyd, S. (1989) *Surviving Child Sexual Abuse*. New York: Falmer.

Hall, L. A., Sachs, B., Rayens, M. K. and Lutenbacher, M. (1993) 'Childhood physical and sexual abuse: Their relationship with depressive symptoms in adulthood', *Image: Journal of Nursing Scholarship*, 25 (4): 317–23.

Hall, Z. and King, E. (1997) 'Group therapy with the NHS V: Patients' views on the benefit of group therapy for women survivors of childhood sexual abuse', *Group Analysis*, 30: 409–427.

Hall, Z. and Mullee, M. (2000) 'Undertaking psychotherapy research', *Group Analysis*, 33 (3): 319–32.

Harper, K. and Steadman, J. (2003) 'Therapeutic boundary issues in working with childhood sexual-abuse survivors', *American Journal of Psychotherapy*, 57: 64–80.

Harrop-Griffiths, J., Katon, W., Walker, E., Holm, L., Russo, J. and Hickok, L. (1988) 'The association between chronic pelvic pain, psychiatric diagnoses and childhood sexual abuse', *Obstetrics and Gynecology*, 71: 589–94.

Harvey, M. R. (1999) 'Memory research and clinical practice: A critique of three paradigms and a framework of psychotherapy with trauma survivors', in L. M. Williams and V. L. Banyard (eds), *Trauma and Memory*. Thousand Oaks, CA: Sage. pp. 19–29.

Hathaway, S. R. and McKinley, J. C. (1967) *The Minnesota Multiphasic Personality Inventory Manual*. New York: Psychological Corporation.

Hayes, S. C. (2004) 'Acceptance and commitment therapy and the new behavior therapies: Mindfulness, acceptance, and relationship', in S. C. Hayes, V. M. Follette and M. M. Linehan (eds), *Mindfulness and Acceptance: Expanding the cognitive-behavioral tradition*. New York: Guilford Press. pp. 1–29.

Hayes, S. C., Strosahl, K. and Wilson, K. G. (1999) *Acceptance and Commitment Therapy: An experiential approach to behavior change*. New York: Guilford Press.

Herman, J. L. (1981) *Father–Daughter Incest*. Cambridge, MA: Harvard University Press.

Herman, J. L. (1992) *Trauma and Recovery*. New York: Basic Books.

Herman, J. L. and Schatzow, E. (1987) 'Recovery and verification of memories of childhood sexual trauma', *Psychoanalytic Psychology*, 4: 1–14.

Herring, R. D. and Salazar, C. (2002) 'Non-western helping modalities', in J. Trusty, E. J. Looby and D. S. Sandhu (eds), *Multicultural Counseling: Context, theory and practice, and competence*. New York: Nova Science. pp. 283–318.

Hesse, E. (1999) 'The adult attachment interview: Historical and current perspectives', in J. Cassidy and P. R. Shaver (eds), *Handbook of Attachment: Theory research and clinical applications*. New York: Guilford Press. pp. 395–433.

Hetherton, J. (1999) 'The idealization of women: Its role in the minimization of child sexual abuse by females', *Child Abuse and Neglect*, 23: 161–74.

Hill, J., Davis, R., Byatt, M., Burnside, E., Rollinson, L. and Fear, S. (2000) 'Childhood sexual abuse and affective symptoms in women: A general population study', *Psychological Medicine*, 30: 1283–91.

Hill, J., Pickles, A., Rollinson, L., Davies, R. and Byatt, M. (2004) 'Juvenile versus adult-onset depression: Multiple differences imply different pathways', *Psychological Medicine*, 34: 1483–93.

Holmes, D. S. (1990) 'The evidence for repression: An examination of sixty years of research', in J. L. Singer (ed.), *Repression and Dissociation: Implications for personality theory, psychopathology, and health*. Chicago: University of Chicago Press. pp. 85–102.

Horowitz, M. J. (1976) *Stress Response Syndromes*. New York: Jason Aronson.

Horowitz, M. J., Wilner, N. and Alvarez, W. (1979) 'Impacts of Event Scale: A measure of subjective stress', *Psychosocial Medicine*, 41 (3): 209–18.

Hunter, M. (1995) *Adult Survivors of Sexual Abuse: Treatment innovations*. Thousand Oaks, CA: Sage.

Hunter, M. and Gerber, P. N. (1990) 'Use of terms victim and survivor in the grief stages commonly seen during recovery from sexual abuse', in M. Hunter (ed.), *The Sexually Abused Male, Vol. 2: Application of treatment strategies*. Lexington, MA: Lexington Books. pp. 79–89.

Hyman, I. E., Husband, T. H. and Billings, F. J. (1995) 'False memories of childhood experiences', *Applied Cognitive Psychology*, 9 (3): 181–97.

Hyman, I. E. and Pentland, J. (1996) 'The role of mental imagery and the creation of false childhood memories', *Journal of Memory and Language*, 35 (2): 101–17.

Ibrahim, F. A. and Ohnishi, H. (2001) 'Posttraumatic stress disorder and the minority experience', in D. B. Pope-Davis and H. L. K. Coleman (eds), *The Intersection of Race, Class, and Gender in Multicultural Counseling*. London: Sage. pp. 89–126.

Jackson, J. L., Calhoun, K. S., Amick, A. E., Maddever, H. M. and Habif, V. L. (1990) 'Young adult women who report childhood intrafamiliar sexual abuse: Subsequent adjustment', *Archives of Sexual Behavior*, 19 (3): 211–21.

Janet, P. (1925/1976) *Psychological Healing*. New York: Macmillan.

Janoff-Bulman, R. (1992) *Shattered Assumptions: Towards a new psychology of trauma*. New York: Free Press.

Jehu, D. (1990) *Beyond Sexual Abuse: Therapy with women who were childhood victims*. New York: Wiley.

Jehu, D., Gazan, M. and Klassen, C. (1988) *Beyond Sexual Abuse: Therapy with women who were childhood victims*. Chichester: Wiley.

Jehu, D., Klassen, C. and Gazan, M. (1986) 'Cognitive restructuring of distorted beliefs associated with childhood sexual abuse', *Journal of Social Work and Human Sexuality*, 4: 49–69.

Johanek, M. F. (1988) 'Treatment of male victims of child sexual abuse in military service', in S. M. Sgroi (ed.), *Vulnerable Populations, Vol. 1: Evaluation and treatment of sexually abused children and adult survivors*. Lexington, MA: Lexington Books. pp. 103–14.

Johnson, D. R. (2000) Creative therapies', in E. B. Foa, T. M. Keane and M. J. Friedman (eds), *Effective Treatments for PTSD*. New York: Guilford. pp. 302–316.

Josephson, G. S. and Fong-Beyette, M. L. (1987) 'Factors assisting female clients' disclosure of incest during counseling', *Journal of Counseling and Development*, 65: 475–8.

Joy, S. (1987) 'Retrospective presentations of incest: Treatment strategies for use with adult women', *Journal of Counseling and Development*, 65: 317–19.

Kasl, C. D. (1990) 'Female perpetrators of sexual abuse: A feminist view', in M. Hunter (ed.), *The Sexually Abused Male, Vol. I: Prevalence, impact, and treatment*. Lexington, MA: Lexington Books. pp. 259–74.

Kendall-Tackett, K. (2003) *Treating the Lifetime Health Effects of Childhood Victimization*. Kingston: Civic Research Institute.

Kendall, P. C., Holmbeck, G. and Verduin, T. (2004) 'Methodology, design, and evaluation in psychotherapy research', in M. J. Lambert (ed.), *Bergin and Garfield's Handbook of Psychotherapy and Behavior Change* (5th edn). New York: Wiley. pp. 16–43.

Kennedy, M. (2000) 'Christianity and child sexual abuse: The survivors' voice leading to change', *Child Abuse Review*, 9: 124–41.

King, M. and Woollett, E. (1997) 'Sexually assaulted males: 115 men consulting a counseling service', *Archives of Sexual Behavior*, 26: 579–88.

Kinsey, A. C., Pomeroy, W. B., Martin, C. E. and Gebhard, P. H. (1953) *Sexual Behavior in the Human Female*. Philadelpha, PA: Saunders.

Kluft, R. P. (1996) 'Treating the traumatic memories of patients with dissociative identity disorder', *American Journal of Psychiatry*, 153 (Suppl.): 103–10.

Kohlenberg, R. J. and Tsai, M. (1991) *Functional Analytic Psychotherapy*. New York: Plenum Press.

Korfmacher, J., Adam, E., Ogawa, J. and Egeland, B. (1997) 'Adult attachment: Implications for the therapeutic process in a home visitation intervention', *Applied Developmental Science*, 1: 43–52.

Krause, E. D., DeRosa, R. R. and Roth, S. (2002) 'Gender, trauma themes, and PTSD: Narratives of male and female survivors', in R. Kimerling, P. Ouimette and J. Wolfe (eds), *Gender and PTSD*. New York: Guilford Press. pp. 349–81.

Kreidler, M. C., Einsporn, R. L., Zupancic, M. K. and Masterson, C. (1999) 'Group therapy for survivors of childhood sexual abuse who are severely and persistently mentally ill', *Journal of the American Psychiatric Nurses Association*, 5: 73–9.

Kuyken, W. and Brewin, C. R. (1999) 'The relation of early abuse to cognition and coping in depression', *Cognitive Therapy and Research*, 23: 665–77.

Lab, D. D., Feigenbaum, J. D. and DeSilva, P. (2000) 'Mental health professionals' attitudes and practices towards male childhood sexual abuse', *Child Abuse and Neglect*, 24: 391–409.

Landis, J. (1956) 'Experiences of 500 children with adult sexual deviances', *Psychiatric Quarterly Supplement*, 30: 91–109.

Laungani, P. (2003) 'Sexual abuse in an Asian family', *Counseling Psychology Quarterly*, 16 (4): 385–401.

Laws, A. (1993) 'Does a history of sexual abuse in childhood play a role in women's medical problems? A review', *Journal of Women's Health*, 2 (2): 165–72.

Lepine, D. (1990) 'Ending the cycle of violence: Overcoming guilt in incest survivors', in T. A. Laidlaw and C. Malmo (eds), *Healing Voices*. San Francisco, CA: Jossey-Bass. pp. 272–87.

Lindsay, D. S. (1990) 'Misleading suggestions can impair eyewitnesses' ability to remember event details', *Journal of Experimental Psychology: Learning, Memory and Cognition*, 16 (6): 1077–83.

Lindsay, D. S. (1994) 'Memory source monitoring and eyewitness testimony', in D. F. Ross, J. D. Read and M. P. Toglia (eds), *Adult Eyewitness Testimony: Current trends and developments*. New York: Cambridge University Press. pp. 27–55.

Lindsay, D. S. and Read, J. D. (1994) 'Psychotherapy and memories of childhood sexual abuse: A cognitive perspective', *Applied Cognitive Psychology*, 8: 281–338.

Linehan, M. M. (1993) *Cognitive-behavioral Treatment of Borderline Personality Disorder*. New York: Guilford Press.

Lisak, D. (1994) 'The psychological impact of sexual abuse: Content analysis of interviews with male survivors', *Journal of Traumatic Stress*, 7: 525–48.

Loftus, E. F. (1993) 'The reality of repressed memories', *American Psychologist*, 48 (5): 518–37.

Loftus, E. F. and Picrell, J. E. (1995) 'The formation of false memories', *Psychiatric Annals*, 25: 720–5.

Longstreth, G. F., Mason, C., Schreiber, I. G. and Tsao-Wei, D. (1998) 'Group psychotherapy for women molested in childhood: Psychological and somatic symptoms and medical visits', *International Journal of Group Psychotherapy*, 48 (4): 533–41.

Low, G., Jones, D., Macleod, A., Power, M. and Duggan, C. (2000) 'Childhood trauma, dissociation, and self-harming behavior: A pilot study', *British Journal of Medical Psychology*, 73: 269–78.

Lubin, H., Loris, M. K., Burt, J. and Johnson, D. R. (1998) 'Efficacy of psychoeducational group therapy in reducing symptoms of posttraumatic stress disorder among multiply traumatized women', *American Journal of Psychiatry*, 155 (9): 1172–7.

Madden, R. G. (1998) *Legal Issues in Social Work, Counseling, and Mental Health*. Thousand Oaks, CA: Sage.

Madill, A. and Holch, P. (2004) 'A range of memory possibilities: The challenge of the false memory debate for clinicians and researchers', *Clinical Psychology and Psychotherapy*, 11: 299–310.

Main, M. (1996) 'Introduction to the special section on attachment and psychopathology: 2. Overview of the field of attachment', *Journal of Consulting and Clinical Psychology*, 64: 237–43.

Main, M. and Goldwyn, R. (1998) 'Adult attachment scoring and classification systems (Version 6.3)'. Unpublished work.

Main, M., Kaplan, N. and Cassidy, J. (1985) 'Security in infancy, childhood and adulthood: A move to the level of representation', in I. Bretherton and E. Waters (eds), *Growing points of attachment theory and research*. Monograph 209 [50 (2–3)] of the Society for Research in Child Development. Chicago, IL: University of Chicago. pp. 66–104.

Main, M. and Solomon, J. (1990) 'Procedures for identifying infants as disorganized/ disoriented during the Ainsworth Strange Situation', in M. T. Greenberg, D. Cicchetti and E. M. Cummings (eds), *Attachment in the Preschool Years: Theory research and intervention*. Chicago: University of Chicago Press. pp. 121–60.

Maltz, W. and Holman, B. (1987) *Incest and Sexuality*. Lexington, MA: Lexington Books.

Martsolf, D. S. (2004) 'Childhood maltreatment and mental and physical health in Haitian adults', *Journal of Nursing Scholarship*, 36 (4): 293–9.

Masters, W. H. and Johnson, V. E. (1970) *Human Sexual Inadequacy*. Boston, MA: Little, Brown.

Matthews, R., Matthews, J. and Speltz, K. (1990) 'Female sexual offenders', in M. Hunter (ed.), *The Sexually Abused Male, Vol. 1: Prevalence, impact, and treatment*. Lexington, MA: Lexington Books. pp. 275–94.

McCarthy, B. W. (1990) 'Treating sexual dysfunction associated with prior sexual trauma', *Journal of Sex and Marital Therapy*, 16 (3): 142–6.

McCauley, J., Kern, D. E., Kolodner, K., Dill, L., Schroeder, A. F., DeChant, H. K., Ryden, J., Derogatis, L. R. and Bass, E. B. (1997) 'Clinical characteristics of women with a history of childhood abuse: Unhealed wounds', *JAMA*, 277 (17): 1362–8.

McNaron, T. and Morgan, Y. (eds) (1982) *Voices in the Night: Women speaking about incest*. Minneapolis, MN: Cleis.

Meichenbaum, D. (1985) *Stress Inoculation Training*. New York: Pergamon.

Meichenbaum, D. (1994) *A Clinical Handbook/Practical Therapist Manual*. Ontario, Canada: Institute Press.

Millon, T. (1994) *Manual for the MCMI-III*. Minneapolis, MN: National Computer Systems.

Moeller, T. P., Bachman, G. A. and Moeller, J. R. (1993) 'The combined effects of physical, sexual and emotional abuse during childhood: Long-term health consequences for women', *Child Abuse and Neglect*, 17 (5): 623–40.

Moncrieff, J., Drummond, D. C., Candy, B., Checinski, K. and Farmer, R. (1996) 'Sexual abuse in people with alcohol problems: A study of the prevalence of sexual abuse and its relationship to drinking behavior', *British Journal of Psychiatry*, 169: 355–60.

Morgan, T. and Cummings, A. L. (1999) 'Change experienced during group therapy by female survivors of childhood sexual abuse', *Journal of Consulting and Clinical Psychology*, 67: 28–36.

Morrison, A. and Treliving, L. (2002) 'Evaluation of outcome in a dynamically orientated group for males who have been sexually abused in childhood', *British Journal of Psychotherapy*, 19 (1): 59–75.

Murray, C. and Walker, G. (2002) 'Reported sexual abuse and bulimic psychopathology among nonclinical women: The mediating role of shame', *International Journal of Eating Disorders*, 32: 186–91.

Nash, M. R., Hulsey, T. L., Sexton, M. C., Harralson, T. L. and Lambert, W. (1993) 'Long-term sequelae of childhood sexual abuse: Perceived family environment, psychopathology, and dissociation', *Journal of Consulting and Clinical Psychology*, 61 (2): 276–83.

National Center on Child Abuse and Neglect (1978) *Child Sexual Abuse: Incest, assault, and sexual exploitation, a special report*. Washington, DC: NCCAN.

O'Toole, A. W. and Welt, S. R. (1989) *Interpersonal Theory in Nursing Practice: Selected works of Hildegard E. Peplau*. New York: Springer.

Paivio, S. C. and Nieuwenhuis, J. A. (2001) 'Efficacy of emotion focused therapy for adult survivors of child abuse: A preliminary study', *Journal of Traumatic Stress*, 14 (1): 115–33.

Paivio, S. C. and Patterson, L. A. (1997) 'Efficacy alliance development in therapy for resolving child abuse issues', *Psychotherapy*, 36 (4): 343–54.

Parker, S. and Parker, H. (1991) 'Female victims of child sexual abuse: adult adjustment', *Journal of Family Violence*, 6 (2): 183–97.

Peake, A. (2003) 'Child abuse: The hidden narrative', *Educational and Child Psychology*, 201: 34–42.

Pecukonis, E. V. (1996) 'Childhood sexual abuse in women with chronic intractable back pain', *Social Work in Health Care*, 23 (3): 1–16.

Perry, B. D. (2001) 'The neuroarcheology of childhood maltreatment: The neuro developmental costs of adverse childhood events', in *The Cost of Child Maltreatment: Who pays? We all do*. San Diego, CA: Family Violence and Sexual Assault Institute. pp. 15–38.

Plant, M., Miller, P. and Plant, M. (2004) 'Childhood and adult sexual abuse: Relationships with alcohol and other psychoactive drug use', *Child Abuse Review*, 13: 200–214.

Polusny, M. A. and Follette, V. M. (1995) 'Long-term correlates of child sexual abuse: Theory and review of the empirical literature', *Applied and Preventive Psychology*, 4: 143–66.

Ponterotto, J. G., Casas, J. M., Suzuki, L. A. and Alexander, C. M. (2001) *Handbook of Multicultural Counseling* (2nd edn). Thousand Oaks, CA: Sage.

Pope-Davis, D. B. and Coleman, H. L. K. (2001) *The Intersection of Race, Class, and Gender in Multicultural Counseling*. Thousand Oaks, CA: Sage.

Powers, B. A. and Knapp, T. R. (1995) *A Dictionary of Nursing Theory and Research*. Thousand Oaks, CA: Sage.

Pribor, E. F. and Dinwiddie, S. H. (1992) 'Psychiatric correlates of incest in childhood', *American Journal of Psychiatry*, 149 (1): 52–6.

Ramsey, J. (1979) 'Dealing with the last taboo', *Siecus Report*, 7: 1–2, 6–7.

Ratna, L. and Mukergee, S. (1998) 'The long-term effects of childhood sexual abuse: Rationale for and experience of pharmacotherapy with nefazodone', *International Journal of Psychiatry in Clinical Practice*, 2: 83–95.

Rausch, K. and Knutson, J. F. (1991) 'The self-report of personal punitive childhood experiences and those of siblings', *Child Abuse and Neglect*, 15 (1–2): 29–36.

Reiter, R. C. and Gambone, J. C. (1990) 'Demographic and historic variables in women with idiopathic chronic pelvic pain', *Obstetrics and Gynecology*, 75 (3, Pt. 1): 428–32.

Reiter, R. C., Shakerin, L. R., Gambone, J. C. and Milburn, A. K. (1991) 'Correlation between sexual abuse and somatization in women with somatic and nonsomatic chronic pain', *American Journal of Obstetrics and Gynecology*, 165 (1): 104–9.

Resick, P. A. and Schnicke, M. K. (1993) *Cognitive Processing Therapy for Rape Victims: A treatment manual*. Newbury Park, CA: Sage.

Richardson, T. Q. and Jacob, E. J. (2002) 'Contemporary issues in multicultural counseling: Training competent counselors', in J. Trusty, E. J. Looby and D. S. Sandhu (eds), *Multicultural Counseling: Context, theory and practice, and competence*. New York: Nova Science. pp. 31–53.

Richter, N. L., Snider, E. and Gorey, K. M. (1997) 'Group work intervention with female survivors of childhood sexual abuse using college samples', *Research on Social Work Practice*, 7 (1): 53–69.

Roberts, L. and Lie, G. (1989) 'A group therapy approach for the treatment of incest', *Social Work with Groups*, 12 (3): 77–90.

Roberts, R., O'Conner, T., Dunn, J. and Golding, J. (2004) 'The effects of child sexual abuse in later family life: Mental health, parenting and adjustment of offspring', *Child Abuse and Neglect*, 28: 525–45.

Robins, C. J., Schmidt III, H. and Linehan, M. M. (2004) 'Dialectical behavior therapy: Synthesizing radical acceptance with skillful means', in S. C. Hayes, V. M. Follette and M. M. Linehan (eds), *Mindfulness and Acceptance: Expanding the cognitive-behavioral tradition*. New York: Guilford Press. pp. 30–44.

Roland, B. C., Zelhart, P. and Dubes, R. (1989) 'MMPI correlates of college women who reported experiencing child/adult sexual contact with father, stepfather, or with other persons', *Psychological Reports*, 64 (3, Pt. 2): 1159–62.

Rothbaum, B. O., Meadows, E. A., Resick, P. and Foy, D. W. (2000) 'Cognitive-behavioral therapy', in E. B. Foa, T. M. Keane and M. J. Friedman (eds), *Effective Treatments for PTSD*. New York: Guilford. pp. 60–83.

Roysircar, G. (2003) 'Counselor awareness of own assumptions, values, and biases', in G. Roysircar, P. Arrendondo, J. N. Fuertes, J. G. Ponterotto and R. L. Toporek (eds), *Multicultural Counseling Competencies 2003: Association for Multicultural Counseling and Development*. Alexandria, VA: American Counseling Association.

Safran, J. D. and Muran, J. C. (2000) *Negotiating the Therapeutic Alliance*. New York: Guilford.

Satir, V. (1988) *The New Peoplemaking*. Mountain View, CA: Science and Behavior Books.

Saunders, B. E., Villeponteaux, L. A., Lipovsky, J. A., Kilpatrick, D. G. and Veronen, L. J. (1992) 'Child sexual assault as a risk factor for mental disorders among women: A community survey', *Journal of Interpersonal Violence*, 7 (2): 189–204.

Saxe, B. J. and Johnson, S. M. (1999) 'An empirical investigation of group treatment for a clinical population of adult female incest survivors', *Journal of Child Sexual Abuse*, 8 (1): 67–88.

Schwartz, M. F. and Masters, W. H. (1993) 'Integration of trauma-based, cognitive behavioral, systemic and addiction approaches for treatment of hypersexual pair-bonding', *Sexual Addiction and Compulsivity*, 1: 57–76.

Sepler, F. (1990) 'Victim advocacy and young male victims of sexual abuse: An evolutionary model', in M. Hunter (ed.), *The Sexually Abused Male, Vol. 1: Prevalence, impact, and treatment*. Lexington, MA: Lexington Books. pp. 73–86.

Sgroi, S. M. (1989) 'Stages of recovery for adult survivors', in S. M. Sgroi (ed.), *Vulnerable Populations, Vol. 2: Sexual abuse treatment for children, adult survivors, and persons with mental retardation*. Lexington, MA: Lexington Books. pp. 111–30.

Sgroi, S. M. and Bunk, B. S. (1988) 'A clinical approach to adult survivors of child sexual abuse', in S. M. Sgroi (ed.), *Vulnerable Populations, Vol. 1: Evaluation and treatment of sexually abused children and adult survivors*. Lexington, MA: Lexington Books. pp. 137–86.

Shalev, A. Y., Friedman, M. J., Foa, E. B. and Keane, T. M. (2000) 'Integration and summary', in E. B. Foa, T. M. Keane and M. J. Friedman (eds), *Effective Treatments for PTSD*. New York: Guilford Press. pp. 359–79.

Sidebotham, P. and the Avon Longitudinal Study of Pregnancy and Childhood Study Team (2000) 'Patterns of child abuse in early childhood, a cohort study of the 'children of the nineties', *Child Abuse Review*, 9: 311–20.

Siegel, D. J. (1999) *The Developing Mind: How relationships and the brain interact to shape who we are*. New York: Guilford Press.

Silver, R. L., Boon, C. and Stones, M. H. (1983) 'Searching for meaning in misfortune: Making sense of incest', *Journal of Social Issues*, 39 (2): 81–102.

Sinason, V. (1998) 'Introduction', in V. Sinason (ed.), *Memory in Dispute*. London: Karnac. pp. 1–16.

Sisk, S. L. and Hoffman, C. F. (1987) *Inside Scars*. Gainesville, FL: Pandora.

Skorina, J. K. and Kovach, J. A. (1986) 'Treatment techniques for incest-related issues in alcoholic women', *Alcoholism Treatment Quarterly*, 3 (1): 17–30.

Smith, D., Pearce, L., Pringle, M. and Caplan, R. (1995) 'Adults with a history of childhood sexual abuse: Evaluation of a pilot therapy service', *British Medical Journal*, 310: 1175–8.

Smolak, L., Levine, M. P. and Sullins, E. (1990) 'Are child sexual experiences related to eating-disordered attitudes and behaviors in a college sample?', *International Journal of Eating Disorders*, 9: 167–78.

Speer, D. C. (1998) *Mental Health Outcome Evaluation*. New York: Academic Press.

Spiegel, D. and Spiegel, H. (1987) 'Forensic uses of hypnosis', in I. B. Weiner and A. K. Hess (eds), *Handbook of Forensic Psychology*. New York: Wiley. pp. 490–507.

Spiegel, J. (2003) *Sexual Abuse of Males: The SAM model of theory and practice*. New York: Brunner-Routledge.

Springs, F. E. and Friedrich, W. N. (1992) 'Health risk behaviors and medical sequelae of childhood sexual abuse', *Mayo Clinic Proceedings*, 67: 527–32.

Stalker, C. A. and Fry, R. (1999) 'A comparison of short-term group and individual therapy for sexually abused women', *Canadian Journal of Psychiatry*, 44 (2): 168–74.

Stein, J. A., Golding, J. M., Siegel, J. M., Burnam, M. A. and Sorenson, S. B. (1988) 'Long-term psychological sequelae of child sexual abuse: The Los Angeles Epidemiologic Catchment Area Study', in G. E. Wyatt and G. J. Powell (eds), *Lasting Effects of Child Sexual Abuse*. Newbury Park, CA: Sage. pp. 135–54.

Struve, J. (1990) 'Dancing with the patriarchy: The politics of sexual abuse', in M. Hunter (ed.), *The Sexually Abused Male, Vol. 1: Prevalence, impact, and treatment*. Lexington, MA: Lexington Books. pp. 3–46.

Sue, D. W., Arrendondo, P. and McDavis, R. J. (1992) 'Multicultural counseling competencies and standards: A call to the profession', *Journal of Counseling and Development*, 70: 477–86.

Sue, D. W. and Sue, D. (2003) *Counseling the Culturally Diverse: Theory and practice*. New York: Wiley.

Sultan, F. E. and Long, G. T. (1988) 'Treatment of the sexually/physically abused female inmate: Evaluation of an intensive, short-term intervention program', *Journal of Offender Counseling, Services, and Rehabilitation*, 12 (2): 131–43.

Swanson, L. and Biaggio, M. K. (1985) 'Therapeutic perspectives on father–daughter incest', *The American Journal of Psychiatry*, 142: 667–74.

Talbot, N. L., Houghtalen, R. P., Duberstein, P. R., Cox, C., Giles, D. E. and Wynne, L. C. (1999) 'Effects of group treatment for women with a history of childhood sexual abuse', *Psychiatry Services*, 50 (5): 686–92.

Taylor, S. E. (1983) 'Adjustment to threatening events: A theory of cognitive adaptation', *American Psychologist*, 38: 1161–73.

Thomas, T. (1989) *Men Surviving Incest*. Walnut Creek, CA: Launch.

Trotter, C. (1995) 'Stages of recovery and relapse prevention for the chemically dependent adult sexual trauma survivor', in M. Hunter (ed.), *Adult Survivors of Sexual Abuse: Treatment Innovations*. Thousand Oaks, CA: Sage. pp. 98–135.

Trusty, J., Looby, E. J. and Sandhu, D. S. (2002) *Multicultural Counseling: Context, theory and practice, and competence*. New York: Nova Science.

Tseng, W. (2001) *Handbook of Cultural Psychiatry*. New York: Academic Press.

Tyrell, C. and Dozier, M. (1998) 'Attachment theory and close relationships', in J. A. Simpson and W. S. Rholes (eds), *Attachment Theory and Close Relationships*. New York: Guilford Press.

United Nations (2003a) 'Demographics and social statistics'. Online, available at: http://unstats.un.org/unsd/

United Nations (2003b) *Trends in Total Migrant Stock: The 2003 revision*. New York: Author.

Urquiza, A. J. and Capra, M. (1990) 'The impact of sexual abuse: Initial and long-term effects', in M. Hunter (ed.), *The Sexually Abused Male, Vol. 1: Prevalence, impact, and treatment*. Lexington, MA: Lexington Books. pp. 105–36.

Urquiza, A. J. and Keating, L. M. (1990) 'The prevalence of the sexual victimization of males', in M. Hunter (ed.), *The Sexually Abused Male, Vol. 1: Prevalence, impact, and treatment.* Lexington, MA: Lexington Books. pp. 89–104.

US Department of Health and Human Services, Administration for Children and Families, National Center on Child Abuse and Neglect (1996) *The Third National Incidence Study of Child Abuse and Neglect.* Washington, DC: Author.

Ussher, J. M. and Dewberry, C. (1995) 'The nature and long-term effects of childhood sexual abuse: A survey of adult women survivors in Britain', *British Journal of Clinical Psychology*, 34: 177–92.

Van der Kolk, B. A. (1996) 'The body keeps the score: Approaches to the psychobiology of posttraumatic stress disorder', in B. A. van der Kolk, A. C. McFarlane and L. Weissath (eds), *Traumatic Stress: The effects of overwhelming experience on mind, body and society.* New York: Guilford Press. pp. 214–41.

Van der Kolk, B. A. and van der Hart, O. (1991) 'The intrusive past: The flexibility of memory and the engraving of trauma', *American Imago*, 48 (4): 425–54.

Van Voorhees, E. and Scarpa, A. (2004) 'The effects of child maltreatment on the hypothalamic-pituitary-adrenal axis', *Trauma, Violence and Abuse*, 5: 333–52.

Walker, E., Katon, W., Harrop-Griffiths, J., Holm, L., Russo, J. and Hickok, L. R. (1988) 'Relationship of chronic pelvic pain to psychiatric diagnoses and childhood sexual abuse', *American Journal of Psychiatry*, 145 (1): 75–80.

Walker, E. A., Katon, W. J., Neraas, K., Jemelka, R. P. and Massoth, D. (1992) 'Dissociation in women with chronic pelvic pain', *American Journal of Psychiatry*, 149 (4): 534–7.

Waller, G. (1991) 'Sexual abuse as a factor in eating disorders', *British Journal of Psychiatry*, 159: 664–71.

Waller, G. (1992a) 'Sexual abuse and bulimic symptoms in eating disorders: Do family interaction and self-esteem explain the links?', *International Journal of Eating Disorders*, 12 (3): 235–40.

Waller, G. (1992b) 'Sexual abuse and the severity of bulimic symptoms', *British Journal of Psychiatry*, 161: 90–3.

Wallis, D. A. N. (2002) 'Reduction of trauma symptoms following group therapy', *Australian and New Zealand Journal of Psychiatry*, 36: 67–74.

Watts, C. and Zimmerman, C. (2002) 'Violence against women: Global scope and magnitude', *The Lancet*, 359: 1232–7.

Wegscheider-Cruse, S. (1985) *Choicemaking.* Deerfield Beach, FL: Health Communications.

Weingardt, K. R., Toland, H. K. and Loftus, E. F. (1994) 'Reports of suggested memories: Do people truly believe them?', in D. F. Ross, J. D. Read and M. P. Toglia (eds), *Adult Eyewitness Testimony: Current trends and developments.* New York: Cambridge University Press. pp. 3–26.

Westbury, E. and Tutty, L. M. (1999) 'The efficacy of group treatment for survivors of childhood abuse', *Child Abuse and Neglect*, 23 (1): 31–44.

Westerlund, E. (1983) 'Counseling women with histories of incest', *Women and Therapy*, 2 (4): 17–31.

Westerlund, E. (1992) *Women's Sexuality after Childhood Incest.* New York: Norton.

White, M. and Epston, D. (1990) *Narrative Means to Therapeutic Ends.* New York: Norton.

Whitfield, C. L. (1989) *Healing the Child Within.* Deerfield Beach, FL: Health Communications.

Wiehe, V. R. (1990) *Sibling Abuse.* Lexington, MA: Lexington Books.

Williams, L. M. (1994) 'Recall of childhood trauma: A prospective study of women's memories of child sexual abuse', *Journal of Counseling and Clinical Psychology*, 62 (2): 1167–76.

Wilson, J. P. and Thomas, R. B. (2004) *Empathy in the Treatment of Trauma and PTSD.* New York: Brunner-Routledge.

Wilson, S. M. and Sandhu, D. S. (2002) 'Multicultural counseling theories', in J. Trusty, E. J. Looby and D. S. Sandhu (eds), *Multicultural Counseling: Context, theory and practice, and competence*. New York: Nova. pp. 129–41.

Wind, T. W. and Silvern, L. (1992) 'Type and extent of child abuse as predictors of adult functioning', *Journal of Family Violence*, 7 (4): 261–81.

Wurtele, S. K. and Miller-Perrin, C. L. (1992) *Preventing Child Sexual Abuse: Sharing the responsibility*. Lincoln, NE: University of Nebraska Press.

Wyatt, G. E., Guthrie, D. and Notgrass, C. M. (1992) 'Differential effects of women's child sexual abuse and subsequent revictimization', *Journal of Consulting and Clinical Psychology*, 60 (2): 167–73.

Wyatt, G. E. and Newcomb, M. D. (1990) 'Internal and external mediators of women's sexual abuse in childhood', *Journal of Consulting and Clinical Psychology*, 58 (6): 758–67.

Yama, M. F., Tovey, S. L. and Fogas, B. S. (1993) 'Childhood family environment and sexual abuse as predicting of anxiety and depression in adult women', *American Journal of Orthopsychiatry*, 63 (1): 136–41.

Yama, M. F., Tovey, S. L., Fogas, B. S. and Teegarden, L. A. (1992) 'Joint consequences of parental alcoholism and childhood sexual abuse, and their partial mediation by family environment', *Violence and Victims*, 7 (4): 313–25.

Zierler, S., Feingold, L., Laufer, D., Velentgas, P., Kantrowtiz-Gordon, I. and Mayer, K. (1991) 'Adult survivors of childhood sexual abuse and subsequent risk for HIV infection', *American Journal of Public Health*, 81 (5): 572–5.

Zlotnick, C., Shea, T. M., Rosen, K., Simpson, E., Mulrenin, K., Begin, A. and Pearlstein, T. (1997) 'An affect-management group for women with posttraumatic stress disorder and histories of childhood sexual abuse', *Journal of Traumatic Stress*, 10 (3): 425–36.

Index